Ernest Dupuy

The Great Masters of Russian Literature in the Nineteenth Century

Ernest Dupuy

The Great Masters of Russian Literature in the Nineteenth Century

ISBN/EAN: 9783337309855

Printed in Europe, USA, Canada, Australia, Japan

Cover: Foto ©ninafisch / pixelio.de

More available books at **www.hansebooks.com**

THE GREAT MASTERS

OF

RUSSIAN LITERATURE

IN

THE NINETEENTH CENTURY

BY

ERNEST DUPUY

TRANSLATED BY

NATHAN HASKELL DOLE

THE PROSE WRITERS

Nikolaï Vasilyevitch Gogol, Ivan Sergéyevitch Turgenief,
Count Lyof Nikolayévitch Tolstoï

WITH APPENDIX

NEW YORK
THOMAS Y. CROWELL & CO.
13 Astor Place

CONTENTS.

It may be said, that the emancipation of literature in Russia dates back scarcely fifty years. All the Russian writers, whether of poetry or prose, with the exception possibly of one or two satirists, were little more than imitators. Some of the most valued authors during the first half of this century, Zhukovsky for example, owed all their fame to translations. Pushkin himself, who, on the recommendation of Merimée, has for some time been admired in France, did not venture far from the Byronic manner. He died, to be sure, just at the moment when he had found his path. He suspected the profit that could be made from national sources; he had a presentiment that a truly Russian literature was about to burst into bloom; he aided in its production. His greatest originality lies in his having predicted, preached, perhaps prepared or inspired Gogol.

NIKOLAÏ GOGOL.

I.

Nikolaï Gogol[1] was born in 1810, in a village of the government of Poltava. His father, a small proprietor with some education, obtained for him a scholarship in the college of Niézhin. Fortunately the young Gogol was able to hold his own in rebellion against the direction of his instructors, and neither the dead nor the living languages brought him any gain. He thus failed of becoming a commonplace man of letters, and consequently had less trouble in the end with discovering his original genius.

In his father's house, on the other hand, he

[1] Nikolaï Vasilyévitch Gogol-Yanovsky, born, according to Polevoï, on the 31st of March, 1809, at Sorotchintsui. See Appendix.

received a priceless education, such as Pushkin, in spite of all his efforts, vainly attempted to obtain. He was imbued with the poetry of the people. His childhood was entertained by the marvellous legends of the Malo-Russians. Gogol's grandfather was one of those Zaparog Cossacks whose heroic exploits the author of "Taras Bulba" was destined to celebrate. He excelled in the art of story-telling, and his narrations had a tinge of mystery about them that brought the cold chills. "When he was speaking I would not move from my place all day long, but would listen, . . . and the things were so strange that I always shivered, and my hair stood on end. Sometimes I was so frightened by them, that at night every thing seemed like God knows what monsters." This fund of mainly fantastic and diabolical legends afterwards furnished the grandson of the Ukraïne village story-teller, with the material for his first original work.[1]

Gogol's first attempts were not original: he began too early. Scarcely out of the gymnasium, he began to write in rhyme; in the morn-

[1] Evenings at the Farm House (*Vetchera na Khutoryé*).

ing trying all the styles in vogue, at evening making parodies upon them. He established a manuscript journal "The Star" (*Zvyezd*). The student intoxicated by reading Pushkin still remained in the trammels of uninspired verse, in the formulas of romanticism. Some characteristics already began to reveal the precocious observer, the brilliant satirist. Thus his prose articles, clandestinely introduced, had a tremendous success never equalled in his ripest years, even by his comedy of "The *Revizor*."

After his studies were ended, Gogol was obliged to conquer the favor of a public less complacent than the rhetoricians and philosophers of Niézhin. He obtained (1830) an exceedingly modest office in the Ministry of Appanages (*Udyélui*). But in the bureau, where, like Popritshchin in the "Recollections of a Lunatic" his service was limited to sharpening dozens of pens for the director, he worked out a comedy on the pattern of Scribe's, and spun a cottony idyl in the German style. The comedy was hissed by the public, and the idyl was so unkindly received by the critics that

Gogol had this attempt withdrawn from the market.[1]

Gogol almost simultaneously shook off the double yoke of bureaucratic slavery and literary imitation. Instead of following, like so many others, in the track of French, English, or German writers, he determined to be himself. He went back over the course of his early years to find in this way in all their freshness the impressions of his childhood; he returned to his first, his real masters, and began once more to get material around the Malo-Russian hearth. He appealed to his mother for recollections; he besought the aid of his friends; he put them like so many bloodhounds on the track of half-forgotten legends, half-vanished traditions; he collected documents of every sort and kind: and when he was sufficiently permeated with savagery to think and speak, if need were, like a Cossack of the last century, he created a work at once modern and archaic, learned and enthusiastic, mystic and refined,—Russian, in a

[1] Hans Küchel Garten—such was the name of the unfortunate idyl—was afterwards placed by the author, not without complaisance, among his *juvenilia*. See Appendix.

word, — and published it under the title "Evenings at the Farm" (*Vetchera na Khutoryé bliz Dikanki*).

This series of fantastic tales, published in the reviews under the pseudonyme of Rudui Panko (Sandy the little nobleman), produced a singular effect. The Russian reader was surprised and charmed in the same way as a French traveller, who, after having visited all the countries and admired all the floras of the world, should discover the banks of the Seine, and declare that he was willing to exchange the splendors of the savannas for a tuft of turf and a bunch of violets. No one was more struck with the value of these tales than Pushkin. He recommended their author to Pletnef, minister of public instruction; and Gogol was appointed professor. The servitude was still more onerous than that of the bureaucracy. The young writer had too much originality to bend under it very long: a second time he escaped, and took his departure for the Ukraïna.

The Zaparog Cossack's grandson used to say that there was material for an Iliad in the exploits of his ancestors. He buried himself in the study of the annals of Little Russia; he collected the traditions; more than all, he picked up the national songs of the Ukraïna,—those kinds of heroic cantilenas composed by the players of the bandura. A modern *diaskenastes*, he constructed a body out of all these poetic remains, joined them together by means of a romantic plot, and renewed the astonishment caused by the appearance of "Evenings at the Farm," by publishing "Taras Bulba." The minister was convinced that a man who could thus revivify history could not fail to be skilled in teaching it: he therefore offered Gogol the chair of mediæval history in the University of Petersburg. The romancer gave only one lecture, his opening lecture. This day he dazzled his audience. The remainder of his course was for both students and professor only a long-continued bore, which ended finally in his losing the place.

Gogol dreamed of a different success. In 1835 he published his comedy, "The *Revizor*" (The Inspector General). It was applauded, and, what was of more value, it was desperately attacked. The author gained as many admirers and enemies as "Tartuffe" cost Molière. At Petersburg, as at Paris, the masterpiece was produced on the stage, and kept before the public, only by a fortunate caprice on the part of the sovereign.

Gogol's health, which had long been failing, caused him about this period to leave Russia. He lived many years in Italy. There he completed his great romance, "Dead Souls" (*Mertvuia Dushi*). The work appeared in complete form in 1841.[1] The author had reached a state of nervous irritation and hypochondria, which was more and more manifested in his correspondence, published in part towards 1846. The last years of Gogol's life were only a long torture. A sort of mystic madness took possession of his brain, exhausted or over-excited by production: death put an end to his nervous disease (1852).

[1] This is a mistake. He completed it, to be sure, but in his religious mania he destroyed the most of the second part: it was completed by another hand. See Appendix.

II.

Dreaminess and banter are the two natural tendencies, the two favorite pleasures, of the Russian mind. They are also the two elements of Gogol's talent. At the beginning of his career as a writer, and during the sprightly years of his youth, it is dreaminess which prevails: the narrator penetrates with enthusiasm into the untrodden paths of the Malo-Russian legends. On the track of witches, of Rusalkas, he finds the unpublished poetry of the forests, the ponds, the wide stretches, and the sky of the steppes. These lovely days pass. With age, this restless spirit grows gloomy and melancholy. The observer's eyes turn from the pacifying spectacle of nature, and attempt only to notice the vexing absurdities of humanity.

The satirical spirit in Gogol is first expressed in verse. He is poetical only in prose; but his prose is equal to the most beautiful verse. In truth, poetry is not rhyme, or metre, or even rhythm : it is the power of touching, of recording its impressions in vivid and genuine images. To feel emotion suitable for poetic expression, there is no need of picturing lofty heroes, or of spreading marvellous landscapes before the eyes. Properly speaking, a Malo-Russian peasant is like a hero in Corneille ; and the imagination of an author, and therefore of his reader, can just as well be stirred by the view of a bit of the flat and naked steppe, as by the sight of the Bay of Naples or a sunset on the ruins of the Coliseum.

Gogol understood this, and, what is far better, made it understood. Instead of preparing his imitation of Werther and his copy of Childe Harold in the fashion of so many others, he had the courage to go to Nature for his models. And in this Russian nature, the wild grace and strange flavor of which he was, so to speak, the first to feel, that which attracts him more than all else is its unostentatious aspect. His field of observation is the village. His heroes are unimportant people, half-barbarous peasants, true Cossack lads, hard drinkers, with circumscribed intellectual training, with superstitious imaginations; in a word, very simple souls, whose artless passions are shown without any veil, but whose very ingenuousness is a deliciously restful contrast to our romantic or theatrical characters, so artificial in their labored mechanism, so insipid and perfunctory in the refinements of their conventionality.

Gogol places his characters in their natural surroundings. It is the hamlet bordering on the steppe, monotonous and infinite, deserted and mysterious. All this country appeals to the writer's imagination, as well as to that of those Malo-Russians, whose history, past and present, he will describe for us in turn. Each shrub inshrines a memory; each winding valley veils a legend. In yonder stretch of water, beset with rushes and starred with nenuphars, the sceptic traveller in his indifference sees only a sort of marsh. The peasant who is here a poet, and the poet who remembers that he was once a peasant, know well who the Rusalka is who has been hiding there these many years. From its surface, on nights when the moon lights up the silvery mist, the queen of the drowned comes forth with her train of virgins, to find and drag into the depths of the water her stepmother, the witch whose evil deeds drove her to suicide.

But to move those whom she has brought forth, this land of the Ukraïna has no need of being wrapped in mystery. Gogol has only to pronounce the name of the Dniépr to arouse a sort of passionate woe, whose expression, unhappily almost untranslatable, equals in beauty the accents of the noblest poetry.

[1]"Marvellous is the Dniépr in peaceful weather, when he rolls his wide waters in a free and reposeful course by forests and mountains. Not the slightest jar, not the slightest tumult. Thou beholdest, and thou canst not tell if his majestic breadth is moving or is stationary. It is almost like a sheet of molten glass. It might be compared to a road of blue ice, without measure in its breadth, without limit to its length, describing its wondrous curves in the emerald distance. How delightful for the burning sun to turn his gaze to earth, and to plunge his rays into the refreshing coolness of the

[1] From A Terrible Vengeance.

glassy waves, and for the trees along the bank to see their reflections in this crystal mirror! Oh the green-crowned trees! They stand in groups with the flowers of the field by the water-side, and they bend over and gaze, and cannot weary of gazing. They cannot sufficiently admire their bright reflection, and they smile back to it, and greet it, waving their branches. They dare not look towards the middle of the Dniépr: none but the sun and the azure sky gaze at it. Some daring bird occasionally wings his way to the middle of the Dniépr. Oh the giant that he is! There is not a river like him in the world!

"Marvellous indeed is the Dniépr on a warm summer's night, when all things are asleep, — both man and beast and bird. God only from on high looks down majestically on sky and earth, and shakes with solemnity his chasuble, and from his priestly raiment scatters all the stars. The stars are kindled, they shine upon the world; and all at the same instant also flash forth from the Dniépr. He holds them every one, the Dniépr, in his sombre bosom; not one shall escape from him, unless, indeed, it perish from the sky. The black forest, dotted with sleeping crows, and the mountains rent from immemorial time, strive, as they catch the light, to veil him with their mighty shadow. In vain! There is naught on earth can veil the Dniépr! Forever blue, he marches onward in his restful course by day and night. He can be seen as far as human sight can pierce. As he goes to rest voluptuously, and presses close unto the shore by reason of the nocturnal cold, he leaves behind him a silver trail, flashing like the blade of a Damascus sword, and then he yields to sleep again. Then also he is wonderful, the Dniépr, and there is no river like him in the world!

"But when the black clouds advance like mountains on the sky, the gloomy forest sways, the oaks clash, and the lightning, darting zigzag across the cloud, lights up suddenly the whole world, terrible then the Dniépr is! The columns of water thunder down, dashing against the mountain, and then with shouts and groans draw far away, and weep, and break out into tears again in the distance. Thus some aged Cossack mother consumes away with grief, when she gets ready her son to take his departure for the army. With many airs, a genuine good-for-naught, he dashes up on his black steed, his hand on his hip, and his cap set jauntily awry; and she, weeping at the top of her voice, runs after him, seizes him by the stirrup, strives to grasp the reins, and twists her arms, and breaks into a passion of scalding tears. Like dark stains in the midst of the struggling waves, emerge uncannily the stumps of charred trees and the rocks on the shelving shore. And the boats moored along the shore knock against each other as they rise and fall. What Cossack would dare embark in his canoe when the ancient Dniépr is angry? Apparently yonder man knows not that his waves swallow men like flies."

The same powerful and charming feeling is found in all the descriptions which are scattered throughout Gogol's work. One must read in "Taras Bulba" the celebrated description of the beauty of the steppe at different hours of the day. What a picture it is of this ocean of gilded verdure, where, amid the delicate dry stalks of the tall grass, shine patches of cornflower with their shades of blue, of violet, or of red; the broom with its pyramid of yellow flowers; the clover with its white tufts; and in this luxuriant flora a corn-stalk, brought thither God knows how, lifting itself with the haughty vigor of a solitary fruit! The warm atmosphere is vocal with the cries of unseen birds. A few hawks are seen hovering; a flock of wild geese sweep by, and the prairie-gull mounts and swoops down again, now black and glistening in the sunbeam. Then it is the evening twilight, with its vapors descending denser and more dense, its perfumes rising more and more penetrating; the jerboas creep out from their hiding-places; the crickets madly chirp in their holes; and "one hears resounding, like a vibrating bell in the sleepy air, the cry of the solitary swan winging its way from some distant lake."[1]

[1] The passage referred to is as follows: "The steppe grew more and more beautiful. The whole South, all the region which includes the New Russia of the present day as far as the Black Sea, was a virgin desert of green. Never had the plough passed through the boundless waves of vegetation. Only a few horses, concealed in it as in a forest, trod it under their hoofs. Nothing in nature could be finer. All the surface of the earth was like a green golden ocean from which emerged millions of varied flowers. Amidst the delicate tall stalks of the grass gleamed azure, purple, violet blue-bonnets (*voloshki*); the yel-

What gives this picturesque and vivid prose a singularly penetrating accent, is the writer's emotion. His admiration has a truly passionate character, and this passion breaks out in cries of joy, even in expletives. "The deuce take you, steppes, how beautiful you are!" There is in this a flavor of savagery which takes hold of us like a novelty, and which must have been as agreeable to the Russian taste as the secretly preferable national dish after too long use of foreign insipidities.

And even for many Russians, this nature which Gogol studied and described, or, more accurately speaking, sang with a sort of intoxi-

low broom lifted on high its pyramidal tower; the white clover, with its umbrella-like bonnets, mottled the plain; a wheat-stalk, brought from God knows where, was waxing full of seed. Under their slender roots the partridges were running about, thrusting out their necks. The air was full of a thousand different bird-notes. In the sky hung motionless a cloud of hawks, stretching wide their wings and fixing their eyes silently on the grass. The cry of the wild geese moving in clouds was heard from God knows what distant lake. From the grass arose with measured strokes the prairie-gull, and luxuriously bathed herself in the blue waves of the air. Now she was lost in immensity, and was visible only as a lone black speck. Now she swept back on broad wings, and gleamed in the sun. The deuce take you, steppes, how beautiful you are!" (*Tchort vas vozmi, styèpi, kak vui khoroshi!*)

cation, was a sort of new world offering every attraction. Nothing is more peculiar than the little Russian landscape with its solitudes, its lakes, its vast rivers, the incomparable purity of its sky, icy and burning in turn. Here there is material to tempt the palette of colorist most enamoured of the untouched (*épris d'inédit*). But what painter's palette has colors sufficiently powerful to express as Gogol has done the profound, ineffable poetry of the sounds and gleams of the night?

[1] "Do you know the Ukraïne night? Oh! you do not know the Ukraïne night. Gaze upon it with your eyes. From the midst of the sky the moon looks down. The immense vault of heaven unrolls wider and still more wide; more immense it has become; it glows; it breathes. The whole earth is in a silvery effulgence, and the marvellous air is both suffocating and fresh. It is full of tender caresses. It stirs into movement an ocean of perfumes.

"Night divine! enchanting night! silent, and as though full of life, the forests rise bristling with darkness; they cast an enormous shadow. Silent and motionless are the ponds: the coolness

[1] From The May Night.

of their darkling waters is gloomily enshrined between the dark green walls of the gardens.

"The cherry-trees and wild plums stretch their roots with cautious timidity towards the icy water of the springs; and from their leaves only now and then are heard faint whisperings, as though they were angry, as though they were indignant, when the gay adventurer, the night wind, glides stealthily up to them and kisses them.

"All the landscape sleeps; and far above, all is breathing, all is marvellous, all is solemn. The soul cannot fathom it: it is sublime. An infinite number of silver visions arise like a harmony in the depths. Night divine! enchanting night! And suddenly all is filled with life, —the forests, the ponds, the steppes. Majestically the thunder of the voice of the Ukraïne nightingale rolls along; and it seems as though the moon drank her song from the bosom of the sky.

"A magic slumber holds the village yonder in repose. Still more brilliant in the moonlight the group of little houses stands out in relief; still more blinding are their low walls in contrast with the shade. The songs have ceased; all is now still. The pious folk are already asleep. Here and there a narrow window shows a gleam of light; on the doorstep of some cottage, a belated family are finishing their evening meal."

Gogol excels not only in picturing the grand aspects of the Ukraïne landscape. He has sketches filled in with adorable detail; and nothing is more curious than the contrast between the lyricism with which he celebrates the seductions of the Malo-Russian sky, and the fine, discreet, restrained tone of so many familiar impressions. The feeling for nature finds in Gogol all manner of expression: he passes in turn through every gradation.

Sometimes it is a vigorous sketch made with a few strokes, at once broad and accurate, dominated by a strange and grandiose theme:—

[1] "In places the black sky was colored by the burning of dry rushes on the shore of some river or out-of-the-way lake; and a long line of swans flying to the north, struck suddenly by the silver rose-light of the flame, were like red handkerchiefs waving across the night."

[1] From Taras Bulba.

Sometimes it is a picture full of detail, whose motives have been strangely brought together and treated delicately, elaborately, as with a magnifying-glass:—

[1] "I see from here the little house, surrounded by a gallery supported by delicate, slender columns of darkened wood, and going entirely around the building, so that during thunder-showers or hail-storms the window-shutters can be closed without exposure to the rain; behind the house, mulberry-trees in bloom, then long rows of dwarf fruit-trees drowned in the bright scarlet of the cherries and in an amethystine sea of plums with leaden down; then a large old beech-tree, under the shade of which is spread a carpet for repose; before the house, a spacious court with short and verdant grass, with two little foot-paths trodden down by the steps of those who went from the barn to the kitchen and from the kitchen to the proprietor's house. A long-necked goose drinking water from a puddle, surrounded by her soft and silky yellow goslings; a long hedge hung with strings of dried pears and apples, and rugs put out to air; a wagon loaded with melons

[1] From Old-time Proprietors.

near the barn; on one side an ox unyoked and chewing his cud, lazily lying down. All this has for me an inexpressible charm."

Here we have a realism anterior to our own, and, if I may be allowed to say so, far superior. Here we do not find, as we do elsewhere, features collected and reproduced with the conscientiousness — or rather the lack of conscientiousness — of a photographic camera: a choice is shown, a soul-felt attention. The observer's notice is that of a poet: the external world is no longer reflected in a glass lens, but is caught by a quivering retina; the image which is transferred to the book is no less alive, and what the writer has felt in this manner the reader feels in turn.

Just so far as purely descriptive description produces an impression of puerility, of unlikeness, and, when it is carried to extremes in the style of our realists, of fatigue and disgust, to the same degree does it here afford interest, picturesqueness, appropriateness. Who could fail to see, or who would refuse to admire, the *pose* of "yonder wooden cottages, leaning to one side, and buried in a thicket of willows, elders, and pear-trees"? They have something better than a physiognomy: they have a language.

"I could not tell why the doors sang in this way. Was it because the hinges were rusted? Or had the joiner who made them concealed in them some secret mechanism? I do not know; but the strangest thing was, that each door had its own individual voice. That of the sleeping-room had the most delicate soprano, that of the dining-room a sonorous bass. As to that which closed the ante-room, it gave forth a strange, tremulous, and plaintive sound, so that by listening attentively these words could be distinctly heard: '*Batiushki!* I am freezing.' I know that many people do not like the squeaking of doors: for my part, I like it very much. And when I happen to hear in St. Petersburg a door crying, I suddenly perceive the scent of the country, together with the memory of a small, low room, lighted by a taper set in an ancient candlestick. Supper is already on the table, near the open window through which the lovely May night looks into the room. A nightingale fills the garden, the house, and the slope to the river gleaming in the gloomy distance, with the glory of his voice; the trees gently rustle. *Bozhe moï!* what a train of memories arise within me!"

We must draw attention to the exclamations which in Gogol serve for the passionate conclusion to his most accurate descriptions. They give us the key to his poetic realism. It is feeling which stored away the impression in the treasure-house of the memory; it is feeling which calls it up again, and places it before the reader, kindled with all the fires of the imagination.

III.

THIS power of resurrection which makes the poet a god, Gogol applies equally to facts and to ideas, to men and to things, to legends and to history. His whole work shows it, but nothing in his work shows it more clearly than his early writings. Here imagination plays the leading part. In the works of his riper years, it is observation which comes to get the mastery, forcing itself everywhere. The part played by poetry, by fancy, grows less and less. The author of "The *Revizor*," of "Dead Souls," no longer takes pains, except rarely, to distinguish by his characteristic touch his models of coarseness, platitude, or ugliness.

The writer of the "Evenings at the Farm" is still content to vivify or revivify in his half-imaginary, half-biographical tales, artless lovers, full of passion and pathos, heroes of epic grandeur, good old folks of the vanished past, of odd exteriors, of ridiculous aspect, but charming by their glances, stirring by their smiles, as in the pale, faded pastels of a bygone age. Such are the figures which Gogol afterwards ceases to depict for us: it is these which we are going to endeavor to take out from his first collection, so as to examine them entirely at our ease.

This collection of "Evenings at the Farm" is divided into two parts, bearing, by way of sub-title, the town names, *Didanka* and *Mirgorod.*

Each part contains two groups of novels. In the "Evenings near Didanka,"[1] the first group contains "The Fair at Sorotchintsui," "St. John's Eve," "The May Night, or the Drowned Girl," and "The Missing Paper." The second group includes "Christmas Eve," "A Terrible Vengeance," "Ivan Feodorovitch Shponka and his Aunt," and "An Enchanted Spot."

The "Evenings near Mirgorod" contain four novels in two groups: in the one, "Old-time Proprietors"[2] and "Taras Bulba" (in its first form; shortly afterwards the author recast it

[1] *Vetchera na Khutoryê bliz Dikanki.*

[2] *Starosvyêtskiê Pomyêshchiki.*

and developed it); in the other, "Vii," which has been translated into French under the title "The King of the Gnomes," and "The Story of how Ivan Ivanovitch and Ivan Nikiforovitch quarrelled."[1]

The novels of the first part have especially a fantastic character. The Devil, who holds such a place in the imagination of the Malo-Russian peasants, is the principal hero of some of the stories, "The Fair at Sorotchintsui" for example. Witches also play a preponderating part in his mysterious tales. But here the witch is not that wrinkled, toothless, unclean being, hiding herself like an abominable beast in some ill-omened hovel. She is generally a beautiful girl, with eyes green as an Undine's, with skin of lily and rose, with long hair yellow as gold or black as ebony, with delicate level, haughty eye-brows. Sometimes, as in "Vii," it is the proprietor's daughter, and those who are impudent enough to stare at her are lost: witness the groom Mikita.

This groom had no equal in the world. En-

[1] *Povyest o Tom Kak Possorilis Ivan Ivanovitch s. Ivanom Nikiforovitchem.*

chanted by the maiden, he becomes a little woman, a rag, the deuce knows what. Did she look at him? The reins fell from his hand. He forgot the names of his dogs, and called one instead of the other. One day, while he was grooming a horse at the stable, the maiden came and asked him to let her rest her little foot upon him. He accepted with joy, foolish fellow! but she compelled him to gallop like a horse, and struck him redoubled blows with her witch's stick. He came back half dead, and from that day he vanished from mortal sight. "Once when they went to the stable, they found instead of him only a handful of ashes by an empty pail. He had burned up, — entirely burned up by his own fire. Yet he had been a groom such as no more can be found in the world."

Artless but not silly sorcery. It is the timid homage, pathetic from its very timidity, which is offered by these barbarous souls to the eternal power of beauty and love.

These witches of Gogol, so bold and novel in their conception, put me in mind of a painting of the Spanish school, attributed to Murillo.

This canvas, which I saw several years ago in a private gallery, is a Temptation of St. Anthony, interpreted in an unlooked-for way. A young man of thirty years, whose features are those of the painter himself, with sunburned face and passionate eyes, bends towards his mistress, a lovely girl with piquant charm, *sal y pimienta*, who is leaning on his shoulder, while her mouth is arched at the corners of the lips in a smile of irresistible seduction.

In these tales of Gogol, the marvellous abounds. But it abounds equally in the life of these Malo-Russians whom the author has wished to depict for us. The supernatural affrights and charms them. If the legends of the Ukraïna are lugubrious, yet they never weary of hearing them told. The young girl who at the first sound of the serenade lifts the latch, steals out from the door, and joins the love-stricken *bandura*-player, desires no other entertainment on the border of the pond which in the uncanny lights of the night reflects in its waters the willows and the maples: [1] "Tell me it, my handsome Cossack," she says, laying her cheek to his face and kissing him: "No?

[1] From The May Night.

Then it is plain that thou dost not love me, that thou hast some other young girl. Speak! I shall not be afraid. My sleep will not be broken by it. On the contrary, I shall not be able to go to sleep at all if thou dost not tell me this story. I shall be thinking of something else. I shall believe — come, Lyévko, tell it." They are right who say that the Devil haunts the brain of young girls to keep their curiosity awake.

Lyévko, however, yields, and unfolds the old legend. It is the story of the daughter of the *sotnik* (captain of a hundred Cossacks). The *sotnik* had a daughter white as snow. He was old, and one day he brought home a second wife, young and handsome, white and rose; but she looked at her stepdaughter in such a strange way that she cried out under her gaze. The young wife was a witch, as was seen immediately. The very night of the wedding, a black cat enters the young girl's room, and tries to choke her with his iron claws. She snatches a sabre down from the wall, she strikes at the animal, and cuts off his paw. He disappears with a yell. When the stepmother was seen again, her hand was covered with bandages. Five days later the father drove his daughter from the house, and in grief she drowned herself in the pond. Since then the drowned girl has been waiting for the sorceress, to beat her with the green rushes of the pond; but up to the present time the stepmother has succeeded in escaping from all her traps. 'She is very wily,' says the poor Undine. 'I feel that she is here. I suffer from her presence. Because of her, I cannot swim freely like a fish. I go to the bottom like a key. Find her for me."

Lyévko the singer hears the drowned girl thus speaking to him in a dream. But this dream is a reality; for when he wakes, Lyévko, who has tracked and caught the stepmother in the circle of the young shadows, finds in his hand the reward of the Queen of the Lake. It is a letter containing an order for the marriage between Lyévko and Hanna, his *fiancée*. The order is given by the district commissioner, to Hanna's father, who has hitherto shown himself recalcitrant. "I shall not tell any one the miracle which has been performed this night," murmurs the happy bridegroom. "To thee alone will I confide it, Hanna; thou alone wilt believe me, and together we will pray for the soul of the poor drowned girl."

IV.

In this collection of "Evenings at the Farm" figures the heroic story of a great character, the life of the atamán Taras Bulba. Gogol afterwards turned this *epopée* into prose, but the after-touches did not change the character of the early composition. The hero of "Taras Bulba" is one of those Zaporog Cossacks who played such an important part in the history of Poland, and later in the history of Russia. After the beginning of the sixteenth century, the Zaporozhtsui, who formed a military republic, or, if the term is preferred, an association of cavalry bandits, became the terror of the neighboring peoples. They had on an island in the Dniépr a permanent camp, the *Setch*, where, even in times of peace, young Cossacks came to perfect themselves in the noble game of war. Women were rigorously excluded from the *Setch*. The men were quartered in divisions, or *kurénui;* each *kurén* had its chief, an *atamán* (*hetman*); the entire camp was commanded by a supreme chief, the *atamán-kotchevói.*

The romance of "Taras Bulba" opens in the most original fashion.[1] The two sons of the Cossack Taras are just back from the divinity school, to which they will not return. The father, a vigorous Zaporozhets, who has grown gray in harness, receives them with sarcastic observations about their long robes. It is a sort of test like that which Don Diego gives his sons in the "Romancero." The eldest of Bulba's sons, Ostap (Eustace), behaves like Rodriguez. "Though thou art my father, I swear to thee, if thou continuest to laugh at me, I will give thee a drubbing."

After an exchange of well-directed blows on either side, Taras kisses effusively his son whose courage and strength he has just experienced; he rudely rallies Andriï (Andrew), the younger, on his gentleness: "Thou art a puppy so far as I can judge. Don't listen to thy mother's words: she is a woman; she knows

[1] For a translation of this portion, see Appendix.

naught. What need have ye of being coddled? A good prairie, a good horse, that's all the delicacies that ye need. See this sabre: behold your mother, lads!"

The poor woman is not at the end of her trials. Taras announces his immediate departure with his sons: she protests amid tears and lamentations; the Cossack ill-uses her, and cuts short her complaints. The two sons spend in their father's house just time enough to give the narrator a chance to describe this interior so characteristic and brilliantly colored. On the wall hang all the exquisite ornaments in which barbarous man delights, — sabres, whips, inlaid arms, reins worked in gold wire, silver-nailed clogs. On the dressers are the products of civilization brought from different corners of the world, — masterpieces of Florentine engravers, of Venetian glass-blowers, of Oriental goldsmiths; and in contrast with all this treasure, the fruit of pillage, piles of wood, the stove made of the enamelled bricks loved by the Ukraïne peasant, and the "holy images" in hieratic posture, these Lares indispensable at every Malo-Russian fireside.

The old Bulba has declared at table, before all the *sotniks* of his *polk*[1] who were present in the village, that he should be off next day. The mother spends the night in tears, crouching by her children's bedside, gazing upon them with a look full of anguish like the swallow of the steppe on her nest. She still hopes that when he wakes, Bulba will have forgotten what he vowed in the exaltation of the bowl.

"The moon from the height of heaven had long been lighting up all the *dvor* filled with sleepers, the thick mass of willows, and the tall grass in which the palisade which encircled the *dvor* was drowned. She sat all night by the heads of her beloved sons: not for a moment did she turn her eyes from them, and she had no thought of sleep. Already the horses, prescient of dawn, had all stretched themselves upon the grass, and ceased to feed. The topmost leaves of the willows began to whisper, and little by little a stream of incessant chattering descended through them to the very base. Still she sat in the selfsame place; she felt no fatigue at all, and she wished in

[1] Regiment.

her inmost heart that the night might last as long as possible. From the steppe resounded the sonorous whinnying of a foal. Ruddy streaks stretched across the sky. Bulba suddenly waked up, and leaped to his feet. He remembered very well all that he had determined upon the evening before."

The preparations for the departure are described in detail with Homeric satisfaction. Bulba commands the mother to give her sons her blessing: "A mother's blessing preserves from all danger on land and on water." The farewell is heart-rending: the poor woman seizes the stirrup of her youngest, Andriï, clings to his saddle, and twice, in a paroxysm of maternal delirium, throws herself in front of the horses, until she is led away. Here we see the features of a painting rapidly sketched by Gogol in another novel. The elements of this scene would, moreover, be found elsewhere still. It goes back to the ancient *dumas*, the cantilenas of the Malo-Russian, the traces of which are constantly found in the epic of "Taras Bulba."

They depart. As they ride along, their minds

are filled with melancholy thoughts. Andriï reviews mentally a romantic adventure, the beginning of which dates from his life at the seminary. At Kief, in order to pay back a joke which had been played upon him, he made his way into the room of a wild Polish girl, the daughter of the voïevod of Kovno. The Polish girl made sport of him as though he were a savage; he put up with his dismissal, but fell in love with her. It is natural to conjecture that this love will have a decisive influence upon Andriï's conduct, and that the beautiful girl will appear again. For the time being, the activity of the adventurous life just beginning drives away these recollections. The Cossacks cross the steppe, and the narrator makes us realize the wholly novel charm of this primitive existence, with its sensations no less strong than simple, in these immense spaces which under apparent monotony are so varied and marvellous.

They reach the Setch, and nothing equals the vigor, the color, the life, of the scenes which the story-teller's imagination brings before our eyes. When they disembark from the ferry-boat, which after a three-hours' passage has brought them to the island of Khortitsa, Taras Bulba and his sons reach the camp by an entrance echoing with the hammers of twenty-five smithies, and encumbered with the packs of pedlers. A huge Zaporozhets sleeping in the very middle of the road, with arms and legs stretched out, is the first spectacle which attracts their admiration. Farther, a young Cossack is dancing with frenzy, dripping with sweat in his winter sheepskin: he refuses to take it off, for it would quickly find its way into the pot-house. The merry fellow has already drunk up his cap, his belt, and his embroidered hilt. You feel that here is a young, exuberant, indomitable race. You have to go back to the Iliad to meet such men, and to Homer to find again this freshness of delineation. Other scenes awaken comparisons such as the author of "Taras Bulba" scarcely anticipated. His hero finds well-known faces, and he asks after his ancient companions in arms. They are questions of Philoktetes to Neoptolemos, and the same replies, followed by the same melancholy regrets: "And Taras Bulba heard only, as reply, that Borodavka had been hanged at Tolopan; that Koloper had been flayed alive near Kizikirmen; that Pidsuitok's head had been salted in a cask, and sent to Tsar-grad (Constantinople) itself. The old Bulba hung his head, and after a long pause he said, 'Good Kazaks were they.'"

I shall not dwell upon the scenes in which Gogol has described for us the customs of the Setch, such as the election of the new kotchevóï; and the wiles of these Zaporogs, in their longing for pillage, to take up the offensive without having the appearance of breaking treaties. From the Ukraïna, news is brought which arrives at the very nick of time. The Poles and the Jews have been heaping up deeds of infamy: the Cossack people is oppressed; religion is odiously persecuted. The whole camp breaks into enthusiastic fervor. They fling the Jew pedlers (*kramari*) into the water. One of them, Yankel, has recognized Taras: he throws himself on his knees groaning; he reminds him of a service which he had once done Bulba's brother; finally he escapes punishment, thanks to this scornful and brutal protection. A few hours later, Taras finds him established under a tent, selling all sorts of provisions, powder, screws, gun-flints, at the risk of being caught again, and "killed like a sparrow."

"Taras shrugged his shoulders to see what was the ruling power of the Jewish race." We catch a glimpse here of that lively humor which is common in Gogol, and that keenness of observation which is always heightened by a satiric flavor.

The Zaporogs invade the Polish soil. They lay siege to Dubno. One night, Andriï sees rising before him a woman's form. He recognizes an old Tartar servant of the voïevod's daughter. She comes in her young mistress's name to beg a little bread. The besieged town is a prey to all the torments of famine. Andriï is anxious instantly to make his way inside the walls. He is introduced by a subterranean passage by which the old woman reached the camp. Andriï sees once again the woman whom he loves, and it is all over with him. "He will never see again the Setch, nor his father's village, nor the house of God. The

Ukraïna will never behold again one of its bravest sons. The old Taras will tear his gray hair by handfuls, cursing the day and the hour when to his own shame he begot such a son."

Here the romance halts to make room for the epos. Help comes to the city almost immediately after Andriï's defection. This news is brought by Yankel, who, true Jew that he is, has succeeded in penetrating the city, in making his escape, in seeing every thing, hearing every thing, and putting a good profit into his pocket. What consoles Taras for Andriï's treason is Ostap's bravery, who is made atamán on the battle-field. One must read the exploits of giants, where the cruelty of the carnage is relieved by the beauty of the coloring. Pictures of heroic grandeur light up these sinister scenes, and the magic of a sparkling palette makes poetical the strong touches of the boldest realism.

Suddenly the news reaches the camp of the Zaporogs, that the Setch has been plundered by the Tartars. The old Bovdug, the Nestor of this second Iliad, proposes a plan which divides the besieging army in such a way as to protect at once the interests and the honor of the Cossack nation. One part sets out in pursuit of the Tartars: the others remain under the walls of the city, with the old Taras as atamán. One would like to quote from beginning to end these lists of heroes, with their Malo-Russian names so nearly uniform in termination. One would like to reproduce these parentheses, these episodes devoted to the complaisant enumeration of the deeds of prowess of all these braves. The separation is marked by a melancholy full of grandeur. The feeling of the solidarity which has grouped all these men, of the brotherhood which unites all these sons of the Ukraïna, is expressed with rare power. Taras perceives that it is necessary to create some diversion for this profound melancholy. He gives his Cossacks the solace of precious wine, and the stimulus of a fortifying word. They drink to religion, the Setch, and glory. "Never will a splendid action perish; and the glory of the Cossacks shall not be lost like a grain of powder dropped from the pan, and fallen by chance."

The battle begins anew; the cannon make

wide gaps in the ranks, and many mothers will not see again their sons fallen this day. "Vainly the widow will stop the passers-by, and gaze into their eyes to see if among them is not found the man whom best she loves in all the world." What an accent in all that, and how we discover in the labored arrangement of the writer, the native force of the primitive song, the depth of the feeling of the people! This arises in fact from the Malo-Russian folk-song; and so also do those challenges which recall those of the heroes of Argos or of Troy, and that sublime death-refrain which each hero murmurs as he dies, "Flourish the Russian soil!" and likewise those rhythmic questions alternating with replies like couplets, "Is there yet powder in the powder-flasks? Is not the Cossack power enfeebled? Do not the Cossacks now show signs of yielding?"—"There still is powder in the powder-flasks; the Cossack power is not enfeebled; the Cossacks do not yet begin to yield."

At the height of the battle, Andriï, who is fighting like a lion at the head of the Poles, finds himself suddenly face to face with Taras

Bulba. Here follows an admirable scene, and long admired, but admired in an imitation. Is not the conclusion of "Mateo Falcone" an invention stolen from Gogol? In the two tales, the father becomes the arbiter of the treason committed by the son; the details of this execution, the accompanying words, the calculated impression of coldness in the account, meant to add to the horror of the deed, — all the resemblances seem to form a literary theft, the traces of which Merimée would have done better not to hide; and we have almost the right to impute to him this intention when we see the part that he took in disparagement of "Taras Bulba."

This tragedy is followed by a new drama still more painful. Ostap is taken prisoner, and carried to Warsaw for execution. Taras, left for dead, is picked up by his followers. He recovers, and, unable to survive his beloved son, goes to risk his life in the attempt to rescue him. Through Yankel's craft he makes his way into Warsaw, but the assistance of the Polish Jews fails to get him within the prison walls. He arrives only in time to see the execution of the Cossacks. Ostap is broken on the wheel before his father's eyes. In a moment of weakness the heroic lad utters the cry of the Crucified on Golgotha: "Father, where art thou? Dost thou hear this?"

"Yes, I hear," replies a mighty voice from the midst of the throng. "A detachment of mounted soldiers hastened anxiously to scan the throng of people. Yankel turned pale as death, and when the horsemen had got a short distance from him, he turned round in terror to look for Taras: but Taras was no longer beside him; every trace of him was lost." A little later on, and Taras has seized his arms, and is making a terrible "funeral mass" in honor of his son. At last he dies, pinned down like Prometheus, and burned alive; but from the midst of the flames he tastes the triumph which his last shout of command has just assured to his soldiers.

V.

WHEN Gogol was spoken of to the great romancer Turgénief, he said simply, "He is our master; from him we get our best qualities." But when Turgénief came to speak of "Taras Bulba," he grew animated, and went on with an accent of admiration which, for my part, I cannot forget, and said, "The day when our Gogol stood the colossal Taras on his feet, he showed genius."

It would have been a very delicate question, to ask Turgénief his opinion of another of Gogol's little masterpieces, "Old-time Proprietors." The question would have seemed indiscreet to the author of "Virgin Soil;" for when this last romance of Turgénief's appeared, all the Russian readers, when they came to the charming chapter where the two old men, Fímushka and Fómushka, come upon the stage, uttered the same cry: "It is Gogol, pure and simple! it is the *Starosvyétskié Pomyéshchiki!*" If the model and the imitation are examined closely, a great quantity of differences in detail are unravelled; and it may be said that here as elsewhere Turgénief is personal, original in his work, in his own fashion. But at first glance one has the right to be struck by the resemblances.

"Old-time Proprietors" is a novel of a number of pages. In this novel there are no intrigue, no abrupt changes, nothing fantastic, no theatrical climaxes, no surprising characters, no unexpected sentiments. Gogol dispensed with all the elements of success: he seems to have wished to reduce the interest to the minimum, and he wrote a masterpiece.

He introduces us to one of those country houses whose appearance alone tells the story of the calm and peaceful life of its inhabitants: "Never had a desire crossed the hedge which shut in the little *dvor.*"

In this habitation of sages, all is friendly, all is kindly, "even to the phlegmatic baying of the dogs." What is to be said of the reception which we meet with at the hands of the owners of the dwelling? The husband, Afanasi Ivanovitch, generally sitting down and bent over, always smiles, whether he be speaking or listening. His wife, Pulkheria Ivanovna, on the other hand, is serious; but there is so much goodness in her eyes and in all of her features, that a smile would be too much, would render insipid her expression of face which is already so sweet.

Afanasi Ivanovitch and Pulkheria Ivanovna had grown up without children: thus they had come to love each other with that affection which is usually reserved for beings in whom one's youthful days seem to bloom anew. Their youth had been full of life, however, like all youth, but it was far away. The husband had served in the army; he had eloped with his sweetheart. But this wild period had been followed by so many days of a calm, secluded, uniform, absolutely happy existence, that they never spoke of the past, and it may be doubted if they ever thought of it either.

These delicious hours are disturbed only by such events as an indigestion, or a pain in the bowels. They are filled only by collations and repasts of greater or less degree. They leave room for no other care than that of varying the bill of fare, of bringing into agreement the most diverse viands, of tempting appetites sated but not satiated.

At first thought, nothing seems more commonplace than such a subject. What poetry, what interest even, could be attached to that complaining belly whose ever-recurring pangs must be lulled to sleep the livelong day and a portion of the night? Herein shines forth all the power of Gogol's talent. He paints egotism for us, double egotism: but he paints it with such delicate shades that the picture excites something more than admiration; it arouses a sort of sympathy.

Gogol knows well that happy people are the best people; that their joy radiates out, as it were, and that it warms, lightens, enlivens, just as sadness, even though legitimate, chills, wounds, warns away, every thing that approaches it. The two old people are happy, not so much by the quality of the pleasures which they taste, or by the value of the goods which they enjoy, as by the assurance which they feel that as long as they live they are not going to see this luxurious abundance disappear, nor these far from ruinous pleasures lose their flavor. Notwithstanding the thefts of the *prikashchik*, of the housekeeper, of the hands, of the visitors, of their coachman, of their valets, "this fertile and beneficent soil produced all things in such quantity, Afanasi Ivanovitch and Pulkheria Ivanovna had so few necessities, that all these depredations could have no injurious effect on their well-being."

These two fortunate people are worshipped for their indulgence, which comes from unconcern; and for their liberality, which takes its rise, if not from the vanity of giving, as La Rochefoucauld would have expressed it, yet at least from the need of feeling further satisfaction, after having taken full enjoyment of what is indispensable, in allowing others to have a certain portion of the superfluous.

In the same way their pity is, above all, a selfish consideration, and a movement of dismay at the idea of falling into such disagreeable or trying situations as they have seen in the cases of others. "Wait," says Afanasi Ivanovitch to each visitor: "we don't know what may happen. Robbers may attack you, or you may meet with rascals." "God protect us from robbers!" said Pulkheria Ivanovna: "why tell such stories when it is night?"

In this association for happiness, which is scarcely any thing else than the joining of two aspirations towards well-being, how did Gogol succeed in bringing about his return to the idea of sacrifice? In point of fact, one of these good old egotists acts to a certain degree in a spirit of self-sacrifice, without ever rising above self-love; becomes partially absorbed in the affection of the companion, who is more indifferent, more inclined to accept fondling without offering return. All love, it has been said, is reduced in last analysis to this: the one kisses, the other offers the cheek. In this case the one who offers the cheek — that is to say, the one who permits the fondling, and limits all manifestations of feeling to not ill-natured but not kindly teasing — is the husband. His wife adores him after her fashion. This adoration it is vain to express in vulgar language, and translate by attentions of far from exalted order: it is real, and it brings to the reader's lips a smile full of indulgence, even at the moment when it compels from the eyes a tear of a rare quality, the discreet witness of the deepest and purest feeling.

This good old woman feels that she is dying; and at the moment when death "comes to take her," she knows only one grief, — that of leaving alone, and, as it were, orphaned, this poor old child for whom she has lived, and who without her will not know what to do with his sad life. With prayers, even with threats, good soul that she is, she intrusts him to a maid-servant old as themselves; and after making all arrangements and dispositions, so that her companion "need not feel too sorely her absence," she goes whither death calls her.

Afanasi Ivanovitch at first is overwhelmed with grief. On his return from the funeral, his solitude comes to him with the sensation of an irreparable void; "and he began to sob bitterly, inconsolably; and the tears flowed, — flowed like two streams from his dull eyes." Is it not striking to find here the expressions of Homer? "He sat down, pouring forth tears like a stream of dark water, which spreads its shady water along the cliff where even the goats do not climb." And is there not here, as in the epic tale of Taras Bulba, the power of the pathetic, the savory freshness of emotion, the secret of which is known only to primitive poetry?

But what is not primitive, what, on the contrary, reveals Gogol as a very well-informed writer, a very watchful psychologist, a satirist whose scheme was well thought out in advance, and whose slightest details are calculated with perfect precision, is the little parable which at the most touching moment of this tale interrupts its thread, and brings out its hidden significance, its moral bearing, its psychological lesson.

Gogol leaves the husband and wife at the very hour of their most touching separation, and tells us rapidly the romance of a young man madly in love with a mistress who is dying. In the effervescence of his grief, the lover twice in succession tries to kill himself: the first time, by a pistol-shot in the head; somewhat later, when he is barely recovered, by throwing himself under the wheel of a passing carriage. Again he recovers; "and a year later," says Gogol, "I met him in a fashionable salon. He was seated at a table, playing *boston*, and was saying in a free and easy tone, 'Little Misery.' Behind him, leaning on his chair, stood his young and pretty wife, toying with the counters in the basket."

The old Afanasi Ivanovitch does not try to kill himself; but he dies slowly day by day from the ever-growing regret for her whom he has lost, from the wound, always more keen and more deep, which has been left in his heart, or, if the expression be preferred, left in his very flesh by the torn cluster of his imperishable habits.

"I have never written from imagination," said Gogol: "it is a talent which I do not possess." "Pushkin," he says in another place, "has hit it right when in speaking of me he declared that he had never known in any other writer an equal gift of making a vivid picture of the miseries of actual life, in sketching with a firm touch the nothingness of a good-for-nothing man." This talent, which will be seen illustrated in such a brilliant way in the great romance of "Dead Souls," already begins to give a striking character to the stories written by Gogol about St. Petersburg. Here he describes in a most fascinating way the mortifications, the humiliations, the tortures even, which he had felt or anticipated at the time of the painful beginning of his literary career, and his wearisome sojourn in the bureaucracy.

"The Portrait," for example, is a fantastic tale which is distinguished from the stories of the former collection by a satiric accent full of bitterness. It is the account of a painter kept in the depths of wretchedness just as long as he takes his art seriously. A happy chance places in his hands a sum of money which allows him to engage rooms on the Nevsky Prospekt. He allows trickery to usurp the place of work. He grows rich from the day when he loses his talent: however, the feeling of having deserted his ideal follows him like remorse, and this remorse leads him straight to madness.

"The Cloak" is the story of a small official, gentle, conscientious, but timid, slow, and absent-minded. The poor devil has a fixed purpose, — the purchase of a cloak to keep him from the cold. This never-to-be-realized idea finally unsettles his somewhat feeble brain.

It is noticeable that the most lugubrious refrains serve for the conclusion of these different moral analyses. "The recollections of a Lunatic," known in France under the title "Les Mémoires d'un Fou," take the reader one step farther into this region of mental trouble, which is explored with a boldness truly disquieting. Involuntarily one thinks of the author's own final insanity; and the tale has the effect of a prelude, or at least of a prognostication.

At the risk of repetition, I lay especial emphasis upon this evolution which took place in the mind and in the work of Nikolaï Gogol. In the "Evenings at the Farm," the satirical note scarcely appears, except in a few details; it is found tempered, and as it were refreshed, by a pure breath of poetry; Nature spoke there almost as much as man, and she spoke a language of very penetrating sweetness and of superb grandeur. In the novels on St. Petersburg, satire has already entirely usurped her place. There is added, to be sure, an element of fancy, and of caprice, which is no longer the poetry of the first novels, but which still draws on the imagination; a troubled, unregulated imagination, which in Gogol shows a physical and moral state sufficiently akin to the hyperæsthesia of seers, of the insane. This period of excitement is followed by several years of rather morose observation and contemplation, during which Gogol writes or plans for his two great works, the comedy of "The *Revizor*," and the romance of "The Dead Souls." Here we are in full satire, and the satire is fully in the domain of reality,—reality often vulgar, and sometimes odious. The author paints only what he sees; and if amid the objects of his contemplation, and his keen pitiless glance, there passes often as it were a shade of illusion, it is only a gloomy illusion, a reflection of melancholy obscuring the real day, and making the colors of things more sombre, the aspect of men more pitiable.

It is not that the romance of "The Dead Souls," and especially the comedy of "The *Revizor*," have not details, or even whole scenes, which are very amusing. There is no satire without gayety; and Gogol understands how to indulge in raillery, that is to say, how to make fun at the expense of another, as perfectly as any satirist that ever lived. But never was laughter more bitter than his, and it never came nearer the ancient definition, "*cachinnus perfidum ridens.*" This bitterness of style is only too well explained by a morbid state of mind, the first manifestations of which can be traced back even to Gogol's infancy, while its tragic end was madness.

VI.

THE comedy of "The *Revizor*" (The Inspector-General) is therefore a satire, — a satire on Russian functionaryism. The action takes place in a small provincial city. The *tchinovniks* of the district have met at the mayor's, for news has just been brought of the approaching visit of the *revizor*. "What can you expect?" asks the mayor[1] with a sigh: "it is a judgment from God! Hitherto it has fallen on other cities. It is our turn now."

Like a prudent man, he has taken his measures, and he advises the other employees to do likewise. "You," he says to the director of the hospital, — "you will do well to take pains that every thing is on a good footing. . . . Let 'em put on white cotton nightcaps, and don't allow the patients to look like chimney-sweeps as they usually do. — And you," he says to

[1] *Gorodnitchi.*

the doctor, "you must look out that each bed has its label in Latin, or some other language. . . . And it would be better not to have so many patients, for they won't fail to throw the blame on the administration." The director of the hospital explains the method of treatment which is adopted. No costly medicines: man is a simple being; if he dies, he dies; if he recovers, he recovers. Besides, any other method would be scarcely practicable with a German doctor who does not understand Russian, and consequently cannot tell at all what his patients say.

"You," he says to the justice of the peace, "pay attention to your tribunal! Your boy brings his geese into your great hall, and they come quacking between the legs of the plaintiffs. . . . And your audience-chamber looks like — the Devil knows what! a horsewhip in the midst of briefs! and the assessor, who always exhales an odor as though he had just come out of a distillery!" But the most serious part of the matter is the rumors of corruption. "A trifle," replies the justice: "a few greyhounds as presents." And he immediately returns allusion for allusion: "Ah! I did not say that if some one had presented me with a five-hundred-ruble *shuba,* and a shawl for my wife" — The mayor interrupts warmly, with that tone of hypocrisy so common to the Russian *tchinovnik,* "That's all right! Do you know why you take presents of dogs? It's because you don't believe in God. You never go to church. I at least have some religion: Fridays I go to mass. But you — Ah! I know you well. When you begin to descant on the way the world was made, your hair stands up on your head.

"And you," he says to the principal of the college, — "you watch over your professors. Their actions are suspicious; there is one who so far forgets himself in his chair as to put his fingers behind his cravat, and to scratch his chin: it is not necessary to teach the young habits of independence." The postmaster remains. The mayor urges him to open a few letters, so as to assure himself that there are no denunciations. "You need not teach me my trade," replies the postmaster: "I have nothing else to do." In fact, it is his daily amusement: he could not do without this reading. Some letters are as well composed as the Moscow journals. He has at this very moment in his pocket a young lieutenant's letter, — reminiscences of a ball, an elegant description. The mayor begs him to hold back every petition of complaint. "There's nothing to fear any other way. It would be a different thing if this were generally the custom; but it's just a little family affair, the way we do it."

Two loungers of the place,[1] two self-important bustlers, in their eager rivalry of tittle-tattle and gossip, run up all out of breath, and, after a great deal of desultory talk, are delivered of the great news. He has come, the government *tchinovnik*, the *revizor;* he saw them eating salmon at the hotel; he cast a terrible look at their plates. "*Akh!* God in heaven," cries the mayor; "have pity upon us, miserable offenders!"

And here follows a general confession, a recapitulation of the most recent sins of moment: an under-officer's wife whipped, prisoners deprived of their rations, wine-shops established in

[1] Bobtchinski and Dobtchinski by name.

open defiance of the law, the streets not swept. "How old is he? He's a young man; then there's more hope than with an old devil. Quick! orders, measures; and let us get ahead of him. My hat! my sword! but the sword is ruined.

"That cursed hatter! He sees that the mayor has an old sword, and does not send him a new one. What a pack of villains! *Akh!* my fine fellows! I am perfectly sure they have their complaints all ready, and that they will rise up right out of the cobble-stones. Let everybody take hold of the street. The Devil take the street! Fetch me a broom, I say, and have the street cleaned in front of the hotel; and let it be well done. — Listen! Take care there, *you!* I know you well. You put on a saintly look, and yet you hide the silver spoons in your boots. You look out! Don't you dare to stir me up! What kind of a job did you concoct at the tailor's? He gave you two arshins of cloth to make you a uniform, and you gobbled up the whole piece. Attention! You steal too much for your rank."

That phrase has taken its place among the

popular proverbs in Russia, and our Molière has not many more pointed. Exactly as in Molière, the situation is spun out and renewed with a liveliness which suffers no loss of force. On the mayor's lips, command follows command; ideas crowd upon one another; words get tripped up; exclamations of fury, of terror, fly out; the note of hypocrisy mingles with his main characteristic, the violence of which forces its way to the surface under false appearances. And this inward trouble is rendered visible, as it were, by stage tricks, not free from vulgarity, but extremely amusing. "You have the hat-box in your hand: here is your hat." All this forms a rude, rough, but new and irresistible element of comedy.

The personage who thus sets a whole city by the ears is a poor devil, himself in a peck of trouble. Kléstakof has left Petersburg, where he is a small official, in order to spend his vacation in the province. On the way he has gambled, has emptied his pockets, and he is waiting for his father to send him a fresh supply of funds to pay travelling expenses and the landlord's bill. We learn all these details from his valet Osip. He it is who, in his description of the situation, gives us the key to his master's character. "One day he lives like a lord, the next he perishes with starvation. But we must have carriages. Every day he sends me to get theatre-tickets. This lasts a week, and then he tells me to bring him his new suit of clothes from the nail. A suit costs him a hundred and fifty rubles. He spends twenty rubles for a waistcoat. I won't answer for the trousers: it's impossible to tell what that amounts to. And the wherefore of all this? the wherefore? I will tell you. He does not attend to his business; he goes for a walk on the *Presh-pektive* (the Nevsky Prospekt). He plays his game. *Akh!* if the old gentleman knew all this business, he would not bother his head whether his son held a place in government: he would take off his shirt, and give him such a drubbing as would warm him up for a week."

In this comedy of "The *Revizor*," the valet Osip fills a comic *rôle* quite like that of the fool in Shakspeare, or the *gracioso* in the Spanish comedy. The Russian buffoon, however, is a clown rather than a joker. He does not enliven the scene with jests: he makes the spectator split his sides by his artless blunders. This smacks of farce, and may seem overdone. But exaggeration in this way is not in the power of every one. It is the splendid fault of Aristophanes, and even of Molière. Let us remember what Fénelon, La Bruyère, and Rousseau said of it. And after all, in spite of the famous definition, is it not the greatest triumph of the comic poet to make the fastidious laugh, and especially smile? An excellent actor of our own time defined the great comedian as one who has only to show his grimace at the opening of a door, to make the whole public shout with laughter. Are not the author and the actor of genius told by the same characteristic? Have not both of them the secret of this grimace?

To return to the analysis of the piece: Klés-takof scolds his valet because he no longer dares to report the traveller's complaints at the office. The landlord treats this stranger as a man who does not pay his bills. After many negotiations he permits him to have some dish-water as apology for soup, and some burned sole-leather in place of the roast. Amid the vociferations wrung from him by such an outrage, Kléstakof beholds Osip returning to announce a call from the mayor. He imagines that the official has come in order to put him in arrest, with which he was threatened only a few moments since; and he endeavors immediately to exonerate himself in the mayor's eyes. His explanations, enigmatical for the still more anxious visitor, clear only for the reader or the audience, have no other effect than to increase the terror of the high functionary, who thinks that he is in the presence of a crafty inspector-general. In the incoherent remarks, full of ingenuous confessions, which the little *tchinovnik* makes to him, the mayor hears only certain portentous words, — the prison, the minister. He is only half re-assured when the conversation offers him a chance to proffer some money and insist on its acceptance.

Kléstakof finally blurts out how matters really stand. "I am here, and I have not a kopek." The mayor sees in this avowal only a further illustration of cunning. He immediately offers his services. The stranger borrows two hundred rubles of him. "Take it," he says eagerly; "don't trouble to count it, it isn't worth while:" and instead of two hundred rubles, he slips four hundred into his hand. And now behold our two sharpers delighted to find themselves so easily in agreement. Kléstakof suspects that there is some misunderstanding, but he takes pains not to say a word which may bring about an explanation. The mayor thinks that he can detect, under Kléstakof's ambiguous actions, an immensely profound plan. "He wants his *incognito* respected. Two can play that game. Let us make believe not know who he is." While the traveller's baggage is transported to a place more worthy of him, — that is, to the mayor's own dwelling, — they drive off in a drozhsky to visit the college and the hospital. They hastily turn their backs on the prison, which offers not the slightest attraction for Kléstakof. "What's the good of seeing the prison? It would be much better to give our attention to institutions of beneficence!"

Here we are now in the mayor's house. They are waiting for Kléstakof; and the entrance of this important personage is very well led up to by two or three scenes of chattering, in which the voices of the mayor's wife and daughter are dominant. At last he appears, followed by the mayor and other *tchinovniks* of the district. They have just returned from visiting the hospital; that is to say, from enjoying a bounteous collation at the superintendent's. The ice is broken: tongues are unloosed; Kléstakof's performs wonders.

First come the exquisite courtesies of the introduction, then the expatiation on the charms of the capital; and instantly there begins a series of inventions grafted by Kléstakof one upon the other.

Here is the summing-up which loses the devil-possessed movement, but not the comic value of the scene.

At the ministry, Kléstakof is the intimate of the *direktor;* on the street, he is recognized as he is out walking; the soldiers leave the guard-house, and present arms; at the theatre, he frequents the green-room; he composes vaudevilles; he is the friend of Pushkin, "that great original;"[1] he writes for the magazines; he

[1] He says that he addresses Pushkin by the familiar pronoun *tui* (thou).

wrote the articles on the "Marriage of Figaro," "Robert le Diable," "Norma." It is he who writes under the signature of the Baron de Brambeus. A book is mentioned: "I wrote it;" the daughter objects that it bears on the title-page the name of Iuri Miloslavski; he replies to the objection [by declaring that there is another book by the same name, which he wrote]. The balls which he gives at Petersburg are marvellous beyond description; he collects around his whist-table the minister of foreign affairs, the ambassadors of France and of Germany. From time to time a glimpse of the truth shines through this tissue of improvised boastings, but he leisurely recalls the phrase imprudently uttered. His importance increases at every new effort of his imagination. Once he had been offered the direction of the ministry: he would have been glad to decline, but what would the Emperor have said? Therefore he accepts the office, and with what hands! He inspires everybody with awe; all bow in the dust before him; the council of state trembles at sight of him; at a moment's notice he will be made field-marshal.

The adventurer would not make any end of speaking, did not intoxication become a factor, and cut short his flow of words. The *tchinovniks*, whose dismay has reached the highest pitch, respectfully assist him to leave the dining-room, to sleep off the effects of his glory and his wine on a bed in a neighboring room. "Charming young man!" say the mayor's wife and daughter in chorus. "Terrible man!" declares the mayor, in an anxious and dubious tone, for he has detected in all this braggadocio some grains of falsehood. "But how can one speak of any thing without a little prevarication? The certain thing is that he makes fools of the ministers, that he goes to court." And while the false *revizor* is snoring peacefully, taking his mid-day nap, they turn to his valet Osip as a make-shift. He also unflinchingly receives flatteries, compliments, and fees.

But now follows the truly new and powerful part of this bold satire. How to wheedle the ferocious inspector? Is he a man to accept money? This attempt at corruption may lead to Siberia. The justice essays the risk with fear and trembling. The bank-note which he held in his hand slips out. To his great dismay, he sees the *revizor* make a dash for the note; to his great delight, he hears the words, "You would do me great pleasure by lending me this." — "Why, certainly, only too much honor." And discreetly he allows another to take his place.

The postmaster enters in great style, and assumes his most official attitude. Kléstakof cuts short the formalities of the interview: "Could you not lend me three hundred rubles?" A new and eager acquiescence; a new and still more eager disappearance.

The college principal appears: Kléstakof, now in good humor, offers him a cigar, indulges in rollicking conversation, all of which completely dumbfounds the poor man's brain, which is already full of perplexity. But a new forced loan of three hundred rubles is accomplished in four words; and the principal takes to his heels, crying, "God have mercy, he has not visited my classes yet!"

The director of the hospitals has hoped to whiten himself at the expense of the other *tchinovniks*. He has brought against them a complaint which our adventurer has but to take action upon. The false *revizor* consents that all the details should be transcribed for him. What the director does not think to proffer is the sum of four hundred rubles; but this is finally demanded of him, and paid over without a word.

It is more difficult to extract a little money from the two gossips who were the first to discover, in the traveller at the inn, the stuff of which an inspector-general is made. This devil of a man nevertheless has the skill to extort a little something from them. They are not *tchinovniks*, to be sure, but how gayly they swell the ranks of the procession! Gogol justifies their visit in showing them up in the capacity of petitioners. The one wants to legitimize a bastard son of his, "born, so to speak, in wedlock," and consequently half legitimate. The other would like to have his name mentioned, on some suitable occasion, before the court and the Emperor: "nothing but these words, 'in such and such a village lives such and such a person;' yes, nothing more,— 'such an one lives in such a village.'"

This train of *tchinovniks* has its counterpart full of eloquent, and even melancholy, humor. Kléstakof has just finished counting his money; he finds the part easy to play, and full of profit. But Osip, whose dull head contains more sense than his master's giddy pate, advises him to have his post-horses put in, and to pack off while yet there is time. Kléstakof admits that his reasoning is good; still, the farce is so pleasant that he cannot refrain from writing to one of his friends, a Petersburg journalist. It is easy to conjecture that this letter will never reach its destination, and that it will serve to bring about the *dénoûment*.

Suddenly voices are heard outside the house. It is the merchants, the hatter at their head, coming to bring their complaints before the *revizor*. The mayor steals from them shamelessly: when they complain, he slams the door in your face, saying, "I will not apply the knout, for that's against the law; but I will make you eat humble pie." A woman comes, complaining that her husband had been forcibly conscripted as a soldier, in place of two others who had escaped service through the aid of bribes. "Your husband is a thief: he is already, or he will be," — that is the excuse offered her by this "blackguard of a mayor."

But it is a real inspector-general's business to perform the functions of his office. Kléstakof has enjoyed the profits, and thinks that he can confine his duties to that. At this moment the sick appear in their hospital dressing-gowns, fever and pestilence in their faces: the false *revizor* rudely drives away all this importunate throng, and shuts the door fast.

In happy contrast to the lugubrious impression of these scenes, the author introduces some inventions of charming buffoonery. The mayor's daughter enters. To beguile the time, Kléstakof makes love to her, kisses her, falls on his knees before her. The mother appears, and expresses her astonishment — but in the fashion of Bélise, in the "Femmes Savantes;" such homage as that is befitting. The daughter departs after a sharp reprimand. The extempore lover, now addressing the mother, continues the wooing which he had begun with the daughter, who returns just as he throws himself on his knees for the second time. The mayor comes in unexpectedly, and almost chokes with surprise to hear an inspector-general ask for his daughter's hand. How can he deny himself such an honor? The agreement is made on the spot, and the two lovers fall into each other's arms.

Just at this moment the valet Osip comes, and, twitching his master by the tail of his coat, announces that the horses are ready. The adventurer, recalled to reality, ventures a brief explanation: a very wealthy uncle to visit, a day's journey distant. The post-chaise departs; and the act ends with the postilion's command to his horses, "Off with you, on wings!"

The *dénoûment* has been unnecessarily anticipated. It has a gayety, a dash, a variety in its detail, which make it amusing, fascinating, rich in surprises. Nevertheless it is only the identical *dénoûment* of our "Misanthrope," the all-revealing letter in which each character of the drama receives his share of epigrams. Gogol's humor is given free play in this series of rapidly sketched portraits, the originals of which are united around the reader, who is spared no more than the rest. The development of the idea has an inexhaustible *verve;* but the idea itself belongs to Molière, and Mérimée long ago ascribed to him all the honor of it.

What belongs to Gogol, what gives the *dénoûment* of "The *Revizor*" an original coloring, is the mayor's comic fury at finding that he has been cheated in such a fine fashion. His new title of father-in-law of an inspector-general had already begun to exalt him, to intoxicate him. He has crushed the merchants with it. He has overwhelmed them with the lightning of his glance. He has dismissed them with one of those deep phrases, such as paint the Russian *tchinovnik* with his redoubtable hypocrisy: "God commands us to forgive: I have no spite against you. You will only be good enough to remember that I am giving my daughter in marriage, and not to the first noble that comes along. Endeavor to have your congratulations suitable to the occasion. Don't expect to get off with a smoked salmon or a sugar-loaf. Do you hear me? Go, and God protect you!" The sly old dog has already begun to dream of a general's epaulets: it can be seen how he is puffed up; he receives with the air of a prince the unctuous compliments of the other *tchinovniks.* Suddenly the pail of milk falls, and the milk is spilt; the balloon bursts! In all that comes to pass, there is only sheer comedy; a skilful sharper, and duped rascals. The one who is most duped of all, the mayor, gives himself up to a storm of the most amusing frenzy. "You great fool!" he says to himself, pounding himself, "idiot! you have taken a dish-clout for a great personage! And this very moment he is galloping off down the road to the sound of the bells. He will tell the story to everybody. Worse than all, he will find some penny-a-liner, some scribbler, to cover you with ridicule! Behold the disgrace of it! He will not spare your rank or your office, and he will find people to applaud him with their voices and their hands. You laugh? Laugh at yourselves, yes. [He stamps with passion.] If I only had 'em! these scribblers! Cursed liberals! Spawn of the Devil! I'd put a bit on 'em! I'd put a curb on 'em! I'd crush the whole brood-of 'em."

And behold what adds a still keener flavor to this adventure.

At the very moment when the mayor, out of his wits at having been capable of mistaking this fop for an inspector-general, is trying to find the one who egged him on to commit this blunder, a policeman enters, and says, "You are requested to repair instantly to the *revizor*, who has come on a mission from Petersburg. He has just arrived at the hotel." The whole company are, as it were, thunderstruck; and the curtain falls on a scene of silence, the arrangement of which Gogol provided for with the minute accuracy of a realistic writer, for whom attitudes and facial expression are the indispensable complement of a moral painting. In point of fact, they are, especially at times when a lively emotion tears away all masks, the faithful and legible translation of character.

VII.

AFTER having laid bare the vices of the Russian administration, in his satiric comedy of "The *Revizor*," Gogol attacked the social question in his romance of the "Dead Souls." He set himself to work at the very moment when the Tsar Nicolas, in a liberal humor, proclaimed in a *ukaz* of prodigious power the principle of the abolition of serfage. Unhappily this liberal policy of the throne was not strong enough to hold its own before the dissatisfaction of the higher classes: the decree was not put into effect. But the impulse was given, and Gogol's satire once more became the echo of the popular feeling.

The very title of the romance was a satiric touch, the significance of which could not escape a Russian, but which for a French reader needs rather a long explanation. At the time of serfdom, a Russian proprietor's fortune was not valued according to the extent of his lands, but according to the number of male serfs which were held upon them. These serfs were called "souls" (*dushi*). The owner of a thousand souls was a great proprietor; the owner of a hundred souls was only a beggarly country squire. The proprietor paid the capitation tax for all the souls on his domain; but, as the census was rarely taken, it happened that he had long to pay for dead serfs, until a new official revision struck them out from among the number of the living. It is easy to see what these dead souls must have cost a proprietor whose lands had been visited by famine, cholera, or any other scourge; and his interest in getting rid of them will be explicable.

What seems more surprising is, that there were people ready to purchase them. But here, again, it is sufficient to lessen the strangeness of the fact, if we accompany it with a simple explanation. There was in Russia, at the time to which Gogol's novel transports us, a sort of bank, established and supported by the State, and directed by the managing boards of certain institutions for orphan boys and girls, deaf-mutes, and others. This bank borrowed money at four per cent, and loaned on deposits. Here a man could pawn his personal property, or mortgage his real estate and his peasants up to ten thousand souls, say at two hundred rubles a head; in other words, up to two million rubles. Here is a reason why the hero of Gogol's romance, Tchitchikof, a former customs officer, dismissed for embezzlement, purchases dead souls. He hopes some day to possess a sufficient number to populate an out-of-the-way estate in a distant province of the empire, and to pawn this domain to the State for a sum large enough to permit him to go and live in grand style abroad.

As can be seen, the motive of the book has lost its point since the abolition of serfage, and this motive never was very interesting except for Russian readers. But this motive serves Gogol only as a piquant pretext for a series of studies of provincial life in Russia. These studies have an originality, a variety, and sometimes a force, so great that it is to be feared lest our analysis can give only a very feeble notion of it.

The hero of "Dead Souls" is a veritable hero of a realistic romance; that is to say, he has nothing which justifies the title of hero. He is neither handsome nor ugly, neither fat nor lean, neither stiff nor pliant; he cannot any longer be taken for a young man. He is more prudent than courageous, more ambitious than honorable, more obsequious than dignified, more scrupulous of his bearing than of his conduct; at once capable of trickery, and guilty of heedlessness; without talent, but not without expedients; with no foundation of goodness, but not without some small change of benevolence; without conscience, but not lacking a certain varnish of decency and gravity. This characterless[1] personage is brought out in a sort of relief by the very frame in which the author has ingeniously placed him. Tchitchikof travels across the province; and Gogol does not separate him from what is his indispensable accompaniment in his outlandish Odyssey, — I mean from his coach, his horses, and his servants.

Petrushka, his lackey, is a blockhead of

[1] *Effacé.*

thirty summers, with a big nose, thick lips, coarse features, and with a skin exhaling an odor *sui generis* which clings to every thing that comes in his vicinity. He speaks rarely, and reads as much as possible; but little difference makes it to him, what the nature of the book may be. He does not bother his head with the subject. "What pleased him was not what he read: it was the mere act of reading. It did not trouble him to see that he was eternally coming upon words the meaning of which the deuce alone knows."

The coachman, Selifan, is a little man, as talkative as Petrushka is silent. He fills the long hours of the journey across the deserted steppe or the monotonous cultivated fields, with monologues laughable in their variety. For the most part, he addresses his incoherent discourse to his horses. With his reproaches, sometimes accompanied by a blow of the whip under the belly or across the ears, he stirs up "Spot," a huge trickster, harnessed on the right for draught, who makes believe pull so that one would think that he was doing himself great injury, but in reality he is not pulling at all. The bay, on the contrary, is a very "respectable" horse: he does his work conscientiously; as does also the light sorrel, surnamed the Assessor because he was bought of a justice. The coachman, Selifan, who understands the spirit of his animals, finds no subject too lofty for their comprehension. He quotes their master's example, who is a man to be respected because he has been in government service, because he is a college councillor;[1] and when once he enters into these abstract and subtile considerations about duty, he goes so far, he soars so high, that he regularly gets lost in the confusing network of Russian roads, and sometimes he finishes his discussion in the bottom of a slough.

As to the carriage, it also has its strange physiognomy, and, so to speak, its national stamp. It is the britchka, with leather flaps fortified with two round bull's-eyes; the britchka, whose postilion, not booted in the German fashion, but simply with his huge beard and his mittens, seated on no one knows what,

[1] *Kollezhsky sovyetnik*, the ninth rank in the civil *tchin*, giving personal nobility.

whistles, brandishes his whip, shouts his song, and makes his team fly over the trembling earth.

In this equipage Tchitchikof reaches the village of N——. He introduces himself to the mayor, to the vice-mayor, to the fiscal attorney, to the *natchalnik* of the court, to the chief of police, to the *vodka*-farmer, to the general director of the crown works. His politeness, his flattering words skilfully accommodated to each of these gentlemen, his air of concern in presence of the ladies, immediately give him the reputation of being a man of the best tone. He is overwhelmed with invitations; he makes his first appearance in the fine society of N—— on the occasion of a party given by the mayor. The throng of functionaries is divided into two classes, — the "slenders" (*fluets*), who hover like butterflies around the ladies, jargon gayly in French, and in three years succeed in mortgaging all their paternal property to the *Lombard;* and secondly the "solids" (*gros*), who *thesaurize* without making any stir, buy estates in the name of their wives, and some fine day go into retirement, so as to go and live like village proprietors, like true Russian *barins*, until their heirs, who are generally the "slenders," come to take possession of the inheritance, and make a single mouthful of it.

In this somewhat monotonous throng, Tchitchikof's attention is attracted by two country gentlemen, — Manilof, a Russian *Philinte*, extremely fair-spoken, assiduous, and sensitive; and Sabakévitch, a colossus of brusque manners, of laconic speech. Both of them invite the new-comer to honor with his presence their dwellings, which are only a few versts distant. Here the novelist's plan becomes apparent. He is going to take his hero and his readers from visit to visit, through all the households of these provincial proprietors, whose foibles he intends to make sport of, and whose vices he intends to scourge. And what the traveller's business will bring under our observation in his peregrinations, will be the condition of the serfs under different masters, — a precarious and ill-regulated condition under the best, lamentable under those who are bad. Thus the importance of the literary value in the romance of the "Dead Souls," whatever it may be, fades before the political and social aim of the conception. Or, rather, here may be seen the new and durable character which Gogol impressed upon the national romance. He applied that form in which fancy reigns to the real description of Russian life: that is to say, he devoted it to the portraying of those abuses of every sort in which the Russian is still, to a certain degree, swaddled; to the expression of the sufferings under which the thinking class, more oppressed to-day than the serfs of yore, feel themselves more and more crushed; finally, to the translation of all those obscure but insistent desires, those vague but ardent aspirations, which are summed up in the old Muscovite cry "Forward!" repeated to-day in a whisper, from one end of the country to the other, like a watchword.

The first household which Gogol brings us to visit, in company with the purchaser of dead souls, is that of the Manilof family. At the very approach to the village of Manilovka, you begin to feel an impression of vulgarity, of vapidness, and of *ennui*. The country is poor, but it does not exclude pretentiousness: in the bottom is a greenish pond, like a billiard-cloth, and on the higher part of the rising ground a few atrophied birches. Under two of these decrepit and consumptive trees stands an arbor with flat roof, with green painted lattice-work, the entrance of which is made by two little pillars with a pediment, on which can be read the inscription: "*Temple de la méditation solitaire.*"

The frame is entirely appropriate to the characters. Manilof is a pale blonde, with eyes blue as faïence. "His ever-smiling face, his ever-sugared words, make you say at first, 'What a good and amiable man!' The next minute you will not say any thing; and the third you ask yourself, 'What the deuce is this man, anyway?'" Above all, he is a man weary of life. He has not a passion, or a hobby, or a fault. He has nothing decisive in his character. At one time he was in the service; and he left in the army the reputation of being a very gentle officer, but a "spendthrift of Levant tobacco." After returning to his estate, he allowed the management of it to go as chance would have it. "When one of his peasants came to find him, and said, scratching the nape of his neck, '*Barin*, let me go and find some work so as to earn enough to pay my *obrok* (quit-rent);'—'All right, go ahead!' he replied, drawing a full whiff from his pipe; and he did not take the trouble to think that this man wanted to get out of his sight so as to have a better chance to indulge in his habits of drunkenness." Manilof himself is continually plunged in a sort of somnolent revery which is like intoxication of the mind. His thoughts do not emerge from the embryonic state, but they come back with the persistence of the fixed idea in the brain of a man who has no ideas. His bureau always has the same book open at the same place. The parlor of his house was hung round with silk and luxuriously furnished many years ago. It has always lacked two arm-chairs, "which aren't done yet;" and this has been so since the first days of his marriage. A bronze candelabrum, which is an object of art, has as a pendant a wretched copper candlestick, out of shape, humpbacked, soiled with tallow.

This disorder disturbs no one in the house.

Manilof and his wife are enchanted with every thing, — with themselves, with their children, with their neighbors, with the city of N——. Every *tchinovnik* is the "most distinguished, the most lovable, the most honorable of men." People so prone to admiration and to praise melt into gush at the visit of their guest. He, in his turn, praises Manilof's merits to the skies, goes into ecstasies over the precocious intelligence of their two sons Alcides and Themistocles; and when he has charmed them all by his delicate attentions, he takes Manilof aside, and asks if he has lost many peasants since the last census. The proprietor, in great perplexity as to what answer to give, summons his *prikashchik*, formerly a peasant, who has cut his beard and thrown his kaftan to the winds, a great friend of the feather-bed and fine down foot-warmers, godfather or relative of all the big-wigs of the village, a tyrant over the poor devils whom he loads down with fees and tasks. The chubby old fellow, who gets up at eight o'clock in the morning, and who gets up simply to put his red-copper *samovar* on the table, and then to tipple his tea like a gourmand for an hour and a half, has no greater knowledge than his master about the insignificant question of the mortality of the serfs. "The number of the dead? That's something we don't take note of. How's that?—the number of the dead? No one has had the idea of counting them, naturally."

Tchitchikof asks to have an exact list made out, with the names, surnames, nicknames, dates of birth, color of eyes, tints of hair. When the *prikashchik* has gone, Tchitchikof comes to the delicate explanation. At first Manilof takes his guest to be crazy; but his face has nothing about it that is not re-assuring. He still hesitates, in the fear of some illegality. The purchaser dispels this fear. The bill of sale will not say any thing about dead souls. "Dead? Never! We will have them entered as living; they are so inscribed on the official registers. No one shall ever induce me to break the law. I respect it. I have suffered enough from my uprightness during my career as a *tchinovnik*. Duty first, the law above all things. That's the kind of man I am, and I shall die the same. When the law speaks, there must be no objections!" Manilof is therefore re-assured; and when he is convinced that the crown has only to gain by this exchange of property, even though it be fictitious, he offers all his dead souls for nothing. He would like to have many other occasions to show his new friend "all the drawing of his heart, all the magnetism of his soul." The friend takes his departure, promising the precocious children some toys; and "when the cloud of dust raised by the britchka had drifted away, Manilof came into the house again, sat down, and abandoned himself to the sweet thought that he had shown his crony a perfect amiability, such as might have been expected from his eminently benevolent and complaisant soul."

Not all his negotiations come to this successful issue with such ease. In driving over to the house of the laconic giant Sabakévitch, the equipage gets off the track, and the carriage is overturned directly in front of a country-house where an old Russian lady, Mrs. Karabotchka, lives. As in the case of Manilof, the appearance of the landscape in some degree gives the clew to the character of the native. The landscape is little else than a nest for poultry. Fowls of every sort fill the court-yard, behind which stretch vegetable-gardens, variegated here and there with fruit-trees protected by great webs of thread. Amid this vulgarly utilitarian nature, rises a pole which ends in a bar shaped like a cross; and on the arm of this cross is nailed a nightdress, surmounted by a damaged bonnet belonging to "the lady and mistress of all this property."

Tchitchikof does not waste so much politeness upon Nastasia Petrovna (these are the lady's given names) as upon Manilof. He is Russian; that is to say, he possesses in perfection all those shades of speech and all those different intonations by which it is possible to show the one with whom you are speaking, veneration, respect, deference, esteem, vulgar consideration, disdainful familiarity, and, descending still lower, all degrees of patronage, even to the extreme limit of scorn. Accordingly he opens his project in free-and-easy style. But the proposition shocks the worthy woman. "What do you want to do with my dead?" she asks, fixing upon him two great eyes streaked with yellow saffron. She suspects some shrewd trick in this business; and her obstinacy, characteristic of the narrow-minded but calculating *baba*, finally exasperates the purchaser, who gets carried away, pounds the floor with a cane-seated chair within his reach, and to the old woman's horror mingles the name of the Devil in his furious exclamations. These violent actions, however, have less effect than a promise deftly introduced into the conversation: "I wanted to buy of you your various farm products[1] because I have charge of various crown contracts." This mention of the crown brings the old blockhead to terms. "*Nu*, yes, I consent. I am ready to sell them for fifty paper rubles. Only look, my father, at that question of supplies. If it happens you want rye-flour or buckwheat, or grits, or slaughtered neats, then please don't forget me." One good turn deserves another. The contract is instantly drawn up; and Mrs. Karabotchka, seeing her guest fetch forth from his travelling outfit a supply of newly stamped

[1] *Khozyaistvennuie produktui.*

paper, arranges to have him leave a package for five rubles in case of necessity.'[1]

All this comedy would be well worth translating word for word. The situation already treated in the preceding canto is here renewed with consummate art. The characters are developed in broad light: the contrasts are forcibly brought out; the drawing is full of freedom in its requisite vulgarity; the coloring is full of brilliancy in its rather trivial boldness. This country scene is itself enclosed between two capital bits of narration, opening and ending the chapter or canto with a symmetry of the most skilful effect.

At the beginning of the episode comes the soliloquy of Selifan the coachman, with his horses, already mentioned; the britchka's wan-

[1] "'*Akhti!* what nice stamped paper you have!' continued she, gazing at him, at his portfolio. And, indeed, there was not much stamped paper to be had then. 'If you would only let me have a sheet! I need it so much. It happens sometimes I want to write a petition to the court, and I haven't any thing fit to write on.'

"Tchitchikof explained to her that this paper was not of that kind; that it was designed for drawing up contracts in regard to serfs, and not for petitions. However, in order to accommodate her, he let her have a few sheets for a ruble" (not five rubles, as M. Dupuy translates it, mistaking the word meaning *price* for *five*). — N. H. D.

derings in a pouring rain, across roads torn up by the storm; finally the catastrophe which sends the whole equipage to the bottom of a ditch into the mud.

At the end of the canto we have the britchka's return guided by a little girl of the neighborhood, a sort of wild Indian with bare legs literally shod with fresh mire. Selifan drives his team with a silent care which makes a pointed contrast with his loquacious spirit the day before. The horses, especially the mottled one, miss his discourses; for he substitutes for them a hail-storm of treacherous goads in the fat, pulpy, soft, delicate, and sensitive portions of their bodies. At last, when the carriage has emerged from the region of mud, and has passed all these roads, running, in every sense of the word, "like crawfish at market when they are allowed to escape from the bag;" and when the coachman has reached the highway, and caught a glimpse of the public house, "he reined in his team, helped the little maiden to dismount, and, as he helped her, he looked at her for the first time. He muttered between his teeth, 'What muddy legs! hu! hu! hu! all the way from here home, she will soil the clean grass!' Tchitchikof gave the little maiden a copper coin, about two kopeks: she turned her back quick as a flash, and off she went, starting with five or six mad gambols; she was enchanted at the splendid gift, still more enchanted at having been allowed to sit on the coach-box of the britchka."

At the public house Tchitchikof falls in with a character whom he has already met at the crown solicitor's at dinner, where his familiarity surprises him, less, however, than his skill at cards, and the suspicious way in which the other players watch his fingers. He is a terrible braggart, and he carries off the traveller willy-nilly. Once again the domain resembles the owner. Nozdref is a great hand for going to fairs, a mighty tippler, a mighty gambler, a mighty liar, or, as they say in Russia of these impudent improvisers, "a mighty maker of bullets." He is always ready to sell all his possessions at a bargain. He sometimes wins at play, and he spends his gains in purchases of every sort. The booths at the fairs in a few hours absorb all his winnings. Generally he loses; and, with the forlorn hope of getting back his money, he casts into the same hole his watch, his horses, and both carriage and coachman. Some friend has to carry him home in a simple short overcoat of Bokharian stuff, despoiled and shorn, but filled only with thoughts of having his revenge next market-day. This imbecile's country-house has nothing more remarkable than his kennels, where beasts of every race growl and bark. As to the mill, the clamp which tightens the mill-stone is missing. The fields lie fallow. Nozdref's work-shop is adorned only with Turkish guns, swords, poniards; add to that, pipes of every clay and of every size, and an old hand-organ. Here the negotiations about dead souls do not run smoothly. Nozdref treats his man as though he were a liar, a sharper: he wants to compel him to a bargain no less preposterous than disadvantageous; then he offers to put up souls at lansquenet. Tchitchikof, in spite of insults, accepts only a part of the queens; and the game has hardly begun before he refuses to play in consequence of the strange pertinacity shown by his adversary's sleeve in pushing forward the cards which are not in the game. Hence a terrible quarrel. Nozdref seizes the suspicious player by the throat, and calls his valets to thrash him. The comedy is changing into a tragedy. The purchaser of souls is paler than one of his dead. At the critical moment a carriage drives up, and from it descends the *deus ex machinâ*, a police-officer, who comes to arrest Nozdref for assault and battery committed by him and some other gentlemen on the person of a Mr Maksimof, whom they had beaten on leaving some orgy.

The procession of vices and absurdities sweeps on. Next to Nozdref, the rascally brutal gambler, appears Sabakévitch, the Russian gormandizer, — a colossus with enormous feet, with a back as wide as the rump of a Viatkan horse, with arms and legs huge as the granite posts which fence in certain monuments; a man capable of wrestling with a bear, himself a bear, as his surname Mikhaïl, which is the nickname of the bear in Russia, sufficiently indicates.[1]

[1] See Mérimée's novel entitled Lokis. — *Author's note.*

After Sabakevitch comes the miser Plushkin, a portrait whose hideous relief outdoes the effect of Balzac's Grandet. The village where he lives still preserves traces of former wealth, rendering more noticeable and more frightful the state of degradation and wretchedness into which the present proprietor has let it fall. The appearance of the miser on his threshold, his sullen reception of the traveller, the characteristics of his dress and his person, the enumeration of the treasures which fill his sheds, the utensils crowding his office, the bric-à-brac loading his what-not, the description of his stingy ways, the contrast with his wise and happy past, the account of his domestic troubles, and of his rapid transformation under the influence of anxiety and loneliness, — all this makes this canto not only a picturesque painting, a most lively comedy, but, more than all, a psychological study as deep as it is novel. In fact, avarice may have been as well described in its effects; it had never before been so studied in its principles, and, as it were, determined in its essence.

Plushkin has sold Tchitchikof all his dead

souls, and all his runaway serfs into the bargain. The list of the different purchases already concluded reaches a respectable length. The names, surnames, nicknames, description, and other particulars, complaisantly noted down by those who sell, give Tchitchikof the illusion of having actual property. His imagination brings all these dead to life. He knows their ways, their faults, their habits, the distinctive characteristics of each. The only thing that is left is to have all the purchases sanctioned by the tribunals. Now or never is the chance to show up in satire the Russian *tchinovnik* and his incurable corruption. The cunning tricks of the clerks, whose slightest service must be bought, the *natchalnik's* collusion, the character of the witnesses, the method of blinding the chief of police as to the nature of the contract, — here would be the material for another comedy in the style of "The *Revizor.*"

Every thing comes out just as Tchitchikof desires. In the village, he marches from ovation to ovation: he seems at the height of his good fortune. But, unhappily for him, Nozdref meets him at the mayor's ball, and publicly and in a loud voice makes sport of him on account of his craze for purchasing dead souls. This mysterious word has its effect. Tchitchikof is shunned as a dangerous man. The tattle of a whole idle village ravins on his reputation. Justice is stirred up: it imputes to him all sorts of misdemeanors and even crimes. True, these imputations almost instantly are shown to be false; but public opinion does not make charges against an innocent man for nothing. Suspicion always hovers about him. Every townsman goes a little farther than what has been already supposed. One day the postmaster comes declaring that Tchitchikof is Capt. Kopéïkin. This Kopéïkin is a robber chieftain, known by his wooden leg and his amputated arm. It is needless to say that Tchitchikof possesses all his limbs.

Finally Nozdref, who has done all the harm, makes partial reparation. He tells Tchitchikof what is thought and said about him in the city of N——. The man of "acquisitions" has his britchka cleaned and greased, straps his valise, and gives Selifan his orders for their departure. Selifan scratches the nape of his neck at this order to depart. What did this expressive pantomime mean? Did he regret the wine-room, and his friends the tipplers, he with the *tulup* thrown negligently over his shoulders? Was he deep in some love-affair, and did he mourn the *porte-cochère*, under the shelter of which he squeezed two whitish hands at the hour when the bandura-player, in red camisole, claws his instrument? Did he merely turn a melancholy glance towards the kitchen with its savory perfume of sauer-kraut, and look with dismay on the weariness of the cold, the wind, the snow, and the interminable roads, following this life of contemplation? "His gesture might signify all that, and many other things; for among the Russians the action of scratching the nape of the neck is not the indication of two or three ideas, limited in number, but rather of an infinite quantity of thoughts."

They depart. A new Odyssey begins; that is to say, a new series of visits, and a new gallery of portraits. This time the author seems to have desired to soften his satire, and to add to the critical portion of his work certain theories, or, at least, certain counsels. Taking as his text Andréi Tentyotnikof, — a sweet-tempered and easy-going gentleman, who is slowly consuming away in the vague torment of a sentimental life, — he propounds his ideas on education, and lays out his programme of studies in the fashion of Rabelais, his favorite author. In contrast to Andréi he places the charming figure of Julienne, daughter of the old general Betrishef. Those who blame Gogol for never having created an elegant and graceful heroine have not read the thirteenth canto of "Dead Souls." Never to be forgotten when once met is the dazzling amazon, whose portraiture thus begins: "The person so suddenly introduced was bathed and caressed by the light of heaven; she was as straight and as agile as a rosewood javelin." Andréi is in love with her. But this romance is scarcely begun before it is hidden from us, and in its place comes satire again.

We fall back into vulgar life, and into the most beastly epicureanism, with the gastronomist Peetukof. This jovial fat-paunch has a splenetic neighbor. With good health, and eighty thousand rubles income, the handsome, gentle, and good Platonof is bored. He has only this word on his tongue: *ennui.* His brother-in-law Konstantin is apparently the only one of these Russian grandees whom Gogol has been pleased to spare. Industrious as an ox, he demands of his serfs constant labor. "I have discovered," he says, "that when a man does not work, dreams come along, his brains run away, and he becomes a mere idiot." This proprietor has, moreover, no claims to noble descent. "He took very little thought about his genealogical tree, judging that the possession of proofs was not worth the labor of research, and that such documents have no application to agriculture." Finally, he contented himself with speaking Russian without going round Robin Hood's barn, and, without any admixture of French, in thorough Russian style.

This wise man has made his property a model domain, and he would like to see the country peopled with good proprietors like himself. He lends Tchitchikof money to purchase an estate in the neighborhood. But we may conjecture that the adventurer will not settle down so soon. In fact, we are yet to see other absurd specimens; for example, the fool Koshkaref, who, though within two steps of ruin, plays with governmental forms. He has transformed his domain into a little state divided into bureaus, with such inscriptions as these: "Depot of Farm Utensils;" "Central Bureau for the Settlement of Accounts;" "Bureau of Rural Matters;" "School of High Normal Instruction;" etc. It is needless to say, that, through the fault of the employees, the bureaus do not work; for the Bureau of Edifices has taken his last ruble, and the poor sovereign's ruin is rapidly drawing nigh.

Finally, the spectacle on which the narrator longest holds our attention is that of the poverty whereto the various faults or vices, touched by our finger in this tale, bring the great majority of the small proprietors of Russia. Klobéyef has been ruined this ten years. He still lives, and his existence is a problem. To-day is a gala day, grand dinner, play by French actors: the next, not a morsel of bread in the larder. Any one would have hung himself, drowned himself, or put a bullet through his head. Klobéyef finds the means of keeping up this alternation of luxury and wretchedness.

He is a well-bred, enlightened, intelligent man: he absolutely lacks common-sense. When he is in trouble, he opens some pious book; and when the compassion of his old friends, or the charity of some strange lady on the lookout for good works, succeeds in rescuing him, for the time being, from the final tragedy, he ascribes praise to Providence, thanks the holy images, and begins to bite off from both ends this fortune come from Heaven.

With this portrait we must end the analysis of "Dead Souls." The impression, as can be seen, is truly heart-rending. According to the author's own statement, "it is a picture of the universal platitude of the country." The story is told, that the scoffer Pushkin, after hearing his friend Gogol read this romance, said to him, in a voice broken by emotion, "Good God! the sad thing is our poor Russia." It is indeed this state of moral wretchedness which Gogol strove above all to make the Russian reader feel, even though he had to do so at the cost of his own popularity.

I shall pass briefly over the last part of the romance, which is only an arrangement drawn from the author's notes. The adventurer is seen for the second time in the clutches of the law. He has forged a will, like Crispin in "Le Légataire;" and he is only released from prison by the intercession of an old philanthropist, who finally succeeds in softening the governor-general's severity. Tchitchikof has agreed to become an honest man, or at least to marry, and to found a line of honest folk.

It has been thought that in this violent but straightforward governor, "animated by healthy hatreds" as Alceste says, Gogol meant to picture the Tsar Nicholas. Gogol belonged, indeed, to an epoch when Russia as yet expected her salvation and delivery from above. However, the tsar is not mentioned here more than elsewhere in "Dead Souls;" and the author, whose patriotism shines forth in so many places in the book, does not seem to have cared, as might have been expected, to personify the country in the emperor. I might adduce, in proof, all the passages where, by way of compensation, words about Russian soil, Russian horsemanship, Russian idiom, etc., bring out, through the ironical and trivial prose of the satire, the poet's passionate lyric utterances which were revealed to us in his first writings. Here is a fragment which deserves to be enshrined in an anthology along with the piece about the Dniépr or the "Ukraine night:"—

"Russia! Russia! from the beautiful distant places where I dwell[1] I see thee, I see thee plainly, O my country! Thy nature is niggardly. In thee there is nothing to charm or to awe the spectator. . . . No: there is nothing splendid in thee, Russia, nothing marvellous; all is open, desert, flat. Thy little cities are scarce visible in thy plains, like points, like specks. Nothing in thee is seductive, nothing even delights the eye. What secret mysterious force, then, draws me to thee? Why does thy song, melancholy, fascinating, restless, resounding throughout all thy length and breadth, from one sea to the other, ring forever in my ears? What does this song contain? Whence come these accents and these sobs which find their echo in the heart? What are these dolorous tones

[1] Gogol was living at that time in Italy. He wrote while abroad the second part of Dead Souls. He left Russia after the publication of the first part. — *Author's Note.*

which strike deep into the soul, and wake the memories? Russia, what desirest thou of me? What is this obscure, mysterious bond which unites us to each other? Why dost thou look at me thus? Why does all that thou containest fix upon me this expectant gaze? My thought remains mute before thy immensity. This very infinity, to what forebodings does it give rise? Since thou art limitless, canst thou not be the mother country of thoughts whose grandeur is immeasurable? Canst thou not bring forth giants, thou who art the country of mighty spaces? This thought of thy immeasurable extent is reflected powerfully in my soul, and an unknown force makes its way into the depths of my mind. My eyes are kindled with a supernatural vision. What dazzling distances! What a marvellous mirage unknown to earth! O Russia!"

IVAN S. TURGENIEF.

IVAN TURGÉNIEF.

I.

Ivan Turgénief was born at Orel on the 28th of October, 1818. This date, given by Turgénief himself in a letter to the Russian journalist Suvarin, corresponds to the 9th of November in our calendar.

His father, Sergéi Nikolayevitch, and his mother, Varvara Petrovna, died early.[1] He was brought up by his grandmother, a Russian lady of the old school, haughty by nature and of despotic disposition. The portrait of this "severe and choleric" *baruina* is found sketched in vigorous outlines in the little story "Punin and Baburin." This story, says Turgénief in the letter which I have just mentioned, "contains much biography."

Turgénief's grandmother lived in the country, on an estate a short distance from the city

[1] This is a mistake. His father died in 1835; and his mother reached the age of seventy, dying in 1850.

of Orel. Here the child became passionately fond of nature. From the age of twelve he entered into intimate relationship with trees and flowers; and he felt, when in contact with them, impressions whose vividness remains after more than forty years in the deeply stirred remembrances of the mature man.

"The garden belonging to my grandmother's property was a large park of ancient date. On one side it sloped towards a pond of running water, wherein lived not only gudgeon and tench, but also *salvelines*, the famous *salvelines*, those little eels which are found scarcely anywhere nowadays. At the head of this pond grew a dense rose-bed; higher up, on both sides of the ravine, stretched a thicket of vigorous bushes, — hazel, elder, honeysuckle, black-thorn, in the lower part encroached upon by tall grass and lovage. Amid the clumps of trees, but only here and there, appeared very small bits of emerald-green lawn of fine and silken grass, prettily mottled with the dainty pink, yellow, lilac caps of those mushrooms called *russules;* and there the golden balls of the great celandine hung in luminous patches.

There in springtime were heard the songs of nightingales, the whistling of blackbirds, and the cuckoos' call. It was always cool there, even during the warmest days of summer; and I. loved to bury myself in those depths where I had my favorite hiding-places, mysterious, known to myself alone—or at least so I imagined."

Prepared by this beneficent influence of colors, perfumes, and the sounds of rustic life, the child's moral education was directed, without anybody's knowledge, and influenced for all time, by the presence of two outlandish servants, flitting members of the high-born lady's household. One of them was a "philanthropic and philosophical plebeian," destined to die in Siberia; the other, a sort of innocent enthusiast, a great reader of Russian epics then out of fashion. The former sowed in the young Turgénief's soul the seeds of a liberalism which will bear fruit in the most manly resolves; the latter kindled in the lad's lively imagination a poetic flame whose heat and glory will shine out in a score of masterpieces.

Towards the age of thirteen, the young Ivan

was removed from these influences. He was given two tutors, one French and the other German. Having obtained his diploma as candidate in philology, he went to Berlin to finish, or rather begin anew, his studies in the humanities; and he brought them to a close by plunging into the current of the Hegelian philosophy. He came back to Russia converted to that "occidentalism" which we shall define later when we study Turgénief's political theories.

He made his *début* as a writer in 1843, with a little poem, "Parasha."[1] The critic Biélinsky gave it such praise that it covered the author with confusion. Towards the end of his life, Turgénief criticised his poetry with a severity that was absolutely sincere. Even at this

[1] Turgénief says in his Recollections: "About Easter, 1843, in Petersburg, an event took place, in itself indeed of small importance, and long ere this swallowed up in perfect oblivion. It was this: A short poem entitled Parasha, by a certain T. L., was published. That T. L. was I. With this poem I began my literary career." He says further that Biélinsky's praise was so extravagant that he felt more confusion than pleasure. "I could not believe it," he adds; "and when in Moscow the late I. V. Kiréyevski came to me with congratulations, I hastened to disown my child, declaring that I was not the author." — N. H. D.

period, he set as little value on his verses as though he had already shown his ability in a prose masterpiece. The masterpiece appeared three years later, in 1846. The first story in "The Annals of a Sportsman,"[1] "Khor and Kalinuitch," was published in the *Sovremennik* ("Contemporary"); and at a single stroke Turgénief's fame reached a height which will never be surpassed by any of his great works.[2]

[Most of] the other stories in Turgénief's first collection were written abroad. The author came back to Russia in 1851, but only to leave it again two years later. He will still have a domicile there, and above all he will come back regularly to keep up his relations, and touch foot to earth; but it may be said that after 1863 he made only flying visits to his country. The Russians have heaped reproaches on Turgénief for this abandonment of his native soil. It has always been easily explained. There was, at least primarily, a sort of state reason. In 1852, owing to an article

[1] *Zapiski Okhotnika.*

[2] Yet Biélinsky wrote him: "'Khor' gives promise that you will be a remarkable writer — in the future." — N. H. D.

on Gogol's death, Turgénief got into difficulty with the imperial censorship, which ended in a month of close imprisonment, and in the writer being interned at his estate. After two years of solitude and work, Turgénief felt the need of "gaining freedom, the knowledge of himself." He acquired these conditions, outside of which it was impossible for him to write and to struggle, at the price of life in a foreign country."[1]

But behold what was not known, and what was revealed only by the posthumous publication of Turgénief's letters. This Russian who made his home abroad, who dwelt twenty years in France, and died in the very heart of Paris,

[1] Turgénief says in his Recollections: "I should certainly never have written The Annals of a Sportsman if I had staid in Russia. I was in a state of mind singularly analogous to Gogol's, who just about this time wrote his best pages about Russia from 'the beautiful distance.'" The article on Gogol's death was not passed by the Petersburg censor, but was admitted by the Moscow censor, and appeared in the Vyédomosti in March, 1852. Nevertheless, the article was construed as a violation of the law: "I was put under partial arrest for a month, and then sent into domicile in the country, where I lived two years. . . . But all for the best. . . . My being under arrest, and in the country, proved to my undeniable advantage: it brought me close to those sides of Russian life which, in the ordinary course of things, would probably have escaped my observation." — N. H. D.

was overwhelmed during his forced or voluntary exile with the blackest melancholy of homesickness, and during the last part of his life suffered even the sharpest torment.

He did not succeed in acclimating himself, either at Baden Baden, in spite of the charm of the situation where his poet's glance first rested; or at Paris, where he was to be enchained by the bonds of love which he himself called "imperishable, indissoluble." It may be asked, in regard to this well-known friendship, whether Turgénief, exiled from Russia by his desire for liberty, succeeded in avoiding all the forms of dependence. It is a problem which I leave to the most inquisitive to settle. I confine myself to pointing out in Turgénief the expressions which now and again betray his weariness of exile, his restlessness as of a Northern bird, a captive swan or eider, languishing, mourning with regret for its cold natal seas. "I am condemned to a Bohemian life, and I must make up my mind never to build me a nest." "In a foreign atmosphere," he writes once more, "I decompose like a frozen fish in time of thaw. . . . I shall certainly come back to Russia in the spring."

During the winter of 1856 Turgénief made this promise to return; and he repeats it many times, as though to assure himself further excuses for keeping it. From that time he knows all the disappointments of a wandering life; and to express the idea of not feeling at home where one is, he uses a word of rare power: "Say what you will, but in a foreign country a man is *dislocated:* you are needful to no one, and no one is needful to you." Far from growing feeble, this painful impression will increase as time goes on; the flame of regret, instead of going out or dying down, will get fresh vigor, and break forth in new developments.

First it is the family instinct, which wakens and which speaks very eloquently at that ambiguous hour when youth begins to withdraw, and when, like the foliage in autumn, one feels a premonitory shiver, harbinger of the wintry winds. "Anenkof married," says Turgénief smiling, "is handsomer than ever." "Get thee a wife," he writes seriously to another of his friends: "it is the one thing needful."

Then there is also the acute feeling of the impoverishment of the creative faculty, the very disturbing realization or apprehension of a sort of literary *anema* due to the deprivation of the desired climate with its inspiring horizons, with its atmosphere filled with vivifying breezes and suggestive sounds. "I will admit, if you please, that the talent with which I was endowed by nature has not grown smaller; but I have nothing on which to set it to work. The voice is rested: there is naught to sing, so it is better to be silent. And I have nothing to sing, because I live away from Russia." "Living abroad," hê says in another place, "the fountain from which my inspiration sprang has dried up."

Finally, more than all, it is the lofty sadness and the noble remorse at not being on hand, at not mingling more intimately in the troublous, dangerous drama which is enacting on Russian soil. "In fact," Turgénief writes his friend the great author, Lyof Tolstoï, "Russia is now passing through serious and gloomy times; but it is for that very reason that at this moment one feels the gnawing of conscience at living like a foreigner."

And so this existence which seemed to be

ruled by a certain indifference, a sort of elegant and fortunate dilettanteism, was early crossed, and to the very end disturbed, by fits of melancholy and splenetic depression, the secret of whose existence few people, I am inclined to think, ever discovered. Who seeing Turgénief unaffectedly smiling, in a humor not exactly sportive, but sweet, even, and obliging, would have suspected that after an interview with his Parisian friends, for whom he saved all the flower of his wit, he would shut himself up to confide his heart-secret to pages destined to fall only under the softened and by no means mocking eyes of his old Russian comrades?

One can easily imagine the sympathy roused in a Polonsky, for example, by passages such as this: "The chill of old age every day penetrates farther into my soul: it takes entire possession of it. The absolute indifference which I find in me makes me tremble for myself. I can now repeat with Hamlet, —

'How stale, flat, and unprofitable
Seems me that life!'[1]

[1] A misquotation, of course, of
"How weary, stale, flat, and unprofitable
Seems to me all the uses of this world!" — N. H. D.

Perhaps this mood will pass; or, if it lasts, perhaps I shall succeed in *lignifying*, and in that case, it is all the same."

Another day he tears out from his private journal this page, the disappearance of which is to be deeply regretted: "Again I am at my table, and in my soul it is gloomier than the gloomiest night. Thus, like a moment, passes the day, empty, aimless, colorless. A space to give a passing glance, and, lo! it is bedtime again. No right to life, no desire to live. Nothing to do, nothing to expect, nothing to hope for. . . . Thou speakest of halos of glory, and of enchanting tones. O my friend! we are the fragments of a vase broken long ago."

When once the straits of old age were crossed, Turgénief enjoyed a few years of relative calm, of less bitter resignation. It was the time of his intimacy with George Sand and Flaubert. They both died. Illness falls upon Turgénief himself, and nails him pitilessly to the land of exile.

From the day when the way of return is cut off, the "occidental" is seized once more with the agony of homesickness for the mother country. His eyes and his heart are fastened immovably on the corner of Russia whither all the memories of childhood and youth draw him. Unable to see his village of Spaskoe, he sends his best friends to it, and establishes them there. He begs them to give him endless details about the peasants, about the women, the school, the chapel, the hospital. He worries about the garden, and urges Mrs. Polonskaïa to look upon its most humble products with "the eyes of the master." He feels more keenly than ever the value of what he has lost. In addition to his ever renewed and lively regrets comes the feeling of bitterness and mourning which is born of the irreparable. His country calls him, and draws him with such force, that he has the sensation of a great "tearing asunder." That is the expression to which it is necessary to hold fast. It is calculated to surprise even those who had the good fortune often to meet Ivan Sergéyevitch; but what regret it ought to cause those who, deceived by the way in which Turgénief persisted in living far away from the Russian land, cruelly upbraided him for having forgotten his country!

Turgénief was so far from forgetting Russia, that he went back almost every year; and he wrote almost all his works there. The critics scarcely had any suspicion of such a thing. They attacked Turgénief's later novels, bringing up against them his residence abroad. "How could he know Russia any more? He no longer lives there." Turgénief was indignant at this objection, which "that old woman called the public" persisted in hurling at him. He answered this argument once for all, in terms which must be quoted: "The objection can only be made to what I have published since 1863. Until that time,—that is, until my forty-fifth year,—I lived in Russia, scarcely going out of the country, except the years from 1848 to 1850. During just those years I wrote 'The Annals of a Sportsman.' On the other hand, 'Rudin,' 'The Nest of Gentlemen,' 'On the Eve,' and 'Fathers and Sons' were written in Russia. But that makes no difference to the old woman. Her mind is already made up."

To be a little more precise, "Rudin" was published in 1855. "A Nest of Gentlemen"[1]

[1] *Dvoryánskaye Gnyezdó*, an untranslatable title. A Nest of Nobles or Courtiers or Gentlemen fairly expresses it.

appeared in 1859 [1858?], and the year 1862 was distinguished by the appearance of "Fathers and Sons." Better than any one, Turgénief understood the necessity of writing nothing without his models before him; and he went to seek for them where they were to be found. Turgénief's correspondence shows these scruples in a score of places, and especially in regard to "Fathers and Sons." Having once conceived the plan of the work, the novelist has no rest until he finds himself in Russia. There only can he imagine, create, or, to speak more accurately, reproduce what he sees in real life. His pen, which refused to move as long as he was abroad, runs and flies over the paper. The sight of familiar landscapes refreshes the parched brain: inspiration flows.

Between the romance of "Fathers and Sons," and that of "Smoke," which was published in 1867, during the period when the Russian writer was an habitual resident of Baden Baden,[1] appeared quite a large number of shorter stories and tales of less pretension, but not of less

[1] "In 1863 Ivan Sergéyevitch bought a plat of land at Baden Baden, built a house on it, and lived there until 1870."—*Polevoï.*

value. There is more than one masterpiece of sentiment or imagination in "Apparitions," in "Strange Stories," "Spring Waters," "Living Relics." Not all these collections preceded "Smoke," but they came shortly before or shortly after it.

Between "Smoke" and "Virgin Soil," Turgénief's last great novel, passes a period of nearly ten years. The cause of this long silence was the alienation which had arisen between the writer and his public. Russian readers had already begun to show their dissatisfaction with "Fathers and Sons," and the causes of this displeasure deserve to be closely examined. We shall return to them in the course of this study. The spitefulness of the critics was let loose against the very satirical romance "Smoke;" other works, such as "The King Lear of the Steppe," did not even have the success of causing scandal, and were "damned with faint praise." "That," said Turgénief, "for an author who is growing old, is worse than a *fiasco*. It is the best proof that it is time to stop, and I am going to stop."

In such a resolution, there were other motives besides pique. Turgénief felt weary, and, as it were, short of inspiration or of subjects. In the intervals between the recuperative journeys which we have mentioned, he was obliged to nourish himself on his own substance. He knew that to suspend them, or even to postpone them too long, was at the risk of losing his strength and wasting away even to consumption. "I am compelled, like a bear in winter, to suck my paw; and thus it is that nothing comes forth."

The weariness disappeared, the pique wore away, and gradually this firm resolution to enjoy rest and absolute silence was shaken. Turgénief finally even found excellent reason for resuming the pen. It was necessary, not to blot out, but to complete, the effect of "Fathers and Sons" by writing another romance, which this time should clear up misunderstandings, and put the author in the position and in the rank that he felt he ought to hold. This romance, "Virgin Soil,"[1] did not appear till 1876; but

[1] *Nov*, the Russian title, means merely *new*, — one of the words, by the way, showing the affinity of Russian with Latin, English, and the other Indo-European languages, — and is suggestive not only of new land, but of new people and new ideas. — N. H. D.

almost two years beforehand Turgénief was talking of it, thinking about it, and working at it. It can be seen in his correspondence, that the work is in some degree taking shape; and under each abstract formula one can already detect the outlines of a character who will be the realization of it.

It is easily understood how Turgénief, who expected so much from this last work, who thought that he had put into it the best of his talent, and reached the culmination of his creative faculty, was disappointed and discouraged to receive once more only reproaches and blame. "This time," he says, "it is my last original work. Such is my decision, and it is irrevocable. . . . I may possibly busy myself still with translations. I am contemplating 'Don Quixote' and Montaigne." In vain opinion calms down, changes base, turns to praise and admiration: he remains firm in his design of staying in retreat, and of "joining the veterans." Indeed, for a few months at least, he seems to drop this implement of the writer, "which he has used for thirty years."

He travels abroad, in England; and quickly

finds himself too well known, too much entertained, too much exhibited. This excess of glory is incompatible with his modesty.

Was it the delight in his visit to Russia in the spring of 1878, was it the joy of renewing long-interrupted relations of intimacy with Count Lyof Tolstoï? At all events, Turgénief again finds literary work to his taste. At first, it is true, he is seen occupying himself only with the work of others. He wishes to do for Tolstoï the same service in France, as for Flaubert in Russia, by popularizing their works in translation. Or he publishes Pushkin's correspondence, and supervises a superb edition of the complete works of his favorite poet.

He writes Bougival his "Song of Triumphant Love," which he regretfully allows to be printed, and which is this time hailed as a marvel. He makes a selection of his "Poems in Prose." He puts some personal reminiscences in the form of short stories; among others, "The Hopeless Man." He already passes beyond the horizon of life, — which is ending for him amid the most cruel sufferings, — by writing that half-real vision entitled "The Morrow of Death."

Turgénief, by these short works, endeavored to get himself into the mood of writing another great work. He was already beginning to speak of it to his friends; he explained the subject; he had, perhaps, blocked out his plan; and since we know his habits of work, and his method, we are safe in adding that he had conceived the principal types, that he had seen the majority of the characters pass and halt before his eyes. In this romance, Turgénief intended to compare the Russian with the French *grévistes* or anarchists. We see it is the subject which Zola had the ambition to take up in "Germinal;" and, in spite of the popularity of the work, I may be allowed to believe that this subject still remains to be treated.

The idea of this great romance must have been suggested to Turgénief's mind, as a consequence of his almost triumphal journey in Russia, on the occasion of the Pushkin festival. A few years had sufficed absolutely to change the feelings of the younger generation in Russia. The popularity which the author of "The Annals of a Sportsman" so suddenly won was restored to him after a pretty long period of alienation, and at last beatified the author of "Virgin Soil." The enthusiastic reception of the Moscow students filled his soul with the emotion of unexpected joy, and the ovation which he received had for him all the value of an improbable result. A Russian who was very near to Turgénief told me that, on this occasion, he found only a few hesitating and broken words to reply to the speeches of the orators, the leaders of this young generation; but he had the moistened eyes and the smile of a happy man.

Full of gratitude for this eleventh-hour homage, he would have been glad to express his thankfulness in his own manner; and doubtless the new work would have translated it. His illness put a stop to his project. On the 8th of April, 1882, Turgénief writes to Mrs. Polonskaïa to inform her of the physician's diagnosis in regard to what they call his *angina pectoris*, or his gouty neuralgia of the heart. The term was not accurate. It is known that Turgénief died of cancer of the spinal marrow. Whatever the trouble was, the torment of it became atrocious, and the suffering which the invalid underwent lasted more than a year. He bore this slow agony with great sweetness. His complaints were rare, and they were for the most part hidden under a veil of irony which robbed them of every shade of bitterness.

Pinched by pain as by a vise, he still found the time and the power to address comforting raillery to those who were sadder than himself. "For your consolation," he wrote to one of his friends, "I wish to quote one of Goethe's remarks, made just before his death. It would seem as if he at least had to satiety all of the happiness that life can give. Think what a pitch of glory he reached, loved by women, and hated by fools; think that he had been translated even into Chinese; that all Europe was setting out in pilgrimage to salute him; that Napoleon himself said of him, 'There is a man!' think that our Russian critics, the Uvarofs and others, burned incense under his nose: and yet, at the age of eighty-two, he declared that during his long life he had not been happy a quarter of an hour all told. Then for you and me it is the will of God, isn't it? Suppose the perfect health which Goethe always enjoyed is lacking to us, still he was bored. . . . But what is to be done about it?"

On the 3d of July, 1883, Turgénief with feeble hand, and at the cost of cruel pangs, wrote in pencil the following unsigned letter to his friend the great novelist Lyof Tolstoï: "It is long since I have written you, for I have been and I am literally on my death-bed. It is impossible for me to recover: it is not within the limits of thought. I write you simply to tell you that I am happy to have been your contemporary, and to express to you my last and most sincere request: my friend, return to literary work! This talent of yours came to you from the source whence come all our gifts. Ah! how happy I should be if my prayer were to have the effect upon you so deeply desired! As for me, I am a dead man. The doctors do not even know what name to give my ailment. Gouty neuralgia of the stomach; no walking, no eating, no sleeping. Bah! it is tiresome to repeat all this. My friend, great writer of the Russian land, hear my supplication. Let me know if you receive this slip of paper, and allow me once more to press you closely in my embrace, — you, your wife, and all your family. I cannot write you more, I am weary."

Turgénief died a month later, on Monday, Sept. 3, 1883.

Turgénief's features are so well known that it seems unnecessary to sketch them in his biography. One of his characters, the gigantic Karlof, thus defined the men of his race: "We are all born with light hair, brilliant eyes, and pale faces; for we have sprung up under the snow." Turgénief himself had a good share of these race characteristics. But in France the majority of people knew the good giant only after he was well along in life, and when he already had the aspect of one of those venerable kings of whom the poet speaks: —

. . . *Nosco crines incanaque menta.*

Turgénief was of a very honest, very obliging, and very affable nature.[1] Those who met

[1] His generosity was more than princely; not even the palpable impositions of his impecunious countrymen caused him to clasp his ever-open purse. It is related that a Russian family residing in Paris made frequent applications to this abundant fountain. Turgénief saw through their wiles, but let the stream still flow. The little daughter of the family showed some musical talent, and Turgénief undertook

him saw him to the best advantage at moments when he allowed himself to talk with a charming frankness. He talked deliciously, with abundance of feeling and a fluency of expression, which went with him even when he spoke in French. He enchanted those who listened to him in his moments of enthusiasm: always lively and original, his conversation then became passionate and brilliant, even lyrical. Listening to this stream of ideas and words hurrying in eager floods, not noisily, from the lips of this old man of heroic mould and structure, one involuntarily thought of some Homeric bard. There was also "the harmony of the cicadas" and "all the sweetness of honey" in the voice of the Nestor of the steppes.

her education. It happened that there was a very exclusive school in Paris; and one fine day the ambitious mother came and besought their Mæcenas to use his influence to have the young girl admitted where no foreigner was allowed. Turgénief was at last a little nettled, and in epigrammatic Russian he said, "Make her either a candle for the Lord, or an ash-scraper for the Devil" (*Bogu svyêtchu ili Tchortu katchergu*). — N. H. D.

II.

Was Turgénief only an artist, only a dilettante?

We must give up this false definition which his enemies wished to become current, and which his friends even have been too willing to let go with contravention. Superficial critics deny in him all capacity, all enlightenment, on the questions of social order: they have gone so far as to say that in these respects he has neither teachings nor opinion. Certain fanatics, young or old, the Písarefs, the Dostoyevskys, have taken it upon them to advance this pretext for denying him the right to write and to print his works, and to be read as they are and more than they are.

It is true to say that Turgénief never laid down, or even sketched out, a programme; that he never made public speeches, that he did not peddle interviews, that he did not lucubrate leading articles for the editorial pages of journals. What am I saying? Perhaps he did not even reply to a sensational toast during his active life! Many persons obtain and grant the title of political man only by this test. In their judgment, Turgénief was not one.

As for believing that Turgénief had in political matters no definite opinions, or keen sympathies, or profound views, or well-digested purposes, it takes a pretty strong dose of passion or of *naïveté* to accept and to promulgate this mistake. Those who have read his works carefully suspected it; those who were in his intimate circle had no question about it: but no scepticism in this regard could withstand the revelations of his correspondence.

We know what popularity the Slavophile party gained from the moment of its birth. The declamations of the Pogodins and the Aksákofs against "occidental rot," their dithyrambs in honor of the virtues of the Slavic race, their childish programmes pretending to put the Russian people on the right track, and to free it from the old vestment of foreign ideas and habits which Peter the Great had swaddled it with, — all this specious rhetoric, flattering at once the national vanity, ignorance, and indolence, found in Turgénief from his early youth a decided enemy. His conviction as an occidental, which was the foundation of all his other convictions, could not be shaken either by the constant effort of years or by the sudden shock of the most varied events.

But what was the characteristic of this occidentalism? Did it go so far as to dislike the special features of the Russian people, and desire to extirpate the individuality of the race, as one would demand the excision of a tumor or the extirpation of a wart? Turgénief was too proud of being a Russian, not to have a legitimate share in the development of these peculiarities of the national type; but, according to his own words, it was repugnant to him "to feel any vanity in this sort of exclusiveness, in whatever sphere it was manifested, pure art or politics." In his eyes, Slavophilism was an artificial entity, a sort of hollow edifice, constructed on foreign models and in imitation of the German genius.

He could not reconcile himself to the idea of artificially isolating Russia from the rest of

Europe, and of shutting her up in a sort of quarantine, where, in order to be free from foreign influences, the result would be that the natal air would not preserve its purity, but would grow vitiated and rarefied. And with still greater reason, he regarded as puerile the thought of giving new life to the European organism by the infusion of the Slavic element. This ambition of grafting the Russian shoot on the aged wood of other races tore from him protestations of very expressive irony. "I cannot accustom myself to this view of Aksákof's, that it is necessary for Europe, if she would be saved, to accept our orthodox religion." Every policy that adopted this narrow principle seemed to him worthy of reprobation, at least in its principle. "In freeing the Bulgarians we ought to be guided to this step, not because they are Christians, but because the Turks are massacring and robbing them." "All that is human is dear to me," he says again: "Slavophilism is as foreign to me as every other orthodoxy."

In bringing these habits of moderation to his judgments of the acts of the government, and of the men who helped, who extolled, who blamed, who clogged its action, Turgénief might have expected to cause dissatisfaction, and to rouse for the most part only murmurs. Early in point of fact, and even to the end of his career, Turgénief is the object of violent attacks from the opposite party. At the very moment when the younger generation of Russians felt that they were travestied by him in "Fathers and Sons," and when Tchernuishevsky, the author of the famous romance "What is to be Done?"[1] turns to his own profit the misunderstandings caused by the appearance of the hero Bazarof; Turgénief, for having created this same Bazarof, for having refused to exaggerate or blacken his character, makes for himself irreconcilable enemies in the reactionary party. He quarrels with Katkof, the officious journalist, the confidant of the heir-apparent, the inspirer of that retrograde policy which has prevailed in Russia of late years. "When I left 'The Russian Messenger' (*Russki Vyestnik*), Katkof sent me word that I did not know what it was to have him for an enemy.

[1] *Tchto Dyêlat*, a translation of which is published by T. Y. Crowell & Co., under the title A Vital Question.

He is trying, therefore, to show me. Let him do his best. My soul is not in his power."

No consideration of interest, no low ambition for popularity, could have decided Turgénief to deviate from this line of conduct. We remember the quite barren movement of agitation started a few years ago by those young people who called themselves, somewhat naïvely, "the new men." A lady who was one of their sympathizers sends Turgénief a bundle of documents: it is the confession of one of the representatives of this progressive generation. Turgénief finds in this jumble of prose and verse only two characteristics,—an intoxicated, delirious self-conceit, and boundless incapacity and ignorance. It is vain to make allowance for time of life, and to attribute a part of their faults to the extreme youth of these individuals puffed up with a mighty sense of their small importance. Under it all there lies "only feebleness of thought, absence of all knowledge, a scantiness of talent verging on poverty." He does not put his unfavorable judgment under any sort of subterfuge or oratorical disguise: his frankness costs him a storm of bitter criticisms.

Yet Turgénief is the very same man who will receive in Paris other young people, with still more trenchant opinions, still more angular forms; and "in their presence," he says eloquently, "I, old man that I am, I open my heart, because I feel in them the 'real presence,' and force, and talent, and mind." These virtues attracted him and disarmed him, no matter in what class of people or in what group of thinkers he found them. Thus he is seen giving the patronage of his name, and the cover of his authority, to the first work on the newspaper *Le Temps* of a young Russian, treated by the home government as a dangerous character. To punish Turgénief for this audacious deed, the minister causes him to be insulted, slandered by a paid scribbler. "Verily, among us," writes Turgénief, "many shameful things are exposed to God's air, like this vile article of the rascally . . . ."

Now, a few days later, on the occasion of the attempted assassination of 1879, behold how the man whom "The Moscow Gazette" (edited by Katkof) affected to confound with the scatter-brains of Nihilism, expressed himself: "The last ignominious news has greatly troubled me. I foresee that certain people will use this senseless outrage to the disadvantage of the party which justly, in the interest of its liberal ideas, places the Tsar's life above every thing; for salutary reforms are to be expected from him alone. In Russia, how can a reform be imagined which does not come from above? . . . I am deeply troubled and grieved. Here for two days I have not slept at the idea of it. I think about it, and think about it; but I cannot come to any conclusion."

Whatever were his apprehensions, he could not foresee with what fury of re-action the Emperor would strive to stem the Liberal current, by which, when he first mounted the throne, he had allowed himself to be carried onward. Turgénief suffered from this aberration of power more than can be told. He foresaw new acts of despair, which would give a color of reason to measures of repression constantly growing more crushing. He attributed this infatuated policy to the influence of Pobyedonostsef, the

Ober-Prokuror of the Holy Synod; and above all to the counsels of Katkof, that former Liberal, that exile converted to the most brutal absolutism. He writes: "Who can tell what is going on at home, *Katkovio regnante?*"

With what passion Turgénief uttered one day before two callers, one of whom was a Frenchman, this expression, which I find also in his correspondence! With what pathetic eloquence he mourned for the days of yore, the days of the old oppression! "We had then a bare wall before us," he writes, "but we knew where it was necessary to make the breach. To-day the door is ajar, but to enter through this narrow opening is more difficult than to undermine and cast down the wall."

I find, among some notes taken down after an afternoon call upon Ivan Turgénief during the winter of 1882, a rather expressive *résumé* of his conversation, which I beg permission to quote in its entirety. "At that time we felt sustained by an auxiliary which allows one to defy, and which finally softens, all the severities of power, — Opinion. We had on our side the two stimuli which lead to victory, — the feeling of duty, the presentiment of success. Who would have believed that the day would come when we should look back with regret upon this period of terror, but of hope; of oppression, but of activity! Indeed, were not the youth of that time happy and enviable compared to those of to-day? What sincere mind can help feeling the deepest pity for that handful of Russians, educated, or greedy for education, whom the misfortune of the times has driven to the most frightful extremes? You might say that every thinker is caught between the anvil of an ignorant populace and the hammer of a blinded power. The Russian people are afraid even of those who, scorning every danger, are laboring to gain them their rights; they are absolutely ignorant, and are afraid of every innovation. They have the anxious look, and the quick flashes of anger, of a wild beast. We have just seen them rush upon the Jews with a sort of frenzy. If the people were not kept like a bear fastened to a chain, they would treat the revolutionists with the same fairness and the same gentleness.

"As to the throne, the end of advance in the

path of absolutism has just about been reached. It is now the formidable ideal of tyranny. During the preceding reign it took the initiative of reform. Alexander II. was carried away by the current of liberal ideas. He ordered measures to be taken; above all, he allowed projects to be elaborated. He wished, for example, to give the district assemblies power enough to struggle against the abuses of the *tchinovniks*, and to put a stop to corruption. But one day he was panic-struck. Karakózof's pistol-shot drove back into the shade that phantom of liberty, the appearance of which all Russia had hailed with acclamation. From that moment, and even to the end of his life, the Emperor devoted himself to the undoing of all that he had done. If he could have cancelled with one stroke the glorious *ukaz* which had proclaimed the emancipation of the serfs, he would have been only too glad to disgrace himself.

"What can be said of his successor, that doting sovereign, that victim nailed to the throne? He shuts himself between four walls, and, what is worse, between four narrow, limited minds, the responsible editors of the policy of an anonymous tsar, the former Liberal and exile, Katkof. It is a war upon ideas, a crusade of ignorance. Russia is having its Inquisition, it has its Torquemada. What other name is to be given to that minister of creeds, or, to speak more exactly, that procuror-general of the Synod, Pobyedonostsef?

"The Tsar sees in Pobyedonostsef the most virtuous and the most saintly man in all the empire. He has for him all the tenderness of Orgon; and you might say that he likes to think, like that pig-headed dupe, —

> 'He teaches me for naught to feel affection,
> My soul from every friendship he estranges.'

"Just as the Tsar loves and venerates Pobyedonostsef, so he shows Katkof *naïve* admiration and respectful deference. In the one he sees science inborn; in the other, religion personified. But the more dangerous of these two fanatics is Katkof, the former Liberal, the companion of Herzen's misfortunes, the ex-professor of philosophy at Moscow. He scorns to hold the reins of power; he likes better to give the word to those who carry the order for him and by him alone. The ministers are his valets; he has even his under-slaves; it would not be interesting to mention all their names. He is the disgraceful Richelieu behind the throne, who terrorizes Russia."

Notwithstanding the very gloomy aspect of the present, Turgénief had unshaken faith in the future. "We must not expect that the future will be all roses. No matter, things will come out all right." And what were the means, according to Turgénief's idea, of realizing this? Give up illusions and fidgeting. Don't imagine that you are going to find a panacea, a remedy for the great evils; and that, to cure the Russian colossus of all his tribulations, it will be sufficient to practise a sort of incantation "analogous to the spells used by old women to calm the toothache suddenly, miraculously." According to Turgénief, the miraculous means alone changes: "sometimes it is a man, sometimes the natural sciences, sometimes a war;" but what is unchangeable is faith in the miracle. That is the superstition which first of all must be extirpated.

Likewise the idea of obtaining without delay

"large, beautiful, and glorious" results, the idea of wishing "to move mountains," must be renounced. It is necessary to know how to pay attention to little objects, to limit one's self to a very narrow circle of action, not to step out of it; and there without glory, almost without result, work incessantly. The only activity that is fruitful was defined by Turgénief, in quoting the two verses of Schiller's old man: "Unwearied activity is that which adds one grain of sand to another." "What!" said he, "you begin by telling me that your constructive work is ended, that the school has just been begun; and, a little farther on, you speak of the despair which takes hold of you! I beg of you, for pity's sake: your enterprise has already had some small result. It is not unfruitful. What more do you want? Let every one do as much in his own sphere, and there will be a grand, a splendid result."

And Turgénief was one of the first to put his doctrine into practice. Just as in his youth he signed the charter for the emancipation of his serfs, with the same pen which wrote the indictment of serfage in "The Annals of a

Sportsman;" so in the time of his old age, notwithstanding his absence, tortured as he was by the horrors of disease, he preached humbleness of aim and constancy of effort, but he preached it by his example. All his cares were directed to the improvement of the material and moral condition of his former serfs. He granted them a fifth of the sum settled upon for the redemption. At his own expense he built a school; he founded a hospital in his village of Selo Spaskoe; he succeeded in diminishing drunkenness, and in spreading a taste for reading in a region where, at the time of his boyhood, an educated, self-taught *muzhik* was a genuine rarity.

His correspondence shows that he was greatly concerned about his estate in the government of Orel: but it was not the revenue of his lands that troubled him; it was the happiness, the moral welfare, of his little people of Spaskoe. Behold the evolution which he wanted to see accomplished from one end to the other of his country, and which, so far as in him lay, he called forth, he prepared.

Any other policy seemed to him useless, dangerous, almost criminal. He hoped that the new reign was going to inaugurate a whole tradition of efforts in favor of the development of the rural classes. That was why he manifested his sympathy with the new Tsar, on the accession of Alexander III.: he applied to him the title, the "Emperor of the *muzhiks*," and, if this was not a name of praise, it was found at least to contain a counsel.

"All that one can say," wrote Turgénief again on the subject of the Tsar, "is that he is Russian, and nothing but Russian. . . . Seeing him anywhere, one would know his country." I do not know whether these words went to the Tsar's heart; but are they not honorable to him who penned them? What Slavophile would have imagined any thing more eloquent in their simplicity? In giving this emperor, "in whose veins runs scarce a drop of Russian blood," his naturalization papers, Turgénief surely thought that he had reached the borders of eulogy.

III.

After reading what has gone before, I trust that no one will be inclined to see a mere paradox in this affirmation: Turgénief was above all things interested in the question of politics and social order, and of this interest were born all his great works. This was the reason that Turgénief's writings so stirred the public: hence the favor of his readers at first was, enthusiastic; hence came notorious alienation, irritation, almost calumnious fury, from the time when the public and the author no longer advanced with equal steps towards progress. For, here is the point to be noted: Turgénief never ceased to make progress; but as long as he walked slowly, with regular steps, like a man who holds aloof from the popular current, and is not dragged along against his will by the rising tide of the throng, the masses of the nation — I mean the majority of the educated classes — no longer regulated his gait, and, seeing him each day a little farther behind them, imagined that he was retrograding or was not following. Turgénief was advancing, and he went to great lengths. Let us see how great was the distance between "The Annals of a Sportsman" and "Virgin Soil."

Turgénief somewhere expressed his sympathy and admiration for Don Quixote. He contrasted him with the dreamer Hamlet, in whom he took little stock. Did not he himself enter the career of letters like a knight-errant (*campeador*) in the lists? From the very beginning, when he had won all the glory of a victor, he gave his young talent to the service of the right and of truth; he turned his pen, like a sword, against egotism, against injustice, against prejudice, — in a word, against the different forms of error. His maiden book, "The Annals of a Sportsman," was not merely a literary event: it brought about a political revolution. This picture of the wretched condition of the serfs contributed in large measure to call forth the *ukaz* that enfranchised Russia.

It was not the first time that fiction had

attacked the social question. Gogol had already struck the first blow against the enemy which Turgénief had the honor of defeating. But the author of "Dead Souls" had laid himself out especially to depict the faults and foibles of the small Russian proprietors; and, while he made it sufficiently evident how miserable was the condition of the serfs under their grotesque or detestable tyranny, his book left the unfortunate *muzhik* in the background. Turgénief's originality consisted in placing this pariah in full light. He dared to show not only his pity but his affection for the Russian peasant, often narrow-minded, ignorant, or brutal, but good at heart. He undertook to reveal to the Russians this being which they scarcely knew.

In the very first pages of his book he showed him with his instinctive qualities; and for this reason he took pains to place him in an exceptional condition, that is to say, in that sort of relative independence occasionally realized in spite of, or by favor of, the law. Khor and Kalinuitch are accordingly almost freed from the actual miseries of serfage, — the first by living in the midst of a swamp, avoiding statute labor by paying a quit-rent (*obrok*); the second by serving as whipper-in for his master, whom he passionately adores. The former is a *muzhik*, who has the feeling of reality, "who is settled in life;" the other is a dreamer, "who sticks to nothing, and smiles at all things." Khor the cautious has carefully observed men and things, and his experiences are expressed with that humorous *naïveté* which gives such a color to the conversation of the Russian peasant. Kalinuitch the enthusiast has the inspired language of a poet. He is largely endowed with mysterious powers. The bees obey him as though he were an enchanter. Both of them are good. The one is devout and gentle; the other, simply cordial and hospitable. There is profit in listening to the former, and pleasure in holding intercourse with the latter. Under these features Turgénief pictured the Russian of the country districts. After showing him, so to speak, in his native state, he went on to explain the deformities from which the type was liable to suffer under the brutalizing influences of serfdom.

The first alteration of the character of the

Russian *muzhik* is a sort of ferocious, even savage, humor, which takes the place of the original reason or ingenuity. The huntsman Yermolaï offers us a curious example of this reversion to barbarism, of this return of the *muzhik* towards the savage state. Emancipated in the manner of an outlaw, of a bandit, he lives in the woods or the marsh, sleeping on a roof, under a bridge, in the crotch of a tree, hunted down by the peasants like a hare, beaten sometimes like a dog, but, aside from these trials, enjoying to the full this strange independence. He does not support his wife or his dog, both of whom he beats with the same brutal indifference. He has all the instincts of the beast of prey in scenting game, in trapping birds, in catching fish. He already possesses the shrewdness of the savage: he would easily acquire his cruelty. "I did not like the expression which came over his face when he applied his teeth to the bird he had just brought to earth."

However precarious and anxious this independent life may be, it appears very enviable when compared to the torment and degradations of slavery. The *muzhik* Vlas walks all the way to Moscow, where he comes to ask a reduction in his quit-rent; for his son who paid it for him is dead, and he himself is old. The *barin* slams the door in his face, with the words, "How do you dare to come to me?" Vlas sadly returns to his hut, where his wife is waiting for him, blowing in her fist from starvation. "His lip is drawn, and in his little bloodshot eyes stands a tear." He suddenly bursts out into a laugh, thinking that they can't take any thing more from him than his life,—"a wretched pledge,"—and that that damned German, the *prikashchik* Quintilian Semenitch, "will shuffle in vain:" that's all he'll get. That tear of anguish, and that desperate laugh, are never to be forgotten.

Here are other impressions not less cruel. The serf Sutchok, now employed at his trade of fisherman, tells how he began by working as a cook; and how, in changing his profession, according as he went from master to master, he found himself successively cook, restaurant-keeper, actor, then back to his ovens again, then wearing livery as sub-footman, then postilion, then huntsman, then cobbler, then journeyman in a paper-mill. These caprices of the mastership which weighs upon the *muzhik* have not only their ridiculous side: there is always something detestable about it. The last owner of this wretch, whose life is only an irksome apprenticeship, is an old maid, who vents her spleen at having been left in single-blessedness by forbidding all her household to marry. This abasement of a human being, condemned by his master to isolation, to barrenness, like a beast, is powerfully shown in the little tale entitled "Yermolai and the Miller Girl."

But what seems still more painful than the slavery itself is to see that it is endured with resignation, and sometimes even upheld, excused, by those who have to submit to it. "How do you live?" is asked of one of these victims of feudal despotism. "Do you get wages, a fixed salary?"—"A salary! *Ekh! barin*, we are given our victuals. Indeed, that's all we need, God knows! And may Heaven grant long life to our *baruina!*" Another has just been tremendously flogged. He treats with very bad grace the stranger who presumes to express commiseration; he takes the part of the master who has so cruelly abused him for a trifle; he is proud of belonging to a man who makes strict use of his seignorial prerogatives. "No, no! there is not a *barin* like to him in the whole province!"

Turgénief does not confine himself to the expression of pity for the *muzhiks:* he is unsparing of the nobles. With what irony he depicts for us their false sentimentality, their detestable selfishness! How he lays his finger on their absurdities! How he scourges their cruelty! How he lays bare their hypocrisy! They all appear in the book, from the narrow and cringing citizen, to the cynically brutal country *pomyeshchik*, from the gentlemen of the steppe (*stepniaks*) up to the vanished nobles, those legendary *vyelmozhui*, personified in Count Alekséi Orlof, so handsome, so strong, so terrible, and at the same time so beloved! "If you were not acquainted with him, you would feel abashed; but after getting wonted to his presence, you felt warmed and delighted as by a beautiful sunrise." The author finds in this vanished aristocracy the rather barbaric form of his own grandfather, and he cannot refrain here from a sort of admiration. It is true, that small men have a sympathy very differently marked for these ostentatious giants of the olden days. Besides, is it not enough that the author of "Annals of a Sportsman" makes no secret of the excesses committed by those of his race? Has he not the right to remember that the form of oppression has merely been changed, and that the serf is not less abused from falling from the mighty hands of the tyrants, into the hooked claws of tyrannical weaklings?

But the true tormentor of the serf was a man whose condition brought him nearest to the *muzhik;* the one who, more often than not, was himself only a *muzhik* polished up, — in other words, the representative of the proprietor, the superintendent (*prikashchik*), the *burmistr.* This subaltern master pays the peasant's quit-rent until the latter, overwhelmed with debts, is absolutely in his power. He becomes his slave, his drudge. Now and then will be found in the woods the corpse of some wretch who has torn himself from this hell, by suicide. But what is the use of complaining? The proprietor receives his revenue, and is satisfied. And then the *prikashchik* has a thousand ways of getting hold of the fault-finder, and the wreaking of his vengeance brings a groan.

Proprietors, *muzhiks*, *priskashchiks*, all these characters strike, move, stir, by their fidelity to the truth. In a subject which lent itself so easily to declamation, the author succeeded in refraining from all excess of fine writing. This self-restraint in form gave greater force to the satire, and added weight to the argument. Besides, under the irony the bitterness was felt, and under the comic fervor was occasionally heard the rumbling of a generous wrath. Turgénief himself explained the feelings which animated him at this period of his life, which I would rather compare to the morning of a battle. He had just left Russia, the atmosphere of which seemed no longer fit to breathe. He went away to get a fresh start, so as to come back with a renewed impetus against his enemy serfage. "I swore that I would fight it even to the death; I vowed that I would never come to terms with it: that was my Hannibal's oath."

From one end of his work to the other, Turgénief never did aught else than thus reflect the feelings of the Russian people, express its hopes, note carefully, proclaim sincerely, all the forward and backward movements of opinion. In every one of his novels, there is to be found one person whose appearance, conduct, and worth may vary, but whose dominant characteristic holds throughout all changes. This personage, however alive he may be, serves to express an abstraction. He is, so to speak, the incarnation of the wishes, the fears, the claims, of the Russian people. Now, in Russia, as elsewhere, and still more than elsewhere, public opinion is undergoing constant modification: the novelist has followed with careful eye, and copied with accurate hand, all these rapid transformations.

In Dmitri Rudin, he depicts for us a lofty but inconsequential generation, eloquent, but lacking in depth, eager for every undertaking, but having no fixed purpose; as the youth of 1840 must have been, who had the power of speech, but were prevented from action.[1]

[1] Písemsky described this same generation in his great story, *Liudi Sorokovuikh Godof* (People of the Forties). — N. H. D.

This was the epoch when there was a passion for words, and especially for words of foreign origin. Hegel's philosophy frothed and foamed in these Russian brains, so little constituted for the digestion of metaphysical nutriment. But the fashion was for cosmopolitanism: they affected to scorn national habits; they dreamed only of going "beyond Russia." Rudin, who personifies this error, was its first victim. At first he carries away, he rouses to enthusiasm, all whom he approaches; then his friends, his disciples, ultimately, sooner or later, turn against him. He succeeds in rousing only hatred, or exciting only distrust. Useless and inactive amid his own people, he goes to perish on a French barricade; and by a supreme but unconscious irony, the insurgent who fights at his side pronounces his funeral oration in these words: "Lo, they have killed our Pole!"

Is it true to say that the Rudins were of no advantage to their country? The author gives us to understand, that their words may have cast the germ of generous thoughts into more than one young soul to whom nature will not refuse the advantage of a fruitful activity.

To this same unfortunate family of forerunners, and to this same sacrificed but indispensable generation, belongs the character of Lavretsky in the romance entitled "A Nest of Noblemen." Unlike Rudin, Lavretsky owes nothing to schooling. Scarcely does he have time for applying his simple and ingenuous mind to the acquisition of knowledge during the period between the moment when he escapes the durance of paternal despotism, and that when he takes upon him the more pleasing yoke of conjugal will. He therefore has remained Russian; he believes in the future of the national genius. He is lavish of himself, and of those of his age; but he admires the tendencies of the young, and he praises their endeavors. Departing from his country, happy, or at least under that delusion, he returns alone and crushed; but he has the consolation of doing his duty, that is to say, cultivating his estate, and improving the lot of his peasants. This unostentatious work of Lavretsky's, better than Rudin's brilliant declamations, pointed out to the rising generations what Russia henceforth expected from her sons: "You must act, and the benediction of us old men will fall upon you."

But this period of action which they seem to be approaching will be postponed before the unanimous wishes of the novelist and the reader. In the book "On the Eve," translated into French under the title "Hélène,"[1] the author's aim is very evident. He contrasts two Russians with a Bulgarian; and the brilliant or solid qualities of the artist Shubin and the student Bersénief yield before the unique virtue of Insarof, a more common nature. This virtue of the barbarian is to go straight ahead; he does not delay for dreaming or discussion; there is nothing of the Hamlet about him. However strange be his ideal, however adventurous his lot, he carries with him Elena's hesitating wisdom, just as Don Quixote overcame Sancho's rebellious good sense. It is this decisiveness, this bold gait, this firm resolution not to fall back, and resolutely to emerge from the beaten path, which the author of "On the Eve" seems to hold up before the Russian people. But it might be said that he despaired of find-

[1] Also under the title *Un Bulgare.* — N. H. D.

ing in his own country the man of action, destined to win the glory to come; and it was thus that the Russian critics explained his significant choice of a Bulgarian for the hero of his romance.

This ingenious explanation is not correct. Insarof and Elena have experienced life. This beautiful young Russian girl, who is anxious to devote herself to a noble cause, and who, not being able to die for her own country, clings to the lot of the foreigner who shows her the path of great sacrifices, was not a creature of Turgénief's imagination. Not only did Elena exist, but there was a throng of Elenas who asked only for a chance to show themselves. This was seen as soon as the romance was published. All feminine hearts throbbed. One might say that the author had placed before the eyes of the virgins of Russia a mirror, where, for the first time, they were allowed to see themselves, and become conscious of their own existence. A few years later Elena would have had a chance to offer herself to Russia. She would have acted like Viéra Sasuluitch, or, not to go outside of fiction, like Marian in "Virgin Soil."

In the famous novel "Fathers and Sons," the young generation for the first time comes upon the scene. It is represented by the medical student Bazarof. Better to bring out his hero by a fortunate contrast, the author has put this brutal but thoroughly original plebeian face to face with a gentleman in whom are united all the qualities and the eccentricities of the conservative nobility. Again, it is German education which has fashioned Bazarof. But Hegel's theories have given place to Schopenhauer's; and Germanic pessimism, grafted on the Russian mind, has brought forth very strange fruit. The young men of whom Bazarof is a type are of the earth earthy, to the same degree as that generation of which Rudin was the shining example showed itself exalted. They have only one aim, action; they admit only one principle of action, utility; they see only one form of utility at the present time, absolute negation. "Yet isn't it necessary to rebuild? — That does not concern us. Before all things we must clear the ground."

Here, clearly formulated, is the theory of Nihilism. This word, invented by Turgénief, and spoken for the first time in "Fathers and Sons," has in short space gone all over the world. We know that all Russian readers, young and old, blamed the author of the novel for slandering them. The older generation could not forgive him for having spurned their prejudices; the rising generation were angry with him for not preaching their errors. What strikes us to-day is that at this moment he was able to remain so clear-sighted and sincere; that he was able to unite so much nobility with Pavel Kirsánof's narrow-sightedness, and so much subtilty with Bazarof's destructive scepticism.

But the character which Turgénief liked best in this romance of "Fathers and Sons" was Bazarof, — in other words, that personage representing the Russian soul with aspiration toward progress, no longer ideal and vague, but violent, and brutal. "What! do *you*, do you say that in Bazarof I desired to draw a caricature of our young men? You repeat (excuse the freedom of the expression), you repeat that stupid reproach? Bazarof! but he is my well-beloved son, who caused me to break with Katkof, for whom I expended all the colors on my palette. Bazarof, that quick spirit, that hero, a caricature!" And he took delight in returning to the definition of this enigmatic personage. He never wearies in commenting on "this harbinger type," this "grand figure," surrounded by a genuine "magic spell," and, as it were, by some sort of "aureole."

The conclusion of the book lies in the ironical and bitter advice given by Bazarof to his friend Arkad: "Take thee a wife as soon as thou canst, build thy nest well, and beget many children. They will certainly be people of brains, because they will come in due time, and not like thee and me."

Thus is the solution of the social problem once more postponed. The rock of Sisyphus falls back as heavily on the new-comers as on their predecessors. The recoil is even so mighty that the observer feels that he too is attacked by pessimism; and if he does not take pride in absolute negation, like Bazarof or his young adepts, he just as surely comes to deny their qualities, to see any sense in their conduct. The romance "Smoke," which is the expression of this new state of mind, roused in Russia all the clamors by which a satire is received. What was entirely overlooked was the feeling of painful compassion hidden under the aggressive form. It was an act of enlightened patriotism, to let daylight into the hollow declamations of the progressists, and to lay the scourge on the stupid folly, the idiotic depravity, of a nobility which had brought itself into discredit. Between Gubaref, that solemn imbecile, and Ramirof, the complaisant husband of a faithless wife, one must go to the hero of the story, Litvinof; that is to say, to the idealized Russia, whose gloomy and painful destiny we have followed across all Turgénief's work, under the features of Rudin, of Lavretsky, of Bazarof. Like Lavretsky twenty years before, Litvinof returns to his country, overwhelmed with domestic troubles, which exasperate all his other feelings, and change the mishaps of his patriotism into despair. The vanity of love makes him find all things vain. In the tumult of the recent years, in the agitation of divers classes, in the words of others, in his own thoughts, he sees mere nothingness, sham, smoke. The desolation of this conclusion was brought up against the author of the book, by his compatriots, with a warmth which almost disgusted him with the *rôle* of political observer, and almost deprived us likewise of a masterpiece in which Turgénief seems to have reached his greatest height, — "Virgin Soil."

The author of "Fathers and Sons" named and defined theoretic Nihilism: in "Virgin Soil," the same author shows us the Nihilists at the very moment when, for the first time, they begin to act. Between the two books a pretty long time elapsed, during which Turgénief kept silent. There is lacking, therefore, among his works, a book which might let us into the secrets of the dark development and mysterious spread of the new theories. In regard to this Nihilist propaganda in its early years, when it was only an attempt at self-instruction, we find, in "Virgin Soil," only hints, allusions. The very character, however, who is going to bring about the crisis, at the risk of destroying every thing along with himself, Markelof, still reads and propagates with naïve assurance the "brochures" which are secretly sent him, and which he passes on "under the mantle" to his other confederates. What subjects were treated in these books so carefully hidden? Those which were worth the trouble of reading were translations of foreign works on political economy; writings attacking, with greater or less ability, the problems of society. But this instruction, good or bad, could not have the least influence on the great mass of the Russian population, which does not read at all.

It was therefore necessary to find more efficacious means of action, and to organize actual preaching. Then it was that a pretty large number of people belonging to the educated classes, students like Nedzhanof, women voluntarily deserting their own rank in life, like Marian, undertook to go down among the people, to dress in their style, to speak their dialect, to lead their rough lives, to gain their confidence at the cost of this labor, to open their minds to the ideas of liberty and progress, to rescue them from the double curse of laziness and drunkenness, and, finally, to bring them into the path of action. The trouble was that these people who preached action did not themselves know where to begin the work. Each of them was waiting for the word of command, which no one could give; for in this concert of wills there was no one to direct, and the most violent efforts, from lack of determined purpose, were obliged to remain without results.

Another insurmountable obstacle lay in the repugnance of the people at emerging from their tremendous inertia. Nedzhanof compares Holy Russia to a colossus, whose head touches the north pole and his feet the Caucasus, and who, holding a jug of *vodka* in his clutched fingers, sleeps an endless sleep. Those who try to struggle against this sleep lose their time and their labor. Discouragement takes hold of them, and some of them, like Markelof, for having desired, having tried by themselves alone, to perform a part which needs the efforts of an army, go forth on the hopeless path by the gate that leads to Siberia; others, like Nedzhanof, having lost faith in this work for the regeneration and enfranchisement of a people to which they believed themselves capable of offering their devotion, throw down violently the double burden of their vain labor and their ridiculous lives. The Russian Hamlet gets rid of his mission by suicide.

This beautiful novel of "Virgin Soil," which must be read through, appeared on the very eve of the great Nihilist suit against the One Hundred and Ninety-three. At first the cry was raised, that the author did not draw a true picture: the author was again slandering Russia. A few days later the critics, dismayed at his power of divination, accused Turgénief of having got into the confidence of the ruling power, and of having had in his hands the entire brief of the preparatory trial.[1] Some Nihilists were already dreaming of more tragic performances. "I also," said one of them, who at this time was a refugee in Paris, "I also am a Nedzhanof; but I shall not kill myself as he did: there is a better way of doing it." This better way was worse. It was

[1] It was reported, and believed by some, that the Russian government paid Turgénief fifty thousand rubles for Virgin Soil.—N. H. D.

assassination in the manner of Solovief, who, having resolved to kill himself, and for the same reasons that influenced Nedzhanof, will inaugurate suicide with a bloody preface.

Since "Virgin Soil," the evolution of Nihilism has made new and rapid strides. The mania of descending among the people, and "being simplified" has given place to other fantastic notions, just as useless, but less innocent. We have said that Turgénief died before he had time to finish the romance in which he would have shown us the agitations of to-day, and possibly pointed out the social reforms of to-morrow.

Who knows what Russia is preparing for us? Hitherto the reforms have been decreed by the throne; and the *ukazes* have remained without effect, because they have not had the support in the lever of the people. The expenditure of energy, starting from above, did not make the nation stir. But now suddenly the nation seems to be shaking off its torpor. The peasants, hitherto deaf to all voices, and stubbornly resistant of all progress, have perhaps found for themselves the way of safety and redemption.

They are assembling in their villages, and they are organizing the league against drunkenness. This strike against the wine-shop is terrifying to the Russian clergy: they see in it a new form of heresy. In their eyes, these water-drinkers are *raskolniks*, and the most dangerous kind. We know the Russian proverb versified by Nekrásof: "The *muzhik* has a head like a bull: when a folly finds lodgement there, it is impossible to drive it out, even with heavy blows of the goad." It is this headstrong obstinacy which seemed to postpone forever, and which may precipitate to-morrow, the settlement of the social question.

IV.

The expressions, "Russian ideal," "representative type of one generation," and other terms of this kind, which one must necessarily use to mark the connection between Turgénief's different works, must not be allowed to give a false idea of the nature of his talent and of his methods in fiction.

He has himself defined his talent. He has explained his methods so far as they were essential. We have, therefore, only to turn to these precious directions. "I will tell you in a few words that I am, so far as preference goes, a realist; and that I am interested, more than all else, in the living truth of the human physiognomy." He says elsewhere, that at no moment of his career has he ever taken for his point of departure in a new creation an abstract idea, but that he has always started with the true image, the objective reality, the characteristic personage observed and living.

Here is the very principle of his æsthetic, as he summed it up in his letter to Mr. King, a novelist just beginning his career: "If the study of the human physiognomy, and of the life of another, interests you more than the promulgation of your own feelings and your own ideas; if, for example, it is more agreeable for you to reproduce accurately the external appearance not only of a man, but also of a simple object, than to express with elegance and warmth what you feel in seeing this object or this man, — then you are an objective writer, and you can begin a story or a novel."

Truth is not disagreeable to those who love it: it gives life to their conceptions. Turgénief's work, the political bearing of which we have already tried to show our readers, is a little world where go and come a thousand people with variously expressive characters and faces. The creator of such living characters as these has been compared to a great portrait-painter. The comparison is unjust to the novelist. Like the great painters of portraits, he seizes a dominant feature, and expresses it powerfully. It is thus that in a book, on the canvas, the resemblance is caught. But the art of a Titian, of a Reynolds, renders the aspect of the face, and reveals, if you like, something more, — the temperament of the model. It goes scarcely beyond that. The novelist expresses, besides, a whole order of hidden facts, a whole internal spectacle, of which the brush scarcely gives us an inkling. There is therefore a double field of studies to go over, a double power of observation to put into use. It is necessary at one and the same time to note the attitude, and interpret the disposition; to catch the expression of the face, and to penetrate the meaning of the character.

Turgénief possessed this double talent to a very high degree. As a general thing, he paints with broad touches; and his portrait, both physically and morally, is finished in few words. Sometimes the detail is more minute, but the accumulation of lines serves only to verify the dominant impression. I refer the reader to the romance of "The Abandoned One," and to that admirable portrait of the old Russian gentleman in the time of Catherine II. What a calling-back of the past is given by this old man of lofty stature, perfumed with ambergris, glacial in doublet of silk with its relief of stock and lace ruffles, a suspicion of powder on his hair brought behind into a cue, and in his hand a gold snuff-box ornamented with the empress's cipher! He always speaks French; he scarcely knows Russian. He reads perforce every day Voltaire, Mably, Helvétius, the *Encyclopédistes;* he has whilom improvised verses in Madame de Polignac's *salon;* he has been among the guests at Trianon; he has seen Mirabeau wearing coat-buttons of extravagant size, and his opinion on our great orator is, that he was "exaggerated in all respects; that, on the whole, he was a man of low tone, in spite of his birth."

It is seen by this example, that Turgénief's portraits often represent a class in an individual. They are the expression of an epoch. In fact, though he studies nature closely, he takes pains not to content himself, as our realists do, with the first model that comes to hand. He carefully seeks for the character whose features are sufficiently marked and original, so that in copying it he shall be sure to reproduce the general type. Thus he discovered Bazarof, the hero of "Fathers and Sons." The idea was given him by the chance which brought to his sick-bed in a small Russian city the "young doctor of the district," who served him for his model. I do not know whether all the characters of "Virgin Soil," without exception, passed under the author's eyes; but I have heard Turgénief tell how he knew, and was able to study, the most characteristic personage of the story, the Nihilist woman, — the upright, solemn, and rather absurd, but strong and sublime Mashurina.

It was by his knowledge of the heart of women, and by the thorough-going fascination of his heroines, that Turgénief left far behind him his great predecessor Gogol. By an inexplicable peculiarity, the author of "The *Revizor*," of "Dead Souls," cared only to paint women who were not women at all, who are lifeless abstractions or caricatures.[1] The most gossiping biographers are embarrassed to explain the reason of this impotence. All that can be said is that

[1] Yuliana Betrishef in Dead Souls is not a portrait: she is a luminous apparition. — *Author's note.*

Gogol dreaded too much the approach of womankind, ever to have the chance to study the sex. On the contrary, Turgénief's heroines are so life-like, that under each portrait his readers have tried to recognize and name some model. All well-informed Russians would have told you in what palace in Warsaw dwelt Iréna of "Smoke," or at the first official reception would have pointed you Mrs. Sipiagina of "Virgin Soil." It certainly seems that all these delicate creations have the irresistible seduction of reality. There is not a romance, not a story, by Turgénief, in which there does not shine forth some feminine face, sometimes of a rather strange grace, but singularly lifelike and touching. Natalia and her sister in "Dmitri Rudin," Liza in "A Nest of Noblemen," Elena in "On the Eve," Marian in "Virgin Soil,"—it would be necessary to name them all.

What rather surprises the French reader is not to find them always beautiful; at least, with that perfect and improbable beauty which our novelists do not hesitate to give their expressionless dolls. One has regular features, a pretty foot, but her hands are too large. Another, at first sight, seems ugly: "She wore her thick chestnut hair short, and she seemed to be fretful; but her whole person gave the impression of something strong, passionate, and fiery. Her feet and her hands were extremely dainty; her little body, robust and supple, reminded one of the Florentine statuettes of the sixteenth century; her movements were graceful and harmonious." What idealized beauty would have this living grace?

Another singularity, which shows us to what a degree the author takes us from our own latitude: in him the women have less originality than the young girls. The indecision and feebleness found in their lovers, the Rudins and the Nedzhanofs, is paralleled by the resolute wisdom, and—let us use the words "graceful virility," in them. They somewhat resemble the Roman girls, and we expect to hear them say in their way the "*Non dolct*" of the illustrious Arria. But no; they have not in the least these rather theatrical attitudes and words. It is the Nedzhanofs who die like impatient Stoics, or perhaps like discouraged Epicureans: Marian continues to live, and without bustle to prepare for the freeing of the country which she loves.

Women raised by noble feeling to the scorn of death are found elsewhere than in Russia. What is more rare, and almost impossible to find, are these fanatical sacrifices, these renunciations worthy of the primitive days of the Church, which associate lovely maidens of sixteen with imbecile vagabonds eaten up by hideous ulcers. Turgénief might have multiplied in his work description of pathological cases ("Strange Stories"); but if his realism is too artistic to delay over what is commonplace, he is too honest to devote himself to exceptions.

The form which best brings out this sincerity of expression is the tale. Turgénief takes little stock in dramatic form, at least in his own case. "I see a subject," he used to say, "only when I have the framework, the portrait, the dialogues, the wanderings, of a narration." In the drama he felt himself bothered by the necessity of collecting, abridging, curtailing, filling in; and his psychology seemed to him warped, when presented in miniature. It is in vain that you brought up in opposition to this modest claim the form of such and such of his stories, which from beginning to end is an uninterrupted scene, a dramatic dialogue.

"That is not dramatic dialogue," said he: he was and had to remain a narrator.

To find finished narration, it is sufficient, indeed, to open at hap-hazard "The Annals of a Huntsman." Nothing is lacking; not character-painting, or lively course of the story, or surprise in circumstances, or development of the situation, or harmony of outline, or feeling for nature, or grace of style, or value of coloring. But one ought to have heard Turgénief, and to have seen him in his character of story-teller, to imagine to what degree all these qualities in him were spontaneous. It was especially in this that his conversation was unlike any one else's: it translated ideas into images, and, without any attempt, created paintings which one would never forget.

Does narration in Turgénief gain by assuming the ampler proportions of the novel? Our French taste is open to suspicion, and I hesitate about replying. Our good novelists are such clever carpenters: they construct so symmetrically works so ingeniously arranged for effect; the interest is kept up with such skill; the action moves along with such a certain step, towards a logical result feared or suspected from the very first word! We find ourselves at first not quite so much at our ease in these Russian novels, which are full of art, but are bare of little artifices; where the developments are like the course of real life; where the characters hesitate, and sometimes remain still; where the action develops without haste; and where the author does not even think it important to come to an end. It is sufficient for him to state facts, and explain characters. This perfect naturalness, at first a trifle dubious, finally comes to have a great charm. There is nothing which is more able to make us reflect on the puerile stress which we lay on the method, and on the often to-be-regretted emptiness of our novels of industrious mechanism.

We should not have given Turgénief his just deserts if we forgot to praise him as a poet worthy of all admiration. I mean, as a poet in prose; for Turgénief was no more successful than Gogol in making good verse. Both of them used a language that was picturesque, infinitely expressive, full of images, and, in the case of Turgénief more than Gogol, of perfect purity and the greatest variety. He feels all the beauties of nature, and expresses them with powerful originality, or a delicate charm which shines through even the rather thick veil of translations. And yet what shadings escape us, what graces are lost for us!

The Russian language has infinite resources. If it is less exact in expressing the relations of action and of time, it brings out the most imperceptible circumstances of action. It outlines with less clearness: it paints with incredible richness of coloring. It is easy to understand what effects a writer who can see and can express — a poet, in a word — is able to make with it. Turgénief's descriptions threw Merimée into despair. One day, when he was trying to put into French a passage where the author had represented the peculiar sound of the rain falling on a sheet of water, the French words *grésillement froid* (cold shrivelling), destined to translate this inexpressible noise, caused the author of "Colomba" to hesitate. "Yet that is it," said he, thinking better of it; "and the thing must be said, or lose the bit of observation, which is perfectly true to nature. The Devil take the pedants! Let us leave the phrase."

How far this poetic realism is from our flat and tiresome enumerations of details heaped up without selection! But the parallel between the Russian realists and the French realists, to which this subject constantly attracts us, would carry us too far. It is sufficient to point out the essential difference. Observation in our realists is systematic and cold; in the Russians, and, above all, in Turgénief, it is always natural, and generally passionate. There is not a novel by Turgénief where the pathetic has not a large part; and sometimes this pathos, by the simplest means, reaches heights neighboring upon the sublime.

I shall only quote one example of it, taken from "Fathers and Sons;" and I have no fear that the reader will charge me with bad taste in cutting out this admirable scene from this novel, extended as it is:—

"Although Bazarof pronounced these last

words with a rather resolute expression, he could not bring himself to tell his father of his departure until they were in the library, just as he was going to bid him good-night. He said, with a forced yawn, —

"'Wait a moment. I almost forgot to let you know. It will be necessary to send our horses to Fyodot to-morrow for the relay.'

"Vasíli Ivanovitch stood stupefied.

"'Is Kirsánof going to leave us?' he asked at last.

"'Yes, and I am going with him.'

"Vasíli Ivanovitch fell back stupefied.

"'You are going to leave us!'

"'Yes, I have business. Have the kindness to send the horses.'

"'Very well,' stammered the old man, 'for the relay. Very good, — only — only — is it possible?'

"'I must go to Kirsánof's for a few days. I shall come right back.'

"'Yes, for several days. Very well.'

"Vasíli Ivanovitch took out his handkerchief, and blew his nose, bending over till he almost touched the floor.

"'Well, be it so. It shall be done. But I thought that you — longer. Three days — after three years of absence. It isn't — it isn't very long, Yevgéni.'

"'I just told you that I would come right back. I must!'

"'You must? Very well: before all things, one must do his duty. You want me to send the horses? Very well; but we did not expect this, Arina and I. She just went to ask a neighbor for some flowers to put in your room.'

"Vasíli Ivanovitch did not add that every morning at daybreak, in bare feet in his slippers, he went to find Timoféitch, handing him a torn bill, which he picked out from the bottom of his pocket-book with trembling fingers. This bill was designed for the purchase of different provisions, principally food and red wine, great quantities of which the young men consumed.

"'There is nothing more precious than liberty; that's my principle. It is not well to hinder people. One should not' —

"Vasíli suddenly stopped, and started for the door.

"'We shall see each other soon again, father, I promise you.'

"But Vasíli Ivanovitch did not return. He left the room, making a gesture with his hand. Coming into his bed-chamber, he found his wife already asleep; and he began to pray in a low voice, so as not to disturb her slumber. However, she waked up.

"'Is it you, Vasíli Ivanovitch?' she asked.

"'Yes, my dear.'

"'You have just left Yeniushka? I am afraid that he is not comfortable sleeping on the sofa. Yet I told Anfisushka to give him your field-mattress and the two new cushions. I would have given him our feather-bed too, but I think I remember that he does not like to sleep too easy.'

"'That's no matter, my dear; don't trouble yourself. He is comfortable. — Lord, have pity on us sinners,' he added, continuing his prayer. Vasíli Ivanovitch did not talk long. He did not wish to announce the tidings that would have broken his poor wife's rest.

"The two young men took their departure the next morning. Every thing in the house, from early that morning, assumed a sad aspect. Anfisushka let fall the plate that she was carrying; Fyedka himself was entirely upset, and finally left his boots. Vasíli Ivanovitch moved about more than ever. He tried hard to hide his disappointment; he spoke very loud, and walked noisily: but his face was hollow, and his eyes seemed always to avoid his son. Arina Vlasievna wept silently. She would have entirely lost her self-control if her husband had not given her a long lecture in the morning. When Bazarof, after having repeated again and again that he would come back before a month was over, finally tore himself from the arms that held him back, and sat down in the *tarantás;* when the horses started, and the jingling of the bells was mingled with the rumbling of the wheels; when it was no use to look any longer; when the dust was entirely settled, and Timoféitch, bent double, had gone staggering back to his lodging; when the two old people found themselves once more alone in their house, which seemed also to have become smaller and older, . . . Vasíli Ivanovitch, who but a few moments before was waving his handkerchief so proudly from the steps, threw himself into a chair, and hung his head on his breast. 'He has left us,' he said with a trembling voice, — 'left us! He found it lonesome with us. Now I am alone, alone,' he repeated again and again, lifting each time the forefinger of his right hand.[1] Arina Vlasievna drew near him, and, leaning her white head on the old man's white head, she said, 'What's to be done about it, Vasíli? A son is like a shred torn off. He is a young hawk: it pleases him to come, and he comes; it pleases him to go, and he flies away. And you and I are like little mushrooms in the hollow of a tree: placed beside each other, we stay there always. I alone do not change for thee, just as thou dost not change for thy old wife.'

"Vasíli lifted his face, which he had hidden in his hands, and embraced his companion more tenderly than he had ever done, even in his youth. She had consoled him in his disappointment."

Were we not right in speaking here of the

[1] A Russian proverb says, "Alone as a finger." — *Translator's note, quoted by author.*

pathetic, and was it not well that we drew the reader's attention to this good old word? It expresses an old idea, which, with no offence to the lovers of the commonplace, is not yet ready to perish. It is the mistake of the French realists,[1] to take coolness for strength, and they claim to be considered very strong men. Turgénief's great superiority consists in his having no pretension, not even to be trivial and common. He does not make it a matter of pride to stay on the hither side of the truth.

[1] It is only just to make exception in favor of Alfonse Daudet. His talent is largely made up of sentiment, and even of sentimentality. — *Author's note.*

V.

In this study of Turgénief, I do not flatter myself that I have pointed out all the aspects of a character so varied, — that I have shown all the traits of a nature so complex. Yet it would be a serious lack if I did not explain Turgénief's relationship to the writers of his country, or if I neglected the great number of criticisms which he has passed, in his letters to his friends, in regard to the literary movement of the last thirty years.

He characterizes the epoch to which he belongs. It is still, in his opinion, an epoch "of transition." He deplores the lack of union, the want of solidarity, in the men who in Russia hold this weapon, — the pen ; and who might, by concentrating their efforts, triumph over so many obstacles against which, in their isolation, they run a-muck and bruise themselves. "Each one sings his own song, and follows his lonely path."

He speaks without too much feeling about his enemies, unless he finds a settled aversion for their work, and for their conception of art. "I am sorry for Tchernuishevsky's dryness, his tendency to crudeness, his unceremonious treatment of living writers; but I find nothing in him corpse-like. I see a living fountain spouting." To be sure, he has little to praise in the man of whom he thus speaks; but malice, arising from personal attacks, could not draw him far from the truth. "These are spring waters," said he in regard to certain injurious writings directed against him. "They will run off, and no trace of them will be left."

It is not the same with him when teachings wound him, and when the literary form disgusts him. After having loved Nekrásof, he goes so far as no longer to recognize any talent in him, so shocked, so disgusted, is he by his intentional brutalities. His verses "leave behind them an after-taste which makes me nauseated." "What a son of a dog!" he says in another place. "He is a vulture, ravening and gorging." But Nekrásof[1] died before him; and he modifies, he explains the judgment which he had passed upon him. "No matter if the young have been infatuated with him, this has done no harm. The chords set in vibration by his poetry (if you can give the name of poetry to what he wrote) are good chords. But when St. ——, addressing these young people, tells them that they are right in placing Nekrásof above Pushkin and Lermontof,[2] and tells them so with an imperturbable smile, I find it hard to restrain my indignation, and I repeat the lines of Schiller:—

'I have seen splendid crowns of glory woven for most common brows.'"

His early sympathy for the novelist Dostoyevsky[3] was soon changed to dislike, owing to

[1] Nikolai Alekseyévitch Nekrásof, born in December, 1821, editor of the *Sovremennik* from 1847 till 1866. Afterwards, when the *Sovremennik* was suppressed, he edited the *Otetchestvennui Zapiski* till his death, which took place in January, 1877. He was eminently Russia's popular poet.— N. H. D.

[2] Mikhaïl Yuryevitch Lermontof, the author of the great poem Demon, and other verses inspired by the Caucasus, was born in 1814, and died in 1841.

[3] Feódor Mikhaïlovitch Dostoyevsky was born in 1822 in Moscow, and died in March, 1881. His life reads like a romance. For a

their differences of opinion. The sharp features in the character of the author of "Crime and Punishment" were not slow to disgust Turgénief. He could not be brought back by the reading of works, the clearly marked tendency of which is sometimes to put a check upon his own. He was not sparing of admiration for the "Recollections of a Dead House." "The picture of the *banya* (bath) is really worthy of Dante. In the character of the various people (that of Petrof, for example), there is much fine and true psychology."

But when Dostoyevsky's faults grow more pronounced; when his qualities become extravagant, and themselves turn to mannerisms; when this keenness, once so fine and delicate, loses itself in subtleties; when the writer's sensitiveness changes into supersensitiveness; when his imagination goes beyond the bounds of reason, and gloats over the pursuit of the horrible, — Turgénief does not hide his disgust, his scorn. "God, what a sour smell! What a vile

short sketch of it, and also for the translation of the scene from his *Zapiski iz Mertvava Doma*, so praised by Turgénief, see appendix. — N. H. D.

hospital odor! What idle scandal! What a psychological mole-hole!" [1]

Turgénief prefers as he debars, he loves as he detests; that is to say, with a passion which is contagious, and carries the reader with him. One should see with what pleasure he receives the works of the satirist Soltuikof, better known and more appreciated under the *nom de guerre* of Shchedrin. What a feast it was for him, when a new "Letter to my Aunt" appeared! With what joy he applauded its satirical features which were "powerful even to gayety"! Soltuikof seems disturbed at the flood of hatred which he stirs up. "If you only had a title of hereditary nobility, nothing of the sort would

[1] A brilliant Russian lady, now in this country, writes to the translator as follows: "I am glad indeed that you escaped the translation of 'Crime and Punishment.' You would never find any readers for such a book in this country. I could never read any of Dostoyevsky's books through. It made me sick. My nerves could not bear the strain on them. I don't believe in pathology in literature. And yet another of my American acquaintances, who is thoroughly versed in Russian, . . . tried to translate 'Crime and Punishment,' but had not time to do it. He says he never read, in any language, any thing so powerful as *Prestuplenie i Nakazanie.* Generally speaking, your countrymen have too healthy a constitution to appreciate such a novel. Let it turn heads among the pessimists in France and Russia, the natives of effete Europe." – N. H. D.

have happened to you. But you are Soltuikof-Shchedrin, a writer to whom it will have been given to leave a deep and permanent impress on our literature: then you will be hated, and you will be loved also; that only depends on the person."

The most striking example of this generosity of Turgénief's is shown us by the spectacle of his relations with his great rival Tolstoï. From the moment when Tolstoï's first book appeared, Turgénief, already famous, distinguishes the young author, welcomes him as a new star, and feels impelled by an irresistible desire to love him. "My heart goes out to you as towards a brother." "Childhood and Youth" appear. Turgénief's admiration is expressed in this fashion: "When this young wine shall have finished fermenting, there will come forth a drink worthy of the gods."

Life separates them; the most diverse mental tendencies still further increase this separation. There is even, at one time, an inopportune meeting, conflict, violent rupture, almost tragic, since a duel narrowly escaped being the result. There are noticeable in Turgénief, from that moment, movements of vexation. The admiration which he was the first to arouse in Tolstoï's favor turns, becomes fashionable, and goes to commonplace unreason: still he continues to be glad that "War and Peace" is praised to the skies; "but it is by its most dubious merits that the public want to regard it as unequalled." In his opinion, there are not such good reasons for falling into ecstasies about "Anna Karénina." "Tolstoï this time has taken the wrong track; and that is due to the influence of Moscow, of the Slavophile nobility, of orthodox old maids, to the isolation in which the author lives, to the impossibility of finding in Russia the requisite degree of artistic liberty."

But excessive strictures are rare in him; and how richly they are compensated by the generous crusade, which, from the year 1878, Turgénief undertakes for the sake of popularizing Tolstoï in France, and of building him a pedestal which at the present time threatens to rise higher than his own! If, unfortunately for French readers, a "Russian lady" had not got ahead of him, he would have translated the masterpiece which he liked the best, which seemed to him to give the highest idea of Tolstoï's great powers, — "The Cossacks."

In last resort, he contents himself with the most active propaganda in favor of another translation, that of "War and Peace." His correspondence shows him to us, going about carrying the book to Flaubert, to Taine, to Edmond About, to those who are capable of enjoying this foreign dish without further advice. He hopes that their articles will enlighten those who need to be told in order to get the taste of it. His illness alone turns him away from this occupation which I have no need of qualifying: it is too characteristic.

At the hour of death, Turgénief's last thought turns to Tolstoï. I beg the reader to go back to that admirable letter, to that short literary will, in which the dying author salutes, and calls back to the arena from which he is just departing, his great rival in talent and in glory.

It would be very strange, if having lived long in France, and having made precious literary friendships, Turgénief had not mentioned names particularly interesting for French readers. He speaks much in his letters of the contemporaneous realistic school, and he judges it favorably, especially at its first beginning. He does more than enjoy the Goncourts and Zolas. He makes arrangements for them with the directors of Russian journals or reviews; he endeavors to have one or two thousands of francs more paid for their manuscripts, by giving them to be translated into Russian before they are published in France.

Especially for Zola did he use his mediatorial influence. He seems very happy to help him; nevertheless, he does not fail to note with his delicate and imperceptible irony certain amusing traits of character. "As far as Zola is concerned, you told me that you would pay more for his manuscript than Stasulevitch. I have informed Zola. . . . His teeth have taken fire at it." "In his last visit to Paris, Stasulevitch, having made Zola's acquaintance, gilded him from head to foot, on the one condition that Zola should belong to him alone. So the European messenger (*Vyestnik Yevropui*) seems in Zola's eyes like the fabulous hen with the golden eggs, which he must guard like the apple of his eye."

The friendship, made of admiration and sympathy, between Turgénief and Flaubert, is well known. It is painted in Turgénief's letters in truly expressive lines: "I have translated one of Gustave Flaubert's stories. It is not long, but of incomparable beauty. It will appear in the April number of 'The European Messenger.' Perhaps two translations of it will appear. I recommend it to you in advance. I have endeavored, so far as in me lay, to reproduce the colors and tone of the original." Flaubert dies. Turgénief is so moved that he breaks with all his habits. He, so sober, so disliking noise, wire-pulling, puffing, puts himself at the head of a demonstration in the Russian journals; and he opens a subscription for a monument to his friend. He speaks with genuine disgust of the low interpretations to which this intervention on his part gave rise. His enemies affected to see in this something like the return of an old actor, who had left the stage, and was tormented by yearning for the scenes.

It would not be well to dwell too strongly on Turgénief's judgment in regard to Victor Hugo. Turgénief was a true poet, but when he wrote in verse he never rose above mediocrity. He knew it, and he criticised this part of his work very severely. The quality of his verses is explained better when it is seen how narrowly and unfairly he judges *La Légende des Siècles.* The epic grandeur and originality of this work escape him: its swing is too powerful, and it wearies him; its brilliancy is too intense, and it blinds him. He judges Victor Hugo as a poet of thirty years ago — Pushkin, if he had come to life — might have done: he did not much rise above the Byronian horizon.[1]

He is, however, more just towards Swinburne, the English Hugo. But here, again, his criticism is superficial: favorable as it is, one can see that he has not had time to find his reasons, and touch bottom.

The critical faculty is evidently less keen in Turgénief than in others of his friends, —

[1] This explains, perhaps, why he did not appreciate Nekrásof. Indeed, Turgénief, though his literary judgments are always interesting, must be taken with a grain of salt: like a true poet, he was not a critic. On the other hand, Tchernuishevsky, whose critical judgments Turgénief affected to despise, was a born critic, and his literary prognostications were greatly in advance of his time. See Appendix. — N. H. D.

Shchedrin, for example. He it was who caused the scales to fall from Turgénief's eyes, and revealed for him what he himself felt somewhat confusedly as to the often artificial and conventional character of our realists. "I would have kissed you with delight, . . . to such a degree what you say about the romances of Goncourt and Zola hits the case, and is true. As for me, it seemed so confusedly, as though I had a heavy feeling over the epigastrium. I have just this moment uttered the *Akh!* of relief, and seen clearly. . . . It cannot be said that they have not talent, but they do not follow the right way: they are already inventing too much. Their literature smacks of literature, and that is bad."

Although he was warned, Turgénief was not the man to wish to put others on the lookout. The success of another did not fill him with any envy. On the other hand, the disappointment of those who were dear to him caused him real pain. After the failure of one of George Sand's dramas, he wrote this charming word: "If I had met her, I should not have said any thing of the *fiasco* of her poor piece: like a respectful son of Noah, I turn away my eyes, and hide the nakedness of my grandam."

He had recovered from his boyish enthusiasm for the work of the illustrious novelist. "I cannot any longer hold by George Sand, any more than by Schiller," he wrote in 1856. But in place of admiration for the diminished and collapsed merits of the writer, there was substituted, especially in latter years, a touching worship for the truly virile virtues of the woman.

This is the way he speaks of her, on the day of her death, in a letter meant for publication: "It was impossible to enter into the circle of her private life, and not become her adorer in another sense, and perhaps in a better sense. Every one felt immediately that he was in presence of an infinitely generous and benevolent nature, in which all the egotism had been long and thoroughly burned away by the ever-ardent flame of poetic enthusiasm and faith in the ideal; a nature to which all that was human became accessible and dear, and from which exhaled, as it were a breath of cordiality, of friendliness, and above all that, an unconscious aureole, something sublime, free, heroic. Believe me, George Sand is one of our saints."

We cannot better finish this review of names loved by Turgénief than by letting the reader rest on this luminous portrait of George Sand. In the virtues which Turgénief ascribed to her, is it not allowed us to find many of his own?

LYOF N. TOLSTOÏ.

LYOF TOLSTOÏ.

I.

Count L. N. Tolstoï was born on the 28th of August, 1828 (O.S.), at Yasnaya Polyana, a village near Tula, in the Government of Tula. He reckons among his direct ancestors one of the best servitors of the Tsar Peter the Great, Count Piotr Tolstoï. Early left an orphan, he studied at the University of Kazan, entered successively the departments of Oriental languages and of law, got tired of both, left the university, returned to his paternal estate, and one fine day set out for the Caucasus, where his eldest brother, Nikolaï Tolstoï, was serving with the rank of captain. He quickly became an officer, took part in the guerilla warfare in Circassia, returned to be shut up in Sevastópol, underwent the siege, was greatly distinguished by his bravery, and resigned at the conclusion of peace.

Count Lyof Tolstoï's works have not been all published in the order in which they were written. "The Cossacks," published after the "Military Scenes," and after "Childhood and Youth," it seems was written, in part, during his stay in the Caucasus. The romantic portion of the work may have been thought out towards the period when the book appeared, but the impressions which fill the book are the first which the writer took pains to note down. It is well to emphasize this fact from the very first moment: in the study of Tolstoï's works, we can make it a starting-point in our investigation of the steps traced in the evolution accomplished by his mind.

The "Military Sketches," collected into a volume in 1856, were produced in the form of articles in the *Sovremennik* ("The Contemporary"). These tales bear the following subtitles: "Sevastópol in December," "Sevastópol in May," "The Felling of the Forest," "The Incursion." They paint at once the energy with which the French invasion was resisted, and the monotony of the siege, more terrible than its dangers. The book narrowly escaped remaining in the censor's hands: this suspicious and petty critic was offended by the most beautiful pages. There is, for example, an admirable passage where the soldiers, in order to escape the irksomeness whereby they have been overcome in the long days, listen with truly infantile excitement to the reading of fairy-stories. According to the censor's opinion, it was a bad example. The author should have depicted the soldiers as engaged in reading some serious work, capable of exerting a good influence on their moral state, on their spirit of discipline. "The attention of the army should be called only to useful literature." Fortunately the book escaped this rolling-mill, and roused the Russian public to enthusiasm.

As regards this album of impressions noted with incomparable vivacity of observation, vigor of tone, and energy of touch, Count Lyof Tolstoï gave another example, which is like a first confession, in his "Childhood and Youth." The material of this biography is family life brought into the exact environment which the Russian nature, when very closely observed and very poetically described, can furnish. On one side external impressions, very accurately and very powerfully retained; on the other, profound reflections upon self, and a very keen view in regard to the most secret and the least explored regions of consciousness: these are the two sides of Tolstoï's talent; these, from the very beginning of his literary career, are the two elements which will combine to form the great novels of the writer's maturity, "War and Peace" and "Anna Karénina."

These masterpieces having been once finished, Tolstoï turned aside from fiction to apply himself to pedagogy. The great painter of men becomes the instructor of children; the creator of heroes undertakes the mission of popularizing the alphabet.

At the present time we see him passing through a new transformation, and from pedagogue becoming preacher. He propagates a new dogma; or, rather, he is on his way to increase the number of Russian sectaries who seek in the Gospels a solution of the social problem.

Soldier, literarian, agriculturist, popular educator, and prophet of a new religion, — Count Lyof Tolstoï has been all these in succession. But the secret of these transformations is no longer far to seek: he has explained it to us in his latest work, entitled "My Confession," the publication of which has been forbidden in Russia by the ecclesiastical censor. The work is read in spite of the interdiction, and it makes converts; copies are hawked about; it will not be slow in following the fortunes of "My Religion:" it will be printed abroad in some sheet edited by exiles, and will be translated, doubtless, in France.

Let us find in this "Confession" the commentary on the strange existence which we have sketched only in broad lines.

Every man has, so to speak, a moral physiognomy; and this physiognomy, like the face itself, is more or less characteristic. In Count Lyof Tolstoï, this characteristic is the need of a fixed principle, of a well-established rule of conduct. This principle has changed, and more than once changed, the formula which expresses the sum of his acts, and explains them, justifies them, which becomes enlarged, transformed, entirely reversed; but what remains immutable is his attachment to some formula, his absorption in the article of faith. Count Tolstoï's soul is, before all things, the soul of a believer.

He begins by believing in the *ego*. He started with a sort of Darwinian conception of the world, of the struggle of individuals, with the conflict of egoisms. For Tolstoï, the ideal at this first period of his life was individual progress. The aim of existence was to get above other individuals, and to subjugate them in some degree by his own superiority. "I tried at first to cultivate the will in me; I laid down rules which I compelled myself to follow. Physically I strove towards perfection by developing, with all sorts of exercises, my strength and my skill, and by wonting myself by privations of every sort, to be neither wearied nor disheartened by any thing." He pitilessly analyzes the feelings which he had at this time; after the fashion of La Rochefoucauld, he tells us to what a degree he was the dupe, the victim, of self-love. Under the pretext of discovering the progress made by the *ego*, and of advancing it towards perfection, "I gave in, above all, to the desire of finding that I was better not in my own eyes, not even in the eyes of God, but above all, but solely, in the eyes of others, in the judgment of the world. . . . And even this desire to seem better to other men quickly yielded to the single desire of being stronger than all others." All these manifestations of individual force so much esteemed by men, and called "ambition, passion for power, cupidity, pleasure, pride, wrath, vengeance," — Tolstoï also admired them, coveted them, and finally realized them to such a degree as to rouse admiration and envy. "Just as in my life I offered homage to strength and to the beauty of strength, so in my works I most often sang all the manifestations of individual force; and yet I pretended to love truth, and boasted of it! In reality I loved only force, and when I found it without alloy of folly, I took it for truth." We shall see in studying "The Cossacks" to what a degree Tolstoï's first ideal, followed and realized especially during his stay in the Caucacus, is reflected in this work, which is the actual product, if not the immediate outcome, of his residence there.

At the age of twenty-six Tolstoï changes his environment: he leaves the army and the bastions of Sevastópol, and passes directly into the circles of St. Petersburg where the famous writers are gathered. He is welcomed, *fêted*, placed at the very first in the front rank. He changes his whole manner of existence; but he changes it in the name of a new faith, the faith in the "mission of the men of thought." This mission consists in teaching other men. "Teaching them what? I had not the slightest idea myself. But I was paid for it in ready money. I had a magnificent table, a sumptuous dwelling. I had women, I had society, I had glory. What I taught could not help being very good." At the end of two or three years of this existence, Tolstoï begins to doubt the infallibility of his literary faith: he applies to the settling of the question his dissolvent analysis. He bethinks himself to discuss also the moral worth of the priests of this faith, of the writers. "They were almost all immoral men;

and the great majority were bad men, of no character, and in no respect less so than the boon companions of yore, of the time when my life was only a round of gayety and disorder." A sort of misanthropy seizes Tolstoï as the result of his inquiry. A new Alceste, he hotly tears himself away from the perverse environment of literary people, and begins to hunt up and down the world for the support of a new conviction.

After having visited foreign lands, interviewed philosophers, questioned the men of "the vanguard," Tolstoï returns to his country, persuaded that progress must be realized, not within himself, but outside of himself. He becomes farmer, judge of the peace, magistrate, instructor; he founds a pedagogical review, and starts a school. "I got upon stilts to satisfy my desire for teaching." In spite of its simple and calm appearance, this existence let all the inward trouble, all the moral anguish, remain. "I left every thing, and I departed for the steppe. I went forth among the Bashkirs to breathe the pure air, to drink *kumis*, and to lead an animal life."

On his return from his visit to the Bashkirs, Tolstoï marries. The joy of family life at first takes all his will, absorbs all his reflective powers. "For a long time his life is centred in his wife and in his children: it is entirely monopolized by the anxiety of increasing their well being." At the end of fifteen years, he finds that he is still the dupe of selfish illusion, that this sacrifice to the greatest advantage of his family has simply turned him aside from the search after the real meaning of life. Is not his present existence, in fact, full of contradictions? Long ago he has become convinced that literary activity is vanity, and yet he continues to write. What impels him to it? "The seduction of glory, the attraction of large pecuniary remuneration." What moral principle is there at bottom of all that? Here begins a period of perplexity, of despondency, of bitter and morbid scepticism. The two questions, "Why?" and "What is to come?" force themselves more and more upon his mind. By reason of attacking the same problem, like dots on the same bit of paper, they finally "make a huge black blot." And Tolstoï's scepticism goes over from theory into practice: it is nihilism in the truest sense of the word. "Before I undertake the charge of my property at Samara, the education of my son, my literary work, I must know what is the good of doing it all. As long as I could not know the reason, I could do nothing. . . . Well, suppose I shall come to possess ten thousand acres and three hundred head of horses, what then? Suppose I become more famous than Gogol, Pushkin, Shakspere, and all the writers in the world, what then? I found no reply." At this moment of strange trouble, Tolstoï seriously considers the question of suicide.

How did he succeed in escaping the entanglement of scepticism? He takes the back track in his ideas in regard to humanity. He had long believed, "like so many other cultivated and liberal minds, that the narrow circle of *savants* and wealthy people to which he belonged constituted his entire world. As to the thousands of beings who had lived, or were living still, outside of him, were they not animals rather than men? I can scarcely realize today, so strange do I find it, that I should have fallen into such a mistake as to believe that my own life, that the life of a Solomon, that the life of a Schopenhauer, was the true or normal life, while the life of all these thousands of human beings was a mere detail of no account." Fortunately for Tolstoï, the taste for country life, and his intercourse with the field-hands, brought him to divine, that, "if he desired to live and comprehend the meaning of life, he must find this meaning, not among those who have lost it, who long to get rid of life, but among these thousands of men who create their life and ours, and who bear the burden of both." Having found only the leaven of doubt or negation among the men of his own society, he goes to ask the germs of faith, the elements of religion, among the poor, the simple, the ignorant, pilgrims, monks, *raskolniks*, peasants. In them alone he finds agreement between faith and works. "Quite contrary to the men of our sphere, who rebel against fate, and are angry at every privation, at every pain, these believers endure sickness and sorrow without any complaint, without any resistance, with that firm and calm conviction that all must be as it is, or could not be otherwise, and that all this is a blessing. The more enlightened we are, the less we comprehend the meaning of life: we see only cruel mockery in the double accident of suffering and death. With tranquillity, and more often with joy, these obscure men live, suffer, and approach death." Seeing these simple souls so unanimous in their interpretation of existence, so obstinately bent on seeking the good by means of calm labor and patience capable of enduring any trial, Tolstoï again begins to feel love for men; and he endeavors to imitate these models. After ten years of initiation into the holy life, he reaches the most perfect renunciation. No longer to think of self, and to love others only, — that is the moral scheme which can alone reconcile us to existence, and reveal to us the good concealed under this apparent evil. The question is, therefore, not to think well, as Pascal said, but to live well. And who shall tell us what it is to live well? "The thousand who create life, and get from it all their faith."

This expression, "create life," must be understood in all its senses. In the moral sense, it is explained only by its contrary. What do the wise men, the Solomons, the Sakyamunis, and the Schopenhauers do? They destroy life; they present it to us as an absurdity and as an evil. The calmness with which the humble, the simple, the pariahs of society, support existence, shows the falseness of the assertions of the thinker; and that which the philosophers in their supercilious speculation claim to anihilate, the modest practice of these virtuous men re-establishes, creates in a certain degree.

Once fixed on the rock of this faith, which seemed to him unassailable, Count Tolstoï felt that it was his duty to study its dogma and formulate its credo. He wrote "My Religion." Later we shall return to this work, in which not only the propensities of the author's mind are revealed, but also the tendencies of a considerable part of the Russian nation. It is enough for us to note here the fundamental article of this religious law, to which Count Tolstoï assents with all his heart, like thousands, nay millions, of his compatriots: "Resist not him that is evil." This saying of Jesus sums up for him all duties, and gives us the secret of all the virtues. We shall see in detail the applications of this principle to the conduct of individual and social life; for the present, let us content ourselves with calling the reader's attention to the path followed by the man whom we are studying. He started with this principle, — the exclusive development of the *ego*. In practice, this principle led him to conflict, to violence, and to hatred. He ended with this principle, — the absolute sacrifice of the *ego*. In practice, this principle leads him to a life of abnegation, of gentleness, and of love.

Between these two extreme limits of his development, we have seen all the mental states through which Tolstoï has passed. These varying dispositions will be found in his literary work. It would be running systemization into the ground to desire to show the writer going through this development, side by side with the man. But it is only just to remark to what a degree Tolstoï's earlier writings, his "Kazaki," for example, express his first ideal, that of the epoch in which he was taken up exclusively with force, and when he worshipped it in himself, giving it the name of truth. Later on in "Anna Karénina," one of his favorite characters, Levin, will closely resemble Tolstoï changed into a farmer, and already, in his drawing towards the rural populace, advancing towards the abandonment of all egotism, towards the spirit of sacrifice, towards that simplicity of virtue personified by the peasant Feódor in the story of "Anna Karénina," and the soldier Platon Karataïef in "War and Peace."

II.

Count Tolstoï's literary life is divided very sharply into three periods; or, if the expression be preferred, his powerful talent, original from the very first, has passed through three phases. He began by writing works which are mainly the working up of reminiscences or illustrations of personal impressions. In the "War Sketches," in "Childhood and Youth," in "The Cossacks," the writer confines himself to narration. Of these three writings, the one that best shows Tolstoï's talent in the first part of his career is the romance entitled "Kazaki," which, to use Turgénief's words, is "an incomparable picture of men and things in the Caucasus." In a detailed analysis of this masterpiece, we shall find the definition of Tolstoï's manner at the time of his forceful youth.

The second period is that of ripe age; it is

filled by the two great novels "War and Peace," and "Anna Karénina." The writer's manner has singularly broadened; even the dimensions of the frame-work of the fiction have taken an almost exaggerated aspect. "War and Peace" makes not less than eighteen hundred pages. "Anna Karénina" appeared in the "Russki Vyestnik," not in the course of months, but of years. It is true that between two parts of the work the author stopped, as though he had lost interest in its publication. But the public did not lose its interest by waiting; and when, after more than half a year, the narrator resumed the broken thread of his story, his readers found themselves, as it were, dazzled by the return of the brilliant characters of the romance, after this long and dismal eclipse.

In the novels of this second period, argument forces its way in under cover of fiction. Thus, in "Anna Karénina," which is the story of an adultery, Tolstoï has not only tried to present us with a very accurate picture of aristocratic customs in Russia; he has not only wished to show as the centre and powerful fascination in this series of pictures, the very subtle, very penetrating, very accurate study of a soul wounded by love, the wound of which becomes more and more painful under the effect of the friction and worriments following her first fault: but he has also wished to attack, to settle in his own way, a problem in the social order; — he wished to express his opinion about marriage, about separation, about divorce, about celibacy, about unions freely agreed upon and religiously maintained.

"War and Peace," likewise, is a sort of semi-military, semi-domestic epos; or, if you like, it is a broad study of Russian life, and especially of aristocratic life, whether in the camps, whether in the parlors, whether in the residences of the proprietors during the first quarter of this century, and more especially at the time of the invasion. But within this ample scope the author expresses his theories on military art, his private opinions on the state of war and on the state of peace, his philosophic doctrine of destiny, or his religious fatalism. Some of the characters in "War and Peace" seem at certain times to give a prophetic hint of the dogma which Count Tolstoï will adopt a little later. In Pierre Bezukhof are seen the aspirations towards the ideal which the author of "My Religion" will soon be preaching to men.

If his teaching at this time encroaches on the romance, still it understood how to use marvellously well that vehicle for dissemination wherever the Russian language is spoken; and we shall see, in analyzing them, that the two works of Tolstoï's second manner show a power and a brilliancy that are truly Shaksperian. But the mysticism, traces of which are found in these works, will develop in their author to such a degree as to make him look upon a novel as an object of scandal, as a "flood of oil thrown on the fire of erotic sensuality." He will therefore renounce the inventions of romance; he will sacrifice fiction, which now he calls "licentious;" he will not take up the pen, except to perform the work of a doctor or an evangelist; he will write "My Confession," "My Religion," the "Commentary on the Gospels." Of these three works which illustrate Count Lyof Tolstoï's third manner, the reader will be interested especially in knowing about the first two. He will even find that we have already said enough about "My Confession," and he will take it kindly if we reserve merely "My Religion" for analysis. In return, he will allow us to dwell upon it, and to speak of it entirely at our ease.

Before entering upon the study of "The Cossacks," it will not be idle to run quickly over a little story which might serve in place of an introduction to a translation of this romance. This story, consisting of only a few pages, is entitled "Recollections of a Scorer."[1] It is the story of a rich young man, who, having full control of his fortune, is led by laziness in a short time to degradation and ruin. Nekliudof falls into the society of debauchees and professional gamblers. They pluck him, and ruin him. At his first appearance in this society, he has a feeble nature, but not vulgar. He had some honor: disgusted by the lowness of one of the gamblers, he demands reparation, calls him a coward when he refuses to fight, and compels him to leave the club forever. He had a sense of shame: on the day following a most debasing night, when he had been made intoxicated and initiated into all the depths of debauchery, he

[1] *Zapiski Markera.*

bursts into tears, declaring that he will never forgive either himself or his companions in the orgie. Passion for gambling keeps him bound to them; he sinks so low that soon he plays, not only with his habitual partners, but with the servant who fills the functions of scorer. One by one he descends all the steps of a sickening and abject degradation. He is ruined, and disappears.[1]

He returns one fine day, enters the club, asks for writing materials, and, having finished his letter, summons the scorer: "I would like to try one more game with you." He gains. "Haven't I learned to play well? Hey?"—"Very well."—"Now go and order my carriage." "He started to walk up and down the

[1] Count Tolstoï himself apparently narrowly escaped a similar fate. His brother-in-law induced him to give up gambling; but, after he went to Teheran, he fell into his old habits, and incurred such debts that he was unable to pay them. He tells how full of despair he was at the thought of a certain note falling due when he had nothing wherewith to meet it. He began to pray; and, as though in answer to his prayer, he received a playfully sarcastic letter from his brother, enclosing the dreaded note which a brother officer had generously refused to press or even collect. Yashvin's passion for the gaming-table, in Anna Karénina, is also a reminiscence of this wild-oats period in Count Tolstoï's life. All true fiction must be fact.—N. H. D.

room. Not suspecting any thing, I went down to call his carriage; but there was no carriage there. I went up-stairs again; and, as I approached the billiard-room, I thought I heard a slight noise, like a knock with a cue. I went in. I noticed a strange smell. I looked around: what did I see? He was stretched out on the floor, bathed in his own blood . . . a pistol near him. I was so terror-struck that I could not make a sound. He gave a few signs of life; he stretched out his legs, gave the death-rattle, and all was over."

If this young Russian had possessed a stronger nature or less enfeebled elasticity, he would have done like Olénin, the hero of "The Cossacks," or like Tolstoï, who is himself represented under that name. He would have torn himself from his habits; he would have started for the Far East: he would have been certain to find there enough new impressions to refresh his weary brain; enough manly occupations or vivifying pleasures to strengthen his nerves, and build up his muscles; enough perils and accidents or proofs of every kind to regenerate his soul, purify it from the tares of vice, and again raise the wheat of more than one virtue.

Tolstoï was not the first of these superficially blasé emigrants who went off to Asia to find a powerful diversion from irksomeness, from the disgust of an idle and disorderly existence. Pushkin had pointed out the road for him; and the author of "The Gypsies" had himself followed the traces already marked through the desert by the *britchka* which carried Griboyédof, and the ox-cart which brought him back.[1]

"On the high river bank," says Pushkin, "I saw before me the fortress of Herhera. Three torrents, with roar and foam, come tumbling down the banks. I had just crossed the river. Two oxen, hitched to an *arba*, were climbing the steep road. A few Georgians accompanied the *arba*. 'Where from?' I asked them. 'From Teheran.' — 'What are you carrying?' — 'Griboyéd.' It was the body of the assassi-

[1] Aleksander Sergeyévitch Griboyédof was born in January, 1795, and died in 1829. He studied law at first, but at the age of seventeen entered the army, and afterwards the college of foreign affairs, the service of which took him to Persia and Georgia, where a part of his great comedy, The Misfortune of having Brains (Gore ot Uma), was written. — N. H. D.

nated Griboyédof, which they were taking back to Tiflis."

More fortunate than Griboyédof, Tolstoï will come back alive, and, like Pushkin, will be able to describe this adventurous existence; but he will describe it without embellishments, above all without exalting it. He will let the people whom he finds there, and whom he studies entirely at his leisure, appear in all the bold relief of their natures. He will not take away the strange grace and the perfume of the wild-flower from this nature in which he feels a voluptuous delight.

The evolution of the romance is rapid and fascinating. We are at Moscow. The night is done. The busy city is waking little by little. The indolent youth are finishing their evenings. At the Hotel Chevallier a light, the presence of which is against the rules, filters through the blinds. A carriage, sledges, and a travelling *troïka*, are before the door, near which the porter, muffled in his *shuba*, and a grumbling lackey with pale, drawn features, are waiting.

In the dining-room three young men are finishing a farewell supper. One of them, in short *shuba*, strides up and down the room, cracking almonds in his strong, thick, but well-cared-for hands. At first glance we feel moved by sympathy for him: there is such an expression of life in his smile, in his heated cheeks, in his brilliant eyes, in his fiery gestures, and in his animated voice. He is off for the Caucasus, in the capacity of *yunker.*[1]

Olénin found himself, without family and without curb, at the head of a great fortune, which at twenty-four he has already half wasted. The dominant trait of his character is scorn for all authority. Yet he remains capable of every impulse, even of the most generous. He has experimented with social relations, with service of the State, with farming occupations, with music, with love. He feels that he is *blasé*, but he believes that he is capable of beginning life anew. He is not one of those men "who, born for the bridle, put it on once, and never take it off till the day of their death." He has the spirit and the vivacity which impel him to pick up and cast far from him all the weight of servitude.

[1] Cadet, or ensign.

After having followed a whole net-work of unknown and obscure streets, after having felt a softening of the heart during this drive, not about his friends, not about his mistresses, but about himself, as though his tears were homage rendered to all that he felt that was still good and beautiful and strong and hopeful in him, Olénin suddenly finds himself before the wide, snow-bound plain. He turns his mind to the past. He thinks about his farming, about his debts, about his follies; and he comes to the conclusion that he is, "in spite of all, a very, very clever young man." Having made the first relay, he endeavors to bring about equilibrium in his budget, so as to pay up his creditors in the briefest possible time; and, his conscience being now eased, he falls asleep. He dreams of Circassian beauties, of battles, of glory, of passionate love, of some wild beauty tamed, civilized, and freed by his hand. His tailor Capelli, whom he owes nearly seven hundred rubles, comes across this gilded dream, which is rudely interrupted by the second relay. His journey is broken or filled only by these halts, by tea served at the station, by watching the rumps of the horses, by a few words with his valet Vanya, by a certain number of indefinite dreams, and, most of all, by the nights of sound sleep, such as is granted to youth alone.

According as Olénin advances towards the Caucasus, calm takes possession of his soul. The evidences of civilization which he sees on the route are a trial to him. At Stavropol he is disagreeably impressed to find fashionable attire, cabs, and round hats. But as soon as he is beyond the city the country assumes and retains a wild and warlike character. In the territory of the Don the air becomes already so mild that he has to ride without his furs. Nothing is so delightful as this unexpected spring. But here is something better: danger begins. At any moment they may be attacked by bandits. Then the mountains rise on the horizon. The first impression, at twilight, and from the distance, and through the clouds, is disappointing; but the next morning at early dawn, in the clearness of the sky, they take a new and superb aspect. "From this moment, all that he saw, all that he thought, all that he felt, took on the new and sternly majestic character of the mountains. All his recollections of Moscow, his shame and his regret, all his idle dreams about the Caucasus, departed, never to return."

It is on the banks of the Terek that Olénin is going to dwell, to struggle, to love, to hate,— in a word, to live,—for a number of seasons. It is this river, therefore, that Tolstoï begins to describe for us, with its heaps of grayish sand, and its border of reeds on the right bank, with its low, steep left bank, gullied and crowned with oaks or "rotten plane-trees." On the right are the villages of the Tcherkes, on the left the *stanitsas* (stations) of the Kazaki. "In old times the majority of these *stanitsas* were on the very bank; but the Terek, moving annually north of the mountain, has washed them away, and now only the traces can be seen of thickly-overgrown ancient ruins, abandoned gardens, pear-trees, lindens, and poplars, woven together with mulberries and wild vines. No one dwells there now; and on the sand only the tracks of stags, wolves, hares, and pheasants, which love these places, can be seen."

A delicious impression of buoyant air and

joyous light fills Olénin's heart as soon as he sets foot in the Novomlinskaïa *stanitsa*, in the midst of the Kazak tribe of Grebna. His arrival in the clear twilight, when the whitish mass of the mountains stood out distinctly against the brilliant rays of the setting sun, is described with a vivacity of coloring which deliciously translates emotions never to be forgotten. "Young girls in tucked-up petticoats, with switches in their hands, ran, merrily chattering, to meet the cattle hurrying home in a cloud of dust and gnats from the steppe. The satiated cows and buffaloes scatter through the streets, followed by the Kazak children in their variegated Tatar tunics. Their loud conversation, merry bursts of laughter, and shouts are commingled with the lowing of the cattle. Here an armed Kazak on horseback, having leave of absence from his outpost, rides up to a cottage, and, leaning down from his horse, raps at the window; and in a moment the pretty young head of the Kazak girl appears, and one hears their gay, affectionate talk. Here comes a ragged, high-checked Nogai laborer back with reeds from the steppe. He turns his creaking *arba* into the captain's broad, clean *dvor*, and throws off the yokes from the shaking heads of the oxen, and talks in Tatar with the *esaul.* Around the puddle which fills nearly the whole street, and by which people, all these years, have forced their way, crowding against the fence, a bare-legged Kazak girl is picking her way, bending under a bundle of fagots, and lifting her skirt high above her white ankles; and a Kazak horseman, returning from the chase, laughingly shouts out, 'Lift it higher, wench!' and he aims at her. The Kazak girl drops her skirt, throws down her wood. An old Kazak, with turned-up trousers and bare gray breast, on his way home from fishing, carries his silvery fish, still flopping in the net, and, in order to take a shorter path, crawls through his neighbor's broken hedge, and tears a rent in his coat on the thorns. Here comes an old woman dragging a dry branch, and the blows of an axe are heard around the corner. Kazak children shout as they whip their tops wherever there are level places in the streets; women crawl through the fences so as to save going round. The pungent smoke of burning dung rises from all the chimneys. In every *dvor* is heard the sound of the increased bustle that precedes the silence of the night."

Amid these new faces, there is one whom Olénin catches a glimpse of the very first thing: it is the girl to whom he is going to lose his heart. How she comes upon the scene, this wild young maiden, with her noble features, her statuesque form, her gloomy and burning eyes, with her red lips, her golden complexion, her supple and nervous muscles, her turbulent blood, her savage heart! She comes in with her cattle, which break their way through the open wicket, following a huge buffalo-cow driven wild by the gnats of the steppe. "Marianka's face is half concealed by a kerchief tied round her head: she wears a pink shirt, and a green *beshmet*, or petticoat." She hides under the pent-house of the *dvor;* and her voice is heard as she gently wheedles the buffalo-cow, which she is about to milk: "Now stand still! Here now! Come now, *mátushka!*" How could Olénin escape the impression of "the tall and stately figure, . . . her strong and virginal form, outlined by the thin calico shirt," of those beautiful black eyes, which at first will shun him, but which later will gaze at him "with childish fright and savage curiosity." Love will be born all the more easily from the fact that Marianka is the daughter of the people with whom Olénin is quartered, and that he will find her in his path at every step.

But this feeling is not destined to be met with return. If Marianka is Olénin's ideal of maidenly beauty, this civilized Russian cannot arouse in the young girl's heart any feeling of admiration, and, in consequence, no love. He is not ill-favored, or a weakling, or foolish, stupid, or cowardly; but he has not the triumphant beauty, or the marvellous vigor, or the ever-watchful shrewdness, or the pitiless courage, of the young Kazak, Lukashka. What woman would not love the latter? He is so tall and so well shaped; he wears his soldier's rig so proudly, his torn kaftan, his woollen cap knocked in behind; he has such elegant weapons, and such unrivalled skill in the use of them! There is nothing sweet, nothing tender about him; but the ardor and the life of all the passions show on his face, with its black brows, with its falcon eyes, with teeth of dazzling whiteness. He appears to us for the first time at the Kazak post, near the Terek. His great hands are laying snares and traps for the pheasants, and he is whistling. His comrade (Nazarka), brings him a live pheasant, not daring to kill it. "'Give it here!' Lukashka took a small knife from under his dagger, and quickly cut the pheasant's throat. The bird struggled, but did not have time to spread its wings before its bleeding head bent over and fell."

Whatever character Tolstoï gave these young figures of Marianka and Lukashka, he does not find that they express all that ideal of strength and power with which at this time infatuated. Accordingly he calls up the image of a more striking savagery, in the person of the old Yeroshka, the colossal huntsman with his voice of thunder, his animal habits, his ogre-like appetites, and his childlike character. "Over his shoulders was thrown a ragged woven *zipún*, and his feet were shod in buck-skin *porshni*, or sandals, fastened by cords, which were twisted about his legs. On his head was a rumpled white fur cap. On his back, over one shoulder, he carried a *kobuilka* [an instrument to catch pheasants], and a sack with pullets and dried meat, to bring back the falcon; over the other shoulder a dead wild-cat was swinging by a strap; behind him, fastened to his belt, were a bag containing bullets, powder, and bread, a horse-tail for keeping off the gnats, a big dagger in a torn sheath, stained with blood, and two dead pheasants." This giant has, for distinctive traits, the discreet and silent way in which he walks in his soft sandals, and the odor which he exhales, "a strong, but not unpleasant odor mingled of fresh wine, of vodka, of powder, and of dried blood." He has an inexhaustible fund of anecdotes, about his past life, his hunting, his exploits, his horse-thefts. Yet he is only a child, compared to what his father was, who carried on his back a four-hundred-pound wild boar, and drank at a draught two buckets of vodka. He likes to repeat this saw of a Western man, whom he knew: "We shall all die, the grass will grow on our grave, and that is all." He is stout and hearty for his seventy years, although a witch had ruined him a little with her spell. On the chase, in the woods, he does not cease to whisper, God knows what mysterious monologue. When he returns, if he finds some host at whose table he can sit, and if he can only have wine furnished according to the measure of his thirst, he gets drunk, until he falls stiff on the floor. Hunting scenes, scenes of love, scenes of ambuscade or of combat, go to make up almost exclusively the matter of all this work. But all these scenes are so variously true, and so profoundly the result of experience, that the romantic thread designed to connect them seems almost needless. What reader, however, would have the courage to disengage it? I should like, for my part, to give by way of analysis, and by short quotations, an idea of the most powerful scenes here pictured. I will present them in the order in which they come.

Here we are in ambush, on the banks of the river: "They were hourly expecting the Abreks—as the hostile Tchetchens were called—to cross and attack them, from the Tatar side, especially during the month of May, when the woods along the Terek are so dense, that a man on foot has difficulty in breaking through, and when the river is so low that it can in many places be forded." The Kazak Lukashka is gazing at the sky, with its flashing of heat lightning. He spreads down his kaftan at the foot of the reeds. "Occasionally the reeds, without any apparent reason, would all begin to wave and to whisper to each other. From below, the waving feathers of the sedge looked like the downy branches of trees, against the bright background of the sky." He listens to all the noises of the night, the murmur of the reeds, the snoring of the three Kazaks who have come with him to keep his secret guard, the buzzing of the gnats, and the rippling of the water, from time to time a far-off shot, the fall of a part of the bank washed away, the splash of some big fish, the crashing of the underbrush as some animal forced its way through. "Once an owl, slowly flapping its wings, flew down the Terek; over the heads of the Kazaks, it turned and flew towards the forest, with faster flapping wings, and then fluttering settled down in the branches of an old *tchinar* (plane tree). At every such unusual sound the young Kazak pricked up his ears eagerly, snapped his eyes, and slowly examined his gun."

Suddenly (it is now almost daybreak) a log with a dry branch floating in the river attracts his attention. He immediately notices that the log, instead of going according to the will of the current, and floating down stream, is crossing the river. Here follows several minutes of strange excitement: the whole inner drama which is enacting in this young savage's soul is expressed with so much truth and force, that you come to follow with him the voice of the ferocious instinct which controls him. He puts his gun to his shoulder and waits, while his heart is violently beating at the thought that he may miss his human game; finally he draws a long breath and shoots, muttering, according to the Kazak custom, the "In the name of the Father and the Son." The tree trunk, rocking and rolling over and over, swiftly floats down the stream, freed from the weight which it carried.

And when the Kazaks come hurrying down, both on foot and on horseback (the first thing, in case of a surprise, was to send for re-enforcements), what a scene is that where the lucky marksman plunges into the water to go and bring his fish from the sandbank, and flings the corpse on the bank "like a carp"! What barbarous coloring in the exclamations of the spectators! "How yellow he is!" says one. "He was evidently one of their best *jigits*," says Lukashka: "his beard is dyed and trimmed." While they are on the spot, the chief claims the *jigit's* gun, one Kazak buys the kaftan for a ruble, another promises two gallons of vodka for the dagger.

But the marvellous fragment of this broad, animated, boldly lighted canvas is this group, this contrast between the living man triumphant in his nakedness, and the corpse lying on the ground, naked also, but rigid and terrible to see under the strange coloration and the disconcerting expression of death. "The cinnamon colored body, with nothing on but wet, dark-blue cotton drawers, girdled tightly about the fallen belly, was handsome and well built; the muscular arms lay stiffly along the sides; the livid, freshly shaven round head, with the clotted wound on one side, was thrown back; the smooth sunburned forehead made a sharp contrast with the shaven head; the glassy eyes were still open, showing their pupils, and seemed to look up beyond them all; a good-natured and shrewd smile seemed to hover on the thin and half-open lips under the reddish, half-cut mustache. The small bony hands were covered with hair; the fingers were clinched, and the nails had a red tinge. Lukashka was not yet dressed; he was still wet; his neck was redder, and his eyes were brighter, than usual; his broad cheeks trembled; and from his white and healthy body there seemed to rise into the cool morning air a visible vapor."

As a reward for this expedition, the Kazaks who took part in. it are permitted to go and spend the day at the village. The victorious Lukashka steps up to Marianka with the same feeling of faith in his strength and in his skill as he had had the evening before while lying in wait for the enemy. He asks her for some of the sunflower seeds which she has; she offers him her apron. He comes close to her, and whispers a request of her: she replies, "I shall not go! I have said so." He follows her by the house, and there he urges her to love him. She laughs, and sends him off to his married mistress. He cries, "Suppose I have a sweetheart, the Devil take her." She does not reply, but breaks the switch which she has in her hands. At last, "I will marry certainly, but don't expect me to commit any follies for you, never!" He tenderly woos her. She leans against him, kisses him on the lips, calls him a sweet name, and, after pressing him warmly to her, suddenly tears herself from his arms and runs away. "You will marry," he says to himself, "but the only thing that I want is that you love me!" He went off to find Nazarka at Yamka's; "and, after drinking a while with him, he went to Duniashka's, where he spent the night."

In this struggle for existence, and in this battle for the possession of the beauty whom both love, why should not Olénin be worsted by Lukashka? The principal obstacle to the triumph of the son of civilization comes from his intellectual advantages and from his moral perfection. Do the best he can, he can never get rid of all his prejudices. He will be able only to approach that barbaric ideal which his rival without effort realizes by his natural gifts. In Marianka's eyes he could have only borrowed virtues, only the graces of a plagiarist.

Olénin cannot change his nature by changing his habits; still more he cannot succeed by formulating a theory of life, in conforming to it in all respects the practical facts of existence. The contradictions which result from this conflict between the past and the present, between long-settled ideas and present convictions, is strongly brought out by Tolstoï in many passages in the novel. Here is one example: The first time that the young Russian goes alone pheasant-hunting, he gets tired, and lies down on the ground in the midst of the forest. Myriads of gnats settle down upon him. The torment of it nettles him, discourages him. He is on the point of retracing his steps; an effort of the will keeps him where he is. Finally the feeling of pain is diminished, and at length it seems to him almost agreeable. "It even seemed to him that if this atmosphere of gnats surrounding him on all sides, this paste of gnats which rolled up under his hand when he wiped his sweaty face, and this itching over his whole body were missing, the forest would have lost for him its wild character and its charm."

From this reflection he passes to others; and, lying "in the old stag's bed," he thinks about his whole surrounding, — the trees, the wild vine, the frightened pheasants, the complaining jackals, the gnats buzzing and dancing amid the leaves. "About me, flying among the leaves, which seem to them immense islands, the gnats are dancing in the air and humming, — one, two, three, four, a hundred, a thousand, a million gnats; and all these, for some reason or other, are buzzing around me, and each one of them is just as much a separate existence from all the rest as I am." It began to seem clear to him what the gnats said in their humming. "Here, here, children, here is some one to eat," they sing, and settle down upon him. And now this taught him that he was not a Russian nobleman, a person in Moscow society, a friend or a relative to this and that person. It came to him that he was just a mere gnat, a mere pheasant, a mere stag, like those around him. The conclusion which he draws from this is quite different from what would be expected. Instead of saying, "Let us struggle like these beings, and like them let us live to triumph, or let us triumph to live," Olénin throws himself down on his knees, and beseeches God to let him live to accomplish some great deed of devotion; for "happiness," he says, "consists in living for others."

What did Tolstoï mean to insinuate? That Olénin was illogical, or that he lacked sincerity? It will be enough for him to find himself in Marianka's presence to forget his vow, and to sacrifice his morals to his instincts.

How much happier the Kazak Lukashka is in having only instincts, and in not entangling them, in not fastening them down in this bird-lime of moral considerations! This is what Tolstoï seems to have wished to be understood in a marvellous scene, an analysis of which cannot give either the bold design or the sombre coloring or the proportions worthy of an epos. It is the wholly Homeric parley about the ransom of the corpse. The brother of the dead man and his murderer are face to face: the former tall, stalwart, with reddish trimmed beard, with an air of royalty under his ragged kaftan, honoring no one with a glance, not even looking at the corpse, and sitting on his crossed legs, with a short pipe in his mouth, doing nothing except occasionally giving an order in a guttural voice to his companion the interpreter; the latter with difficulty restraining the exultation into which he is thrown by the promise which has just been made of giving him the cross, and, in spite of his face reddened with pleasure, striving to preserve an impassive attitude, and whittling a stick of wood, out of which he will make a ramrod.

The Tchetchenets has merely asked, as he takes his departure, where the murderer is; and the interpreter points out Lukashka. "The Tchetchenets looked at him for a moment, and then, slowly turning away, fixed his eyes on the other bank. His eyes expressed, not hatred, but cold disdain." They get into the boat; they rapidly push through the stream. Horsemen are waiting for them; they put the dead body across a saddle on a horse, which shies. Lukashka is told what a curt threat the Tchetchenets made as he went away. "You have killed us, but we will crush you." Lukashka bursts out laughing. "Why do you laugh?" asked Olénin. "If they had killed your brother, would you be glad?" The Kazak looked at Olénin, and laughed. He seemed to have comprehended his idea, but he was above all prejudice. "Well, now, mayn't that happen? Isn't this necessary? Haven't they sometimes killed some of our men?"

The time passes. Instead of drinking, of playing cards, of flirting with the Kazak women, of all the time calculating his chances of promotion, like the majority of the Russian *yunkers* in the Caucasus, Olénin plunges into the solitudes of the woods, and gathers indelible impressions. His love for Marianka has imperceptibly developed until it presents all the phenomena of a genuine passion. He has even blurted out a few hints of his affection, which a strange timidity or a scruple of candor keeps him from putting into more direct form; but at night he comes to the door of the room where the young girl is sleeping, in order to listen to her breathing.[1] What shall he do? To take her for his mistress would be "horrible; it would be murder." To marry her would be worse.

"Ah! if I could become a Kazak like Lukashka, could steal horses, could drink *tchikhir* wine, could sing songs, shoot people, creep under her window at night when drunk, without any thought of what I am, or why I exist, that would be another matter. Then we might understand each other; then I might be happy. . . . What is the most terrible and the most delightful thing in my position is the feeling that I understand her, and that she will never under-

[1] M. Dupuy, in his condensation of the story, loses the perspective. Olénin taps lightly on the window. "He ran to the door, and actually heard Marianka's deep sigh and her steps. He took hold of the latch, and shook it softly. Bare, cautious feet, scarcely making the boards creak, drew near the door. The latch was lifted: the door was pushed ajar. There was a breath of gourds and marjoram, and suddenly Marianka's full form appeared on the threshold." But the prospective interview is broken by the appearance of Lukashka's friend Nazarka, who has to be bought off. The next day Olénin writes a letter, which, being more like a diary, he does not send, "because no one would understand what he meant to say." In this letter occurs the passage which M. Dupuy quotes. — N. H. D.

stand me. It is not because she is below me that she does not understand me : no, she could not possibly understand me. She is happy. She, like nature itself, is beautiful, calm, and absolutely self-contained." What is to be done, then? Give her up? Sacrifice himself? What folly! Live for others? Why? It is the fate of men to love only the *ego;* that is to say, in this case, to conquer Marianka, "and live her life." Olénin then makes himself drunk like a Kazak; and, in the madness of intoxication, he offers to marry the young girl. She perceives clearly that that is only the wine that speaks: she drives the wooer away, and escapes him.

Yet she feels somewhat moved in consequence of this offer; and on the day of the *stanitsa* festival she is rude to Lukashka, though she has already become his acknowledged "bride." But a tragic event is about to bring forth abundantly the feeling which fills this young soul to overflowing. All Marianka's deep love for Lukashka will suddenly gleam out with unexpected brilliancy, like the gloomy sheet of the Terek in the flashes of the storm.

The Kazaks have started out on an expedition against the Abreks. Olénin follows the band which is directed, but not commanded, by Lukashka. The engagement takes place. The Abreks are sitting in a swamp at the foot of a hillock of sand. The Kazaks approach them behind a cart loaded with hay. At first they do not reply to the enemy's shots. They wait till they are within five paces from the Abreks, then they rush upon them. Olénin joins them. "Horror came over his eyes. He did not see any thing distinctly, but perceived that all was over. Lukashka, white as a sheet, had caught a wounded Tchetchenets, and was crying, 'Do not kill him. I will take him alive.' The Tchetchenets was the red-bearded Abrek, the brother of the one whom he had killed, he who had come to ransom his body. Lukashka was twisting his arms. Suddenly the Tchetchenets tore himself away, and his pistol went off. Lukashka fell. Blood showed on his abdomen. He leaped to his feet, but fell back again, swearing in Russian and Tatar. Still more blood appeared on him and under him. The Kazaks hurried up to him, and began to loosen his belt. One of them — it was Nazarka — for some time before coming to him could not sheathe his *shashka.* The blade of the *shashka* was covered with blood."

"When Olénin came back to Marianka, and wanted to speak of his love for her, he found her grieving. She looked at him silently and defiantly.

"Olénin said, 'Mariana, I have come.' . . .

"'Stop,' she said. Her face did not change in the least, but the tears poured from her eyes.

"'What is the matter? What are you crying for?'

"'Why?' she repeated in a hoarse, deep voice. 'They have been killing Kazaks, and that's what the matter is!'

"'Lukashka?' asked Olénin.

"'Go away. I don't want to see you.'

"'Mariana,' said Olénin, coming nearer to her.

"'You will never get any thing from me!'

"'Mariana, don't say so!'

"'Go away, you hateful man!' cried the young girl, stamping angrily, and starting towards him with a threatening gesture. Such anger, scorn, hatred, were expressed in her face that Olénin instantly saw that he had nothing more to hope for."

He therefore goes away. The scene of his farewell with the old uncle Yeroshka has that exquisite pathos where smiles are mingled with tears. As a friendly gift at this solemn moment of separation, the old Kazak gives the young Russian some advice which will save his life in battles. He casts ridicule on the customs of the orthodox soldiers. "When you have to go into battle, or everywhere, — I am an old wolf, you see, who has seen every thing, — when they fire at you, don't go into a crowd where there are many men. You see, when your fellows are a bit afraid, they all crowd together; and though it's more sociable in a crowd, it is more dangerous, because a crowd gives a good mark. . . . I say sometimes, when I look at your soldiers, "I wonder at 'em. How stupid! They go straight on, all in a mass; and, what is worse, they wear red. How can they help getting killed?" And he breaks into tears as he kisses this young, "ever-wandering fool;" but he manages to extort from him a gun, to keep as a remembrance of him.

"Olénin looked round. Dyadya Yeroshka and Marianka were talking, evidently about their own affairs; and neither the old Kazak nor the young girl were looking at him." (With these simple but pathetic words, the story ends.)

III.

An analysis mingled with characteristic quotations might be able to give some slight idea of the romance "Kazaki," might give the reader a hint of its interest, its color, and its flavor of originality. An analysis of "War and Peace" can have no other aim, no other pretension, than to point out Tolstoï's design in this colossal work, and separate the moralist's tendencies from the story itself, which every one will want to read, and read again, in detail.

In "War and Peace," amid a multitude of thoroughly interesting figures, there are three heroes who in some measure occupy the foreground, and who stand out clearly against a background of great variety, carefully studied, and peopled with living beings. These three characters are Andréi Bolkonsky, Nikolaï Rostof, and Pierre Bezhúkhof. The last mentioned is not at first glance the one who is most attractive in outward appearances; but it is the one whose moral nature is most curious, the one in whom the author has expressed his own inmost views, the one who, in his eyes, best illustrates the striking faults and the fundamental virtues of a Russian nature. Bezúkhof's qualities are exactly those of the men of the Slav race: he is good, gentle, loyal, compassionate; his faults are indolence, apathy, fickleness in his tastes, incapability of following a given course, inaptitude in realizing his own volitions.

Thus after having given his word not to attend a *soirée* at Prince Anatol Kuragin's, Pierre Bezúkhof goes there, becomes intoxicated, then with the aid of another gay spirit, Dolokhof, fastens a police-agent to the back of a tame young bear, and throws them both into the river. Dolokhof is degraded; Pierre escapes with a few months' exile from the capital. In the same way Bezúkhof is perfectly convinced that Elen Kurágina's beauty and the dazzling whiteness of her shoulders do not hinder her from being dangerous on account of her coquetry; he has heard mysterious rumors concerning her equivocal relations with his brother, the last of the debauchees; he is perfectly convinced that it would be foolish to the last degree to marry this admirable character, and that the best way of not committing this folly is to give up seeing her charming face, her seductive snowy complexion. Unhappily for him, her marble shoulders, neck, and bosom, one evening, came close to his poor near-sighted eyes, and all "is so near to his lips that he had scarcely to bend a hair's breadth to impress them upon it." Pierre Bezúkhof does not depart more: he allows himself to be married, partly through infatuation, partly through feebleness.

The marriage almost from the very first turns out ill. The rake Dolokhof has returned, and never leaves Bezúkhof's house. Pierre long puts up with a situation, the meaning of which he does not suspect: the inevitable anonymous letter comes to open his eyes. At first he refuses to believe what he has been told; but at the club where he meets Dolokhof, it is sufficient for him to find himself face to face with his wife's lover, for his jealousy to burst forth with a flash like a discharge of electricity. The first pretext gives Pierre cause for a quarrel, and a duel follows. Dolokhof is a crack marksman: he has no sort of feebleness. Pierre Bezúkhof is near-sighted, awkward: he has never fired a pistol in his life. But, as if by judgment of God, it is Dolokhof who falls.

Returning home, Pierre Bezúkhof tries vainly to sleep, so as to forget all that has just passed. He cannot close his eyes. "He got up, and began to pace up and down the room with uneven steps. Now he thought of the early days of their marriage, of her beautiful shoulders, of her languishing, passionate gaze; now he pictured Dolokhof standing by her, handsome, impudent, with his diabolic smile, just as he had seen him at the club dinner; now he saw him pale, shivering, vanquished, and sinking on the snow.

"'And, after all, I have killed her lover," he said to himself; 'yes, my wife's lover! How could that be? 'It happened because you married her,' said an inward voice. 'But in what respect am I to blame?'—'You are to blame because you married her without loving her,' continued the voice; 'you deceived her, since you willingly blinded yourself.' At this instant, the moment when he said with so much difficulty, 'I love you,' came back to his memory. 'Yes, there was the trouble. I felt then that I had not the right to say it.'"

If any one wishes to be assured of the passage which I have just quoted, he must open "My Religion," and there read the commentary on adultery, and the condemnation of divorce according to the books of Matthew (xix.), Mark (x.), Luke (xvi.), and Paul's First Epistle to the Corinthians. According to Tolstoï, marriage is indissoluble. Nothing, not even a wife's unfaithfulness, authorizes a man to repudiate her; and, if he puts her away, he cannot marry another without himself committing the crime of adultery. We shall see this theory more clearly brought out in the romance of "Anna Karénina;" but even here Tolstoï makes his hero Bezúkhof conform to it. He will not allow him to claim the hand of another woman until the day when Elen's unexpected death shall have broken the bond which he had imprudently allowed to be tied. He exalts this imprudence into a crime. He thinks that the chief culprit was he who did not fear to contract a loveless marriage, or to seek in this marriage mere gratification of pride and lust.

But Pierre acknowledges his fault to no purpose: his conscience will not speak as soon as his wrath is again stirred up by his wife's impudent cynicism and truly mad provocations. Elen comes into her husband's library in a rich and brilliant dishabille, with her calm and imposing air, "though on her slightly prominent forehead a deep line of fury was drawn." She reproaches her husband for the scandal which he has caused, twits him as though he were an imbecile, and declares that the man of whom he was jealous was a thousand times his superior. She claims that she has the right to berate him; "for I can say up and down that a woman with such a husband as you who would not have a lover would be a rare exception, and I have none." Pierre, as he listens, feels a moral discomfort, which torments him, the sting of physical pain.

"'We had better part,' he said, in a choking voice.

"'Part? By all means, on condition that you give me enough of your fortune,' replied Elen.

"Pierre leaped to his feet, and, losing control of himself, flew at her.

"'I will kill you!' he cried; and seizing a piece of marble from the table, he made a step towards Elen, brandishing it with a force which even startled himself.

"The countess's face was frightful to see: she yelled like a wild beast, and fell back. Pierre felt all the fascination, all the intoxication, of fury. He threw the marble on the floor, breaking it into fragments, and advanced towards her with uplifted arms.

"'Get out,' he cried, in a voice of thunder, which sent a thrill of terror throughout the house. God knows what he would have done at that moment had Elen not fled.

"A week later Pierre left for Petersburg, having made over to his wife the full control of all his property in Russia proper, which constituted a good half of his fortune."

In going from Moscow to Petersburg, Bezúkhof stops at Torzhok for relays, but horses are not to be had. He spends the night at the post-station. The bitterest reflections crowd upon his mind. "What is wrong? what is right? Whom must you love? whom must you hate? What is the end of life?" "Every thing within him and without seemed to him confused, uncertain, distasteful; but this very feeling of repugnance gave him an irritating sense of satisfaction." At this moment a stranger arrives, an old man, whose "grave, intelligent, piercing gaze" strikes Pierre, and troubles him, in spite of its fascination. The new-comer knows Bezúkhof by sight, and has heard of his domestic grief. He expresses to Pierre his deep regret at this "misfortune." Pierre, confused at the pity shown him, turns the conversation to the subject of a death's-head ring which he notices on the stranger's finger: he recognizes in it the mark of Free Masonry. The conversation takes up the moral views and the religious doctrine of those who belong to the order. The old man urges the young man to take a different view of life from that of looking at it with horror; not to escape from it, but to change it. "How have you spent your life? In orgies, in debauchery, in depravity, taking every thing from society, and giving nothing in return. How have you employed the fortune that was put into your hands? What have you done for your fellow-men? Have you thought of your tens of thousands of serfs? Have you ever helped them, morally or physically? No! Is it not true that you profited by their labor to lead a worthless life? That is what you have done. Have you striven to employ your abilities for the good of others? No, you have passed your life in idleness. Then you married. You undertook the responsibility of being a guide to a young woman. How did you acquit yourself? Instead of aiding her to find the path of truth, you cast her into an abyss of falsehood and misery. A man insulted you: you killed him. And you say that you don't believe in God, that you look upon your life with horror. How could it be otherwise?"

In this programme of a new life sketched out by the old Free Mason, we recognize the one followed by Tolstoï himself, at a certain epoch of his life between the period of relentless struggle, of implacable egotism, and the period of absolute sacrifice, of humble renunciation.

Pierre accordingly allows himself to be initiated into the order. I forbear to quote all the picturesque details of the ceremony. The novelist, using his rights, does not fail to throw a curious light on the mystic customs of the Russian aristocracy at the beginning of this century. What concerns us to note here, is the immediate benefit which Pierre Bezúkhof draws from this first transformation of his life. The simple prospect of devoting himself "to the regeneration of humanity" was sufficient to put meaning into a life which seemed to him impossible to travel. Unfortunately, in practice, his accomplishments fall below his dreams. He contents himself with giving his overseer orders concerning the emancipation of his serfs, the cessation of corporal punishment, the reasonable regulation of labor, the building of hospitals and schools. The overseer, who sees through his master's *naïveté*, constantly plays it upon him, and imposes upon him in regard to the effect of the measures prescribed, but which he carefully refrains from undertaking. Pierre is not the man to descend to the details of the reform which he has vowed to carry out: he is, above all, not the man to make a bold stand against the difficulties of execution. At bottom, he would be very sorry if they had not been concealed from his sight. Accordingly he contents himself with a few apparent results, and is very careful not to look too closely into the lack which these appearances cover.

Besides, his new faith receives a terrible blow the day when he tries to make one of his friends, Prince Andréi Bolkonsky, share in his conviction. He encounters his bitter scepticism, which is the fruit of heredity (Andréi's father having been a "grand seigneur," of sharp temper and despotic soul), but it is also the result of the most painful collisions in life. Like Pierre Bezúkhof, Andréi Bolkonsky had been the husband of a woman whom he did not love. He always treated her like a brainless doll, and never showed any other feeling in her presence than lassitude. His only attitude towards her was that of disdain. This child, whom he did not have the patience to make into a helpmeet, died in child-birth. His young wife's death has left in Andréi a sense of irremediable injustice, and he loves better to blame fate than himself; although at times he is seized with such a violent wish to repair his fault, that he is driven by it almost to express his belief in immortality. He hesitates to utter his assent to the dogma of the future life; but his wounded heart allows the exclamation to escape, "Oh, if it were so!"

To realize the distance traversed by Count Tolstoï since the time when he put this language into Bolkonsky's mouth, we must look in "My Religion," at the place where the writer — rather, let us say, the apostle — engages in such a vigorous combat with the doctrine of the resurrection of the dead, which he condemns as heresy. "Strange as it may seem, it is impossible to refrain from saying that the belief in a future life is a very low and degrading conception, founded on a confused notion of the resemblance between sleep and death, a notion common to all savage peoples. The Hebrew doctrine (and much more the Christian doctrine) was far above this conception."

Prince Andréi Bolkonsky, as soon as he enters the stage, strikes us as one of the most distinguished examples of that Russian aristocracy to which Tolstoï belongs, and which he wished to make known to his readers in "War and Peace." He has for his dominant features a clear, sharp, penetrating mind, and all the elegancies of his race, including a super-eminent pride. During the peace, and when his best qualities are not called into action, he wears some "affectation of indifference and *ennui*." In time of war, and when "the weight of serious and real interests" will leave him no "leisure to consider the impression which he makes on others," he will deserve all Kutuzof's praise by his solidity, his desert, and his attachment to his duty. He will give offence by his disdain, but he will win over to his side the majority of the Russian officers; for his birth gives him a certain superiority over his chiefs, which they themselves tacitly acknowledge. Finally, he has a few rare friends, whom the distinction of his character has carried even to passionate admiration.

Andréi Bolkonsky's faults and virtues are found, with more striking features, and exaggerated till they give an impression of humorous terribleness, in his father, the old proprietor,

Nikolaï Bolkonsky. With his powdered wig, his withered hands, his arms of steel, his bushy, grizzled brows, under which shine his youthful and brilliant eyes; with his manias for mathematics, for turning wooden snuff-boxes, and for putting up buildings; with his brusque speech, his sardonic smile, his yellow teeth, his ill-shaven chin, his Tatar boots of soft leather, his arm-chair tainted with a musty odor of tobacco,—this despot is not to be forgotten. He teaches his daughter, the Princess Marya, the sciences. Before she goes into the room where her father is, to give him the morning greeting, the young woman, as she leaves the vestibule, "crossed herself, and prayed that courage would be given her." On the day when his son Andréi comes to announce that he is going away to enter the service, and that he leaves in his father's care his young wife, who is pregnant, and much troubled by a prediction which had been made to her after a dream, "the king of Prussia," as the old man is nicknamed, replies only with the words, —

"'Bad business, hey;' and he smiled. . . .

"'What is bad business, father?'

"'Your wife,' replied the old man bluntly, accenting the word.

"'I don't understand you.'

"'Well, my dear fellow, you can't do any thing, you see; you can't get unmarried. Don't worry, . . . I won't tell any one: but — you know it as well as I do — it's the truth.' He seized his son's hand with his lean, bony fingers, and pressed it, while his piercing eyes seemed to look to the very bottom of his being. His son answered with a silent confession, — a sigh."

The weight of this paternal dictatorship, which constantly crushes the Princess Marya, has an effect upon her which it is important to note. She is thrown into a sort of mysticism, somewhat like that which we have seen come over Tolstoï himself. She has frequent interviews with beggars, pilgrims, the poor in spirit; she listens to them, and gets instruction, not from their coarse anecdotes about the wonder-working Virgin whose cheeks sweat blood, but from their resignation at the torments of life. Thus she succeeds in forgetting her most bitter disappointments, or at least in bearing them with a steadfastness which no stoicism can approach. She also gets from her faith, her gentleness in judging those who come near her.

"*Akh*, Andréi," she says to her brother, "what a treasure of a wife you have! — a real child, gay, animated. How I love her!" Andréi had taken a seat by his sister: he did not speak; an ironical smile played on his lips. She noticed it, and went on: "Her little weaknesses call for indulgence. . . . Who is there without some? . . . To understand every thing is to forgive." And she forgives every thing, even the most cruel insult, even the wound inflicted on the most sensitive part of her sensitive nature, — of her loving heart. The handsome Anatoli Kuragin comes with his father, Prince Vasíli, to ask her hand in marriage, she being an heiress. While waiting to carry off this dowry with a high hand, he plays, in the Bolkonsky house, as everywhere else, his game of seduction; and he has rendezvous with the *demoiselle de compagnie*, a young and pretty French girl. Marya catches them accidentally. She refuses the marriage which she had eagerly anticipated. "I shall be called to some other good fortune. I shall be happy in devotion, and in making others happy." She dreams of seeing the man whom she loved marry the one who has so shamefully insulted her. "I should be so glad to see her his wife: she is so sad, so lonely, so abandoned! How she must love him when he forgets her so! Who knows? Perhaps I should have done the same."

Andréi goes to war; and Tolstoï takes us with him into a world of action, which he describes with rare power. We are dazzled at first by the brilliant art with which the novelist moves armies, carries out the combinations of tacticians, shows the troops with their passionate dash or their senseless terrors, represents their leaders with their hesitations or their unconscionable activity, but all alive, true, recognizable, from the humblest of the German officers to Napoleon the great captain. We are singularly struck by certain of his preferred methods; like that, for instance, of being true to fact in his painting of what is always idealized. Napoleon has vulgarities of character and expression, and the unexpected meeting with them gives us at first a shock of admiration.

Instead of saying simply, "What realism!" we exclaim, "What reality!" Yet I do not hesitate to consider this portion of "War and Peace" as inferior to others. The historian in Tolstoï inspires me with a certain feeling of distrust: it seems to me that the painter of battles, with his first-class ability, here and there takes advantage of our fairness. There is a tinsel effect in his painting; the details are far too numerous, and there is not so much variety among them as one would think.

What is incomparable in the war part of the romance are the descriptions of military customs, the scenes of camp-life, the impressions of certain hours of day and night, the reminiscences of evening conversations, the effects of groups lighted up by the weird light of the bivouac, the heart-rending aspects of the battlefield or the hospital-wards. The marvellous beauty of all this wealth of feelings felt and experienced adds its glory to the more commonplace and less valuable woof of the historical narration. Turgénief, who understood this, noted somewhere or other this difference; but there are very few readers who can thus bethink themselves, and take account of their illusions.

Wounded at Austerlitz, and taken to the French hospital, Andréi sees Napoleon approach his bedside; that is to say, he sees the one who, in his eyes, represents the ideal, the superhuman man, the hero, the demigod. At death's door, Andréi sees all things in a light which reduces them to their real proportions. To him all Napoleon's acts, all his words, all the motives which make him act and speak, seem empty of interest. He turns from the sight of what is only human, and, with his eyes fixed solely on the medal which Marya hung around his neck on the day of his departure, he endeavors to believe "in that ideal heaven which alone promises him peace."

Scarcely recovered from his wound, Andréi returns to his father's home, which he reaches in time to be present at his wife's confinement. There is here an admirable scene, which will be surpassed only by the birth-scene described in the romance of "Anna Karénina." All that is dramatic, august, mysterious, in the opening flower of maternity has been expressed by

Tolstoï in these two passages. That of "Anna Karénina" is famous. We feel nothing of the equivocal impressions and the lugubrious effects, which, under the pretext of realism, the author of "La Joie de Vivre" will put into a similar description. But a parallel between the realism of Tolstoï and the realism of Zola would carry us too far from our subject.

The impression left upon Andréi Bolkonsky by the death of his wife has in no small degree contributed to develop in him the tendency toward dissatisfaction with life. But one day a young girl comes into the circle of shadow, and he instantly allows her to usurp its place. The memory of a luminous vision is brought into the depths of his soul. All the apparently sleeping springs of affection in his nature are stirred up by the appearance of Natasha Rostova. Chance brings Andréi to the young girl's paternal mansion: he falls in love with her, and with this new love begins the renewal of life.

The house of the Rostofs is the third of the seignorial homes which Tolstoï opens to us, and it is the one where it is the easiest thing to forget one's self. Songs only are heard, merry laughter, the chatter of fresh voices. The head of the family, Count Rostof, is a great proprietor, ostentatious, but free from arrogance, and is carelessly hurrying to his ruin; but no one better than he understands the duties of hospitality. His wife is a sweet, good woman, adoring her family, and by her family adored. There are two sons in the house. The youngest, Petya, is a child at the beginning of the story; but he will be seen in the ranks of the Russian army before the end of the book. And Tolstoï, in describing his heroic death, will write a few pages, the beauty and noble sadness of which, without any sense of detriment, recall Virgil and the episode of Euryalus dying beside Nisus. The elder brother, Nikolaï Rostof, is the typical young noble, born for military life, for whom the profession of soldier is the first in the world, who is too sound in mind, too healthy in body, not to carry everywhere with him his good-humor and his off-hand manners. But he returns to camp as to a second *home*, and weeps with joy to see his comrades again; and he has no regret when he is once more in his tent, and he submits to the yoke and habits of military life with the same sensation of pleasure that a weary man feels when at last he has the chance to lie down and go to sleep. Tolstoï makes use of Nikolaï Rostof just as he does of Prince Andréi, in order to make us present with him during a portion of the deeds of war which he wishes to relate. Rostof's impressions are not, however, like Bolkonsky's: they recall pretty closely the memories noted in the "Military Sketches" of Sevastópol. It is evident that Tolstoï, who has very largely put himself into each of his characters, has reflected himself in this peculiar side in this one.

In the house of the Rostofs, there is a whole swarm of young girls,—the prudent Viéra, methodical and tiresome; the gentle Sonya, a poor relation, who is loved by the son, and who worships him, even to sacrifice: she will forego marriage with him, so that he may be rich and happy. But a luminous face, dazzling with its freshness, gayety, and grace, is that shown us in Natasha, Andréi Bolkonsky's "bride." Natasha is so beautiful, that no one can see her without loving her. She is willing to be loved without returning it. Happy in the effect caused by her beauty, she mistakes all her coquettish, maidenly caprices for honest, serious sentiments. She has imagined that she was in love with her brother Nikolaï's friend Boris, then with Denisof, then with Prince Andréi, all in succession; but her passion has never yet been really awakened. It is waiting for the appearance of the last aspirant, the only one unworthy of being chosen; and then it bursts forth with frightful violence. Natasha meets Anatoli Kuragin: she yields to the fascination of his beauty, his boldness. He shamelessly addresses a few coarse, flattering words to her; and she is intoxicated by this unrefined incense more than by delicate homage. She forgets that she is plighted to Prince Andréi: she allows herself to listen to words of love. She loves; and she loves so passionately, that, without hesitation, she consents to all that her seducer has planned to lead her to irretrievable ruin. She is willing to elope. A providential chance prevents her departure. Pierre Bezúkhof arrives in time to reveal to the unfortunate young woman that Kuragin is married:

he gives him a pretty rough experience of his giant hand, and compels Lovelace to return Natasha's letters, and to pack off.

Natasha[1] falls ill with sorrow, shame, and remorse. The doctors cannot get the better of this moral suffering. Religion alone puts an end to it. A lady who lives in the country near the Rostofs comes to Moscow during Lent, and takes Natasha with her to perform their devotions. Each morning before daybreak they set out, and go to kneel before the Virgin, "the blackened painting of whom is lighted up by the candles and the first rays of the dawn." Natasha prays with fervor, with humility. She feels that she is gradually becoming somewhat regenerated; and on the day when she is to receive the communion, she finds herself "at peace with herself, and reconciled to life."

"'Count,' asked Natasha of Pierre, as she paused, 'do I do wrong to sing?' And she raised her eyes to his, and blushed.

"'No. Wherein would lie the harm? . . . On the contrary. But why should you ask me?'

[1] She takes a dose of arsenic, but prompt means save her life.—N. H. D.

"'I don't know, I'm sure,' replied Natasha, speaking hurriedly. 'But it would grieve me to do any thing which might displease you. I saw,' she went on, without noticing that Pierre was embarrassed, and reddening in his turn, 'I saw his name in the order of the day. . . . Do you think that he will ever forgive me? Do you believe that he will always be angry with me? Do you?'

"'I think,' continued Pierre, 'that he has nothing to forgive. If I were in his place'— And the same words of love and pity which he had spoken to her once before were on his tongue's end, but Natasha did not give him time to finish.

"'*Akh!* you? That is a very different thing,' she cried enthusiastically. 'I don't know a better and more generous man than you. Such a man does not exist. If you had not helped me then and now, I do not know what would have become of me.' Her eyes filled with tears, which she hid behind her music; and, turning around abruptly, she began to practice her *solfeggi*, and to walk up and down."

Thus begins the last romance in Natasha's

life. She loves Pierre Bezúkhof, not with the fanciful love which she felt for Andréi, nor the mad passion which Kuragin inspired in her, but with a pure, moral affection, founded on esteem, on the similarity of thoughts and feelings. This union is the only one which Tolstoï wishes to realize for Bezúkhof, for it is the only kind which seems to him legitimate. But, before it can be accomplished, it must needs be that the man to whom Natasha had plighted her troth should be no longer between her and the one whom she is to marry. Accordingly we are brought to witness Andréi Bolkonsky's death.

The French invasion of 1812 has roused all the powers of Russia. From the *muzhik* to the *velmozh*, every one has felt the impulse of self-sacrifice. The Rostofs, whose second son Petya desires to go as a hussar, are surprised in the midst of moving, by the arrival of wounded, whom it is impossible to transport farther. They have some of the furniture unloaded, and arrange a train of wagons. Among the mortally wounded whom they have thus received is Prince Andréi. He was struck by a bursting shell on the same day as Kuragin, and chance has so brought it about that the wounded man can behold on his bed of agony the man who stole Natasha's heart from him. This is a most powerfully dramatic scene. It is not the only one offered by this part of the book. Natasha discovers, during the journey, that Prince Andréi is in one of the wagons. She makes her way out during the night, and comes to kneel by his bedside. Natasha and the Princess Marya meet at this death-bed. The analysis of the wounded man's last feelings and sensations at the supreme moment is a marvel of divination: the ecstasy of the evening hours, the delirium of the moments of somnolence, are expressed with a power of imagination which makes one shudder.

Meantime, beside the Rostofs' carriage walks a man of lofty stature, in laborer's attire. It is Pierre Bezúkhof, who also has desired to find a chance to sacrifice himself. He did not join the army, like Andréi Bolkonsky, Nikolaï Rostof, Petya, and the others. Does he think, then, like the author of "My Religion," that he has no right to kill a man, even though it were an enemy of his country? He stays in Moscow, with vague projects, which Fate, that mighty actor in the dramas of mankind, according to the author of "War and Peace," prevents him from putting into execution. He is captured by the French, and endures a most trying nomad captivity. But he finds among his comrades in misfortune a poor soldier with wounded feet, and body devoured by vermin, and from him he learns the great secret of existence. Platon Karataïef, in spite of his pitiable exterior, personifies the moral and religious ideal, which, as we have already seen, Count Tolstoï definitely came to accept. As soon as the hero of "War and Peace," Pierre Bezúkhof, has reached this limit of his development, the story has only to proceed of its own inertia to the conclusion. I feel that there is no necessity of delaying over the final scenes. The Princess Marya, whose father is now dead, marries Nikolaï Rostof, who had saved her life by quelling a revolt among the serfs of Luisuia Gorui, the Bolkonsky's domain. Bezúkhof, at last a widower, is free to marry Natasha.

IV.

As in "War and Peace," so in "Anna Karénina," we shall find Count Lyof Tolstoï himself just as his own confessions have allowed us to point him out. As in "War and Peace," all the chief personages will have some of his characteristics, and Vronsky and Konstantin Levin, in turn, represent him in some peculiar aspect, in the same way as Nikolaï Rostof, Prince Andréi, and Count Pierre. Thus, in the discourse where Count Vronsky proposes a re-organization of his landed property, and claims that it must be based on the agreement between the *muzhik* and his former lord, Count Tolstoï propounds a theory which he long held, but which he has since gone beyond; for, as we shall soon see, he has reached Communism.

In the same way we recognize the ideas of "My Religion" in Levin's resistance of the patriotic outburst, or, to use his language, the unreflecting enthusiasm which rouses the Russian youth, and drives one of the characters of the story, Vronsky, to enlist of his own accord for the defence of the Serbian cause. While protesting by his own abstention, and also by his tirades against the Slav committees and the enlistment, Konstantin Levin is already applying the doctrine which Count Tolstoï will formulate in the maxim, "Do not engage in war," and on which he will make the following comment: "Jesus has shown me that the fifth temptation that deprives me of my welfare is the distinction made by us between our compatriots and foreign nations. I must believe in that. Consequently, if in a moment of forgetfulness I experience a feeling of hostility against a man of another nationality, I must not fail to recognize, in my thoughtful moments, that this feeling is false. No longer, as formerly, can I justify myself by the superiority of my people to others; by the ignorance, the cruelty, or the barbarity of another people. I cannot refrain, at the first opportunity, from endeavoring to be more affable to a foreigner than to one of my countrymen." And if Vronsky behaves differently from Konstantin Levin, it is not because Tolstoï wishes to offset the conduct of the one to the views of the other. In reality, it is not from conviction, it is from despair, that Vronsky enlists. He goes away so as to forget, amid the excitement — or, as Pascal said, the *divertissement* — of a soldier's life the impression of the inward drama which has disturbed his soul to its foundation, and which, by a fatal, but unexpected, conclusion, has just bespattered him with blood.

The romance of "Anna Karénina" is the history of an adulterous amour: the climax of the amour is suicide. Is this suicide in the novelist's mind a moral penalty? That would be a wholly barbarous conception, a sort of divine judgment such as would have been imagined by a story-teller in the Middle Ages, and Tolstoï seems to have wished to forestall such a vulgar interpretation of his narrative. There are in the romance other criminal amours, and it is without any sign of punishment that the wholly immoral relationship between the Princess Betsy and her lover leads them to scandalous conduct. On the other hand, the passion which unites Anna Karénina and Vronsky is a sincere, profound, almost solemn passion, in spite of the illegality of their behavior. The hearts of these two lovers are culpable but lofty. Besides, the more sympathy the author of the romance shows in their presentation, the more powerful is the lesson which he desires to draw from their moral torment. All the plan and all the interest of the work are here. What agonies of remorse this illegal union, so passionately desired, brings upon the guilty woman! What deep mortifications and what vulgar discomfitures, what deadly humiliations and what prosaic irksomeness, spring from this false situation, and ultimately make it so odious, so painful, that way of escape has to be found by an act of madness in a moment of despair!

Yet never were more conditions united to facilitate this union outside the law. Vronsky's rank is too lofty for him to fear public opinion: he makes it, as it were, a point of honor to defy it, and he instals his mistress in his splendid domain as though she were his legitimate wife. Without much apparent difficulty, he makes his friends and his family treat his *liaison* with respect. Anna Karénina, on her part, loves Vronsky with a perfect passion, which is only intensified and not chilled by the feeling of sacrifices undergone. All that she asks from her lover in return is to be loved by him. She has made it a point of honor on her part to refuse the advantages of a divorce which her husband, Alekséi Karénin, at first offers to have pronounced against himself. She refused from a double reason of delicacy: she did not wish to add this gratuitous insult to the wrongs of which she is guilty towards this disagreeable, but upright, man; above all, she does not wish that a suspicion of calculation should cast its shadow over the feeling which she has towards the count.

A divorce, however, would put an end to many sentimental doubts causing misunderstandings, and to many subtleties of behavior resulting only in collisions. Vronsky demands the divorce with all the strength of his generous pride. Anna Karénina scouts the idea of it with such jealous anxiety as a naturally noble woman can feel in preserving the remains of her dignity, which a shock of passion has thrown down and broken to fragments like a costly vase. This antagonism creates between the two lovers a secret source of bitterness. There are other latent troubles. By her marriage, Anna Karénina has a son from whom she is separated, whom she worships; and the slightest remembrance of him causes her heart to thrill with that same strange feeling which is the precursor of motherhood. In consequence of her amour with Vronsky, she has a daughter. By a singular anomaly she does not love the child of the man whom she loves: she is vexed with her daughter for occupying in some measure a place usurped, for monopolizing with her the maternal cares which it seems to her that the other child so grievously needs. If as a mother she has her whimsical but touching fits of jealousy, as a woman she has other fears, the absurdity of which does not prevent them from being very painful. She spends her time and gnaws her heart in trying to divine her lover's attitude towards her. She knows that for her sake he has renounced a most brilliant future; she is afraid that she cannot fill his objectless existence; she sees in each attempted return to any occupation, to any distraction whatsoever, a proof of weariness, a confession of irksomeness, a sign of regret.

Vronsky, who has made absolute renunciation without thought of return, at last begins to suffer from this distrust: the more it grows, the more disappointment and secret vexation he feels. Here the loftiness of character which attaches him to his mistress, and which has made it easy for him to brave every thing for her, turns against the unfortunate woman, and impels him to resist the efforts which she makes to get fuller possession of him. It is easy to imagine what will be the outcome of this incessant struggle. Each day the angles become sharper, feelings become more touchy, actions rankle more painfully; these two beings, starting on the bright and free pinnacles of love, have descended, without being themselves aware of it, into the dark and suffocating regions of hate. The result of this inevitable decay of passion is made not less cruel, but more evident, by a wholly external complication. The divorce which at one time Alekséi Karénin had offered, he refuses when his wife, weary of such suffering, at last decides to ask him for it. Here it is that the future author of "My Religion" appears with his precise theory of the immorality of divorce. The group of mystics to which the deserted husband has been led to ask consolation of a religious kind declare, through the mouth of the Countess Lidia Ivanovna, that Alekséi Karénin cannot accede to his wife's wishes, and grant her liberty, without falling himself into a state of mortal sin.

From the day when they learn of his refusal, Anna Karénina and Vronsky, in spite of themselves, rush straight towards separation. Anna, in her dread of it, precipitates it. Vronsky is nettled at her ever increasing restlessness; and before what seems to him pure ingratitude, he affects an indifference which he does not feel. Discussions, once rare, come in quick succession, and become quarrelsome. This daily conflict brings about an explosion, followed by a rupture.

Vronsky leaves her. He goes to his mother,

the natural enemy of his mistress. As soon as she is alone, Anna Karénina feels as though torn in every fibre of her being: he must come back; she will fall on her knees before him; she will humiliate herself like a naughty child. She has written him to return, but she has not the strength to wait for him; she hurries to meet him, and stops at an intermediate station, when by a telegram she informs him of her arrival. The train arrives. Only the count's valet appears, bringing a note in which Vronsky dryly announces that he is coming back. The tone of the note is interpreted by Anna as a new proof of the death of a love which in her alone has grown with time and possession. She tells herself that there is no more reason to live, and a series of fatal circumstances unite at this critical moment to hasten her to her death. She wishes to escape the inquisitive eyes of the loiterers at the station, who are struck by her strange behavior: she leaves the platform, and steps down upon the track. She remembers the terrible accident which a train-hand had met with at Moscow on the very day of her first meeting with Vronsky. A sort of reflex action takes place in her brain: a freight-train is coming along; she goes to meet it.

"She looked under the cars, at the chains and the brake, and the high iron wheels; and she tried to estimate with her eye the distance between the fore and back wheels, and the moment when the middle would be in front of her.

"'There,' she said, looking at the shadow of the car thrown upon the black coal-dust which covered the sleepers, 'there in the centre he will be punished, and I shall be delivered from it all, — and from myself.'

"Her little red travelling-bag caused her to lose the moment when she could throw herself under the wheels of the first car: she could not detach it from her arm. She awaited the second. A feeling like that she had experienced once, just before taking a dive in the river, came over her, and she made the sign of the cross. This familiar gesture called back to her soul memories of youth and childhood. Life, with its elusive joys, glowed for an instant before her, but she did not take her eyes from the car; and when the middle between the two wheels appeared, she threw away her red bag, drawing her head between her shoulders, and, with outstretched hands, threw herself on her knees under the car. She had time to feel afraid. 'Where am I? What am I doing? Why?' thought she, trying to draw back; but a great, inflexible mass struck her head, and threw her upon her back. 'Lord, forgive me all!' she murmured, feeling the struggle to be in vain. A little *muzhik* was working on the railroad, mumbling in his beard. And the candle by which she read, as in a book, the fulfilment of her life's work, of its deceptions, its grief, and its torment, flared up with greater brightness than she had ever known, revealing to her all that before was in darkness; then flickered, grew faint, and went out forever."

Certainly when one reads this brutally frightful *dénouement* in the light of the motto of the book, "Vengeance is mine, I will repay," one might be tempted to interpret Jesus' word in its Judaic sense. Yet it would be a serious mistake. It is very certain that this sudden and tragic end in the novelist's mind was meant for Anna Karénina's deliverance: out of pity for her, he granted her the favor of death. Death alone could put an end to the torment of this soul, and this torment began with the sin. Here is the true punishment of guilty love: all the illusion which exalted the senses, as long as they are pastured in "love's shadow," as one of Shakspeare's characters calls it, vanishes as soon as one is sated of love itself.

"What had been for Vronsky for nearly a year the only and absolute aim of his life, was for Anna a dream of happiness, all the more enchanting because it seemed to her unreal and terrible. It was like a dream. At last the waking came; and a new life began for her, with a sentiment of moral decadence. She felt the impossibility of expressing the shame, the horror, the joy, that were now her portion. Rather than put her feelings into idle and fleeting words, she preferred to keep silent. As time went on, words fit to express the complexity of her sensations still failed to come to her, and even her thoughts were incapable of translating the impressions of her heart. She hoped that calmness and peace would come to her, but they held aloof. Whenever she thought of the past, and thought of the future, and thought of her own fate, she was seized with fear, and tried to drive these thoughts away.

"'By and by, by and by,' she repeated, 'when I am calmer.'

"On the other hand, when during sleep she lost all control of her imagination, her situation appeared in its frightful reality: almost every night she had the same dream. She dreamed that she was the wife both of Vronsky and of Alekséi Aleksandrovitch. And it seemed to her that Alekséi Aleksandrovitch kissed her hands, and said, weeping, 'How happy we are now!' And Alekséi Vronsky, he, also, was her husband. She was amazed that she could believe such a thing impossible; and she laughed when she seemed to explain to them that every thing would simplify itself, and that both would henceforth be satisfied and happy. But this dream weighed on her spirits like a nightmare, and she always awoke in a fright."

That is the moral punishment. What keen psychology! What an admirable commentary, and what a powerful interpretation of the "*surgit amari aliquid!*" And it is not only her punishment as a woman which Tolstoï has described, it is also her punishment as a mother, when the separation, long postponed by the husband's own will, becomes indispensable to the two paramours, both of whom have returned from the doors of death, and returned more morbidly, more hopelessly, in love with each other than ever before.

During the first part of this separation, Anna Karénina had wonted herself to think that it was her duty to give up all that had hitherto gone to make her happiness, and to leave in her husband's hands as a compensation, such as it was, all the elements of her past happiness which she had exchanged for another kind. "I give up all that I love, all that I appreciate most in this world,—my son and my reputation!" She succeeds for some time in lulling, in deceiving, the maternal sentiment, in substituting in place of her affection for her son her tender and constant care for the daughter, the child of her *liaison* with Vronsky. But Vronsky is obliged suddenly to leave Italy where they have been together; he and Anna reach Petersburg; the mother is again in the neighborhood of the house where her son is living; she wishes to enter it, to see him; she begs for permission, and it is harshly refused; she determines to go to her husband's at any cost, and make her way to the child by bribing the servants. The reader will not blame me for quoting this admirable scene.[1]

"She went to a neighboring shop and purchased some toys, and thus she formed her plan of action: she would start early in the morning before Alekséi Aleksandrovitch was up; she would have the money in her hand all ready to bribe the Swiss and the other servants to let her go up-stairs without raising her veil, under the pretext of laying on Serozha's bed some presents sent by his god-father. As to what she should say to her son, she could not form the least idea: she could not make any preparation for that.

"The next morning, at eight o'clock, Anna got out of her hired carriage and rang the door-bell of her former home.

[1] M. Dupuy adds, that he borrows "the inelegant but expressive translation of this scene" from the *Journal de Saint Pétersbourg*. In the present case, as in nearly all other quotations in the book, the originals have been used, which will account for greater or less variations from the literal version of the French text. — N. H. D.

"'Go and see what is wanted! It's some *baruina*,' said Kapitonuitch, in overcoat and galoshes, as he looked out of the window and saw a lady closely veiled standing on the porch. The Swiss's assistant, a young man whom Anna did not know, had scarcely opened the door before Anna thrust a three-ruble note into his hand.

"'Serozha — Sergéi Aleksiévitch,' she stammered; then she went one or two steps down the hall.

"The Swiss's assistant examined the note, and stopped the visitor at the inner glass door.

"'Whom do you wish to see?' he asked.

"She did not hear his words, and made no reply.

"Kapitonuitch, noticing the stranger's confusion, came out from his office and asked her what she wanted.

"'I come from Prince Skorodumof to see Sergéi Aleksiévitch.'

"'He is not up yet,' replied the Swiss, looking sharply at the veiled lady.

"Anna had never dreamed that she should be so troubled by the sight of this house where she had lived nine years. One after another, sweet and cruel memories arose in her mind, and for a moment she forgot why she was there.

"'Will you wait?' asked the Swiss, helping her to take off her *shubka.* When he saw her face, he recognized her, and bowed profoundly. 'Will your ladyship[1] be pleased to enter?' he said to her.

"She tried to speak; but her voice failed her, and with an entreating look at the old servant she rapidly flew up the stairs. Kapitonuitch tried to overtake her, and followed after her, catching his galoshes at every step.

"'Perhaps his tutor is not dressed yet: I will speak to him.'

"Anna kept on up the stairs which she knew so well, but she did not hear what the old man said.

"'This way. Excuse it if all is in disorder. He sleeps in the front room now,' said the Swiss, out of breath. 'Will your ladyship be good enough to wait a moment? I will go and see.' And opening the high door, he disappeared.

[1] *Vasha prevoskhoditelstvo;* literally, Your Excellency.

"Anna stopped and waited.

"'He has just waked up,' said the Swiss, coming back through the same door.

"And as he spoke, Anna heard the sound of a child yawning, and merely by the sound of the yawn she recognized her son, and seemed to see him alive before her.

"'Let me go in—let me!' she stammered, and hurriedly pushed through the door.

"At the right of the door was a bed, and on the bed a child was sitting up in his little open nightgown; his little body was leaning forward, and he was just finishing a yawn and stretching himself. His lips were just closing into a sleepy smile, and he fell back upon his pillow still smiling.

"'Serozha!' she murmured as she went towards him.

"Every time since their separation that she had felt an access of love for the absent son, Anna looked upon him as still a child of four, the age when he had been most charming. Now he no longer bore any resemblance to him whom she had left: he had grown tall and thin. How long his face seemed! How short his hair! What long arms! How he had changed! But it was still the same, — the shape of his head, his lips, little slender neck, and his broad shoulders.

"'Serozha!' she whispered in the child's ear.

"He raised himself on his elbow, turned his frowzy head around, and, trying to put things together, opened wide his eyes. For several seconds he looked with an inquiring face at his mother, who stood motionless before him. Then he suddenly smiled with joy; and with his eyes still half-closed in sleep, he threw himself, not back upon his pillow, but into his mother's arms.

"'Serozha, my dear little boy!' she stammered, choking with tears, and throwing her arms around his plump body.

"'Mamma!' he whispered, cuddling into his mother's arms so as to feel their encircling pressure. Smiling sleepily, he took his hand from the head of the bed and put it on his mother's shoulder and climbed into her lap, having that warm breath of sleep peculiar to children, and pressed his face to his mother's neck and shoulders.

"'I knew,' he said, opening his eyes; 'to-day is my birthday; I knew that you would come. I am going to get up now.'

"And as he spoke he fell asleep again. Anna devoured him with her eyes. She saw how he had changed during her absence. She would scarcely have known his long legs coming below his nightgown, his hollow cheeks, his short hair curled in the neck where she had so often kissed it. She pressed him to her heart, and the tears prevented her from speaking.

"'What are you crying for, mamma?' he asked, now entirely awake. 'What makes you cry?' he repeated, ready to weep himself.

"'I? I will not cry any more — it is for joy. It is all over now,' said she, drying her tears and turning around. '*Nu!* go and get dressed,' she added, after she had grown a little calmer, but still holding Serozha's hand. She sat down near the bed on a chair which held the child's clothing. 'How do you dress without me? How' — she wanted to speak simply and gayly, but she could not, and again she turned her head away.

"'I don't wash in cold water any more; papa

has forbidden it: but you have not seen Vasíli Lukitch? Here he comes. But you are sitting on my things.' And Serozha laughed heartily. She looked at him and smiled.

"'Mamma! *dúshenka, golúbtchika!*' [dear little soul, darling], he cried again, throwing himself into her arms, as though he now better understood what had happened to him, as he saw her smile.

"'Take it off,' said he, pulling off her hat. And seeing her head bare, he began to kiss her again.

"'What did you think of me? Did you believe that I was dead?'

"'I never believed it.'

"'You believed me alive, my precious?'

"'I knew it! I knew it!' he replied, repeating his favorite phrase; and, seizing the hand which was smoothing his hair, he pressed the palm of it to his little mouth, and began to kiss it."

"Vasili Lukitch, meantime, not at first knowing who this lady was, but learning from their conversation that it was Serozha's mother, the woman who had deserted her husband, and whom he did not know, as he had not come into the house till after her departure, was in great perplexity. Ought he to tell Alekséi Aleksandrovitch? On mature reflection he came to the conclusion that his duty consisted in going to dress Serozha at the usual hour, without paying any attention to a third person — his mother, or any one else. But as he reached the door and opened it, the sight of the caresses between the mother and child, the sound of their voices and their words, made him change his mind. He shook his head, sighed, and quietly closed the door. 'I will wait ten minutes longer,' he said to himself, coughing slightly, and wiping his eyes.

"There was great excitement among the servants; they all knew that the *baruina* had come, and that Kapitonuitch had let her in, and that she was in the child's room; they knew, too, that their master was in the habit of going to Serozha every morning at nine o'clock: each one felt that the husband and wife ought not to meet, that it must be prevented.

"Kornéi, the valet, went down to the Swiss to ask why Anna had been let in; and finding that Kapitonuitch had taken her up-stairs, he reprimanded him severely. The Swiss maintained an obstinate silence till the valet declared that he deserved to lose his place, when the old man jumped at him, and shaking his fist in his face, said, —

"'*Da! Vot!* you would not have let her in yourself? You've served here ten years, and had nothing but kindness from her, but you would have said, "Now, go away from here!" You know what policy is, you sly dog. What you don't forget is to rob your master, and to carry off his raccoon-skin *shubas!*'

"'Soldier!' replied Kornéi scornfully; and he turned towards the nurse, who was coming in just at this moment. 'What do you think, Marya Yefimovna? He has let in Anna Arkadyevna, without saying any thing to anybody, and just when Alekséi Aleksandrovitch, as soon as he is up, will be going to the nursery.'

"'What a scrape! what a scrape!' said the nurse. 'But, Kornéi Vasilyevitch, find some way to keep your master, while I run to warn her, and get her out of the way. What a scrape!'

"When the nurse went into the child's room, Serozha was telling his mother how Nádenka and he had fallen when sliding down a hill of ice, and turned three somersaults. Anna was listening to the sound of her son's voice, looking at his face, watching the play of his features, feeling his little arms, but not hearing a word that he said. She must go away, she must leave him : this alone she understood and felt. She had heard Vasíli Lukitch's steps, and his little discreet cough, as he came to the door, and now she heard the nurse coming in ; but unable to move or to speak, she remained as fixed as a statue.

"'*Baruina! Golúbtchika!*' [mistress, darling], said the nurse, coming up to Anna, and kissing her hands and her shoulders. 'God sent this joy for our birthday celebration! You are not changed at all.'

"'*Ach!* nurse [*nyanya*], my dear : I did not know that you were in the house,' said Anna, coming to herself.

"'I don't live here ; I live with my daughter. I came to give my best wishes to Serozha, Anna Arkadyevna, *golúbtchika.*'

"The nurse suddenly began to weep, and to kiss Anna's hand.

"Serozha, with bright, joyful eyes, and holding his mother with one hand and his nurse with the other, was dancing in his little bare feet on the carpet. His old nurse's tenderness towards his mother was delightful to him.

"'Mamma, she often comes to see me; and when she comes'—he began; but he stopped short when he perceived that the nurse whispered something in his mother's ear, and that his mother's face assumed an expression of fear, and at the same time of shame.

"Anna went to him.

"'My precious!' she said.

"She could not say the word 'farewell' [*proshchái*]; but the expression of her face said it, and he understood.

"'My precious, precious Kutik!' she said, calling him by a pet name which she used when he was a baby. 'You will not forget me; you'—but she could not say another word.

"Only then she began to remember the words which she wanted to say to him, but now it was impossible to say them. Serozha, however, understood all that she would have said: he understood that she was unhappy, and that she loved him. He even understood what the nurse whispered in her ear: he heard the words 'always at nine o'clock;' and he knew that they referred to his father, and that his mother must not meet him. He understood this, but one thing he could not understand: why did her face express fear and shame? . . . She was not to blame, but she was afraid of him, and seemed ashamed of something. He wanted to ask a question which would have explained this circumstance, but he did not dare: he saw that she was in sorrow, and he pitied her. He silently clung close to her, and then he whispered, 'Don't go yet! He will not come yet awhile.'

"His mother pushed him away from her a little, in order to see if he understood the meaning of what he had said; and in the frightened expression of his face she perceived that he not only spoke of his father, but seemed to ask her how he ought to think about him.

"'Serozha, my dear,' she said, 'love him; he is better than I am; and I have been wicked to him. When you have grown up, you will understand.'

"'No one is better than you,' cried the child, with sobs of despair; and, clinging to his mother's shoulders, he squeezed her with all the force of his little trembling arms.

"'*Dúshenka*, my darling!' stammered Anna; and, bursting into tears, she sobbed like a child, even as he sobbed.

"At this moment the door opened, and Vasíli Lukitch came in. Steps were heard at the other door; and, in a frightened whisper, he exclaimed, 'He is coming,' and gave Anna her hat.

"Serozha threw himself on the bed, sobbing, and covered his face with his hands. Anna took them away to kiss yet once again his tear-stained cheeks, and then with quick steps hurried from the room. Alekséi Aleksandrovitch met her at the door. When he saw her, he stopped and bowed his head.

"Though she had declared a moment before that he was better than she, the swift glance that she gave him, taking in his whole person, awoke in her only a feeling of hatred and scorn for him, and jealousy on account of her son. She hurriedly lowered her veil, and, quickening her step, almost ran from the room. She had entirely forgotten in her haste the playthings which, on the evening before, she had bought with so much love and sadness; and she took them back with her to the hotel."

In such scenes, in such moral analyses, as these, it is necessary to look for the meaning and the drift of "Anna Karénina." There is also in the conduct of the husband, the statesman, Alekséi Karénin, a constant lesson and significance which it would be easy to verify with "My Religion" in hand. He is punished for having sacrificed every thing to his ambition, even the love and the care of her whom he took to be his wife. He does not fight a duel with Vronsky because he lacks courage, but, above all, because religion lays it upon him as a duty not to strive to kill his neighbor. He hates his guilty wife, even to the point of wishing for her death, and of feeling disappointment when he finds her alive after the travail which she dreaded so keenly; but his heart softens at her delirium, at the words of repentance which she speaks at the moment which she thinks is her last: he forgives her. From the day when he has tasted the divine sweetness of mercy, he is another man: he has found the meaning of life. Henceforth he will apply the doctrine of Jesus: "'I offer my other cheek to the smiter; I give my last cloak to him who has robbed me; I ask only one thing of God, that he will not take from me the joy of forgiving.' . . . Karénin rose: sobs choked his voice. Vronsky rose too, and standing with bowed head and humble attitude, looked up at Karénin without a word to say. He was incapable of understanding Alekséi Aleksandrovitch's feelings; but he felt that such magnanimity was above him, and irreconcilable with his conception of life."

V.

The astonishment felt by Vronsky at hearing Karénin's words, we also have some right to feel in reading Tolstoï's work entitled "My Religion." This work is a socialistic and communistic interpretation of the gospel. The censorship has put an end to the publication and sale of it; but it cannot prevent the manuscript from passing from hand to hand; and, when it shall have succeeded in destroying it, it will be forever unable to suppress the state of mind of which this work is only a manifestation, and which will possibly be before long the state of mind of a whole people.

It is possible now, if it ever was, by looking towards Russia, to find in the spectacle of the moral phenomena there going on an answer to the question, "How are dogmas born?"

It was remarked long ago that all the great convulsions of a nation are followed by an increased tendency towards mysticism: this is manifested in Russia more than elsewhere. For example, after the invasion in 1812, a sort of sectarian eruption followed the patriotic fever. The *muzhik* had bravely burned his harvest, and had taken arms to drive out the foreigner. He had done a man's work, and had been given to understand, that, as soon as the enemy were out of the way, the grateful country would recognize him as a son and give him his freedom. The French, burned out by fire, cut down by frost,[1] retire, sowing the path of their journey back with corpses. But the hour of liberty does not yet strike. The affairs of Europe must be put in order before taking hold of the *muzhik's*. After the treaties have been signed, after the armies have gone home, the rights of the *muzhik* remain neglected, and his complaints are stifled. His despair is seen in emigrations, in deeds of violence, in his affiliation with existing sects, in the formation of a new social and religious dogma. At that

[1] The Russians, after the retreat of the French, conferred the epaulets on Jack Frost: it was said that General *Morozof* won the victory for them. — N. H. D.

moment we see arise for the first time the *bogomól*, or praying men.

In the last quarter of the century, Russia has experienced a storm more tremendous than that of the invasion of 1812: it might be said that the face of the country was transformed by the upheaval in the condition of the people.

The single reign of Alexander II. saw such facts accomplished as the abolition of serfdom; the redivision of the land; above all, the increase in the taxes, which has touched the people in a very different way from all the reforms. The dominating influence of wealth has grown more and more; a great net-work of railroads has extended over the country; the maxim of *laissez faire* and *laissez passer* has made its way into the Russian village. None of these changes has fully succeeded, or, in better words, none has succeeded as yet. In periods of transition, it is the feature of inconvenience that, above all, attracts attention, and more often than not causes the advantageous to be overlooked. Now, here, the ill has often surpassed the good. Thus in the regulation of landed property, the insufficiency of the lots of land granted the *muzhik*, and the lack of proportion between the revenue and the tax imposed, have quickly brought the small cultivator back into dependence upon the great proprietor, and serfage has re-appeared in disguise. 

As to the administrative reforms, the *zemstvo*, the tribunal, the school, all this has scarcely made any impression upon the people except as bringing an increase in the tax, expressed by the immemorial formula *so much per soul.* The taxes coming in much less than the increase in the rates, extreme measures have to be taken to obtain the payment of them. The *muzhik* has only one way of escaping prosecution, and that is to give himself over, body and soul, to the usurer. In short space of time the misery is universal. A single man gets rich at the expense of all the others: it is the *kulak* (the fist), the monopolist.

Bread is lacking in many places. In its place they eat, not cake, but preparations of straw, bark, or grass, all that which is called by the expressive term *cheat-hunger.*[1] It is plain

[1] The word *podspórye* might be rendered by the much less expressive periphrasis "the *succedanea* of bread." — *Author's note.*

to see that the *muzhiks*, reduced to these extremities, lose their interest in a society which treats them a little less kindly than if they were common cattle. All that they know of public affairs is that it is necessary to pay the tax. The most palpable advantage which they get from the time spent in discussing the common interests is the bumper of *vodka* with which discussions are kept alive: thus they forget themselves for a few hours.

Then, in hatred of the present, minds turn back to the past, and, above all, yearn eagerly for the future. The peasant's *naïve* imagination is consoled by his dreams; the ardor of his desires is spent in Utopias. The idea of *free lands* haunts these enthusiastic minds. The story is secretly whispered about of the promises made by the Shah of Persia to emigrants who will come and settle in his dominions: his subjects shall pay no taxes and have no superiors. Solid masses of people set out suddenly, and depart for "the country of the white waters." There it is that the popular ideal is to be realized. Many outlaw themselves without leaving their residences, and refuse to answer any of their obligations towards the commune or the *mir*. Others take refuge in the neighboring forest, go and settle in the desert, in the steppe. A considerable number go on pilgrimages to the holy places. Finally, there are those who go to swell the class of true Nihilists ; that is to say, people who make their lives even a bold negation of all that is accepted, affirmed, around them, — the class of wanderers, or that of occults.

The attitude of these refractory men and women strikes the people, and is not slow to inspire them with a respect which is thus explained. The Russian people's heads are stuffed with legends. One of the widest spread is that of the centenarian who lives in the desert, taking no other food than a consecrated wafer once a week ; and, though he has not the slightest notion of the alphabet, yet he reads the Holy Book, the book with the leaves of gold, where is found the answer to every question, the rule for all conduct. We see now how reality and legend can come to be confounded. In the lonely hut where this hermit dwells apart, fitted as he is ordinarily by his intelligence and his will for the exceptional part which he is going to perform, he allows himself endlessly to reflect on all sorts of subjects. He ruminates at his leisure, in the solitude, over all the difficulties of the life from which he has torn himself away. He gropes after his definition of things good and of things evil; he slowly builds up his solemn casuistry.

The peasants one after another take the road to his hermitage. They are sure of bringing away good advice about disputed cases. Their cases include every subject, — family affairs, commune affairs, church affairs. Every thing is discussed, exposed to the cenobite's criticism, to his interpretation. It is a matter of course that religious questions fill a large part in this programme, worked up by the anxieties of the throng, and the prophetic explanations of the hermit. But the programme also takes up economic or social questions. It prepares for the coming of a new law. This law is the outcome of a duty, and this duty is summed up in the formula, "To live according to justice;" or, in other words, "according to the will of God."

The schisms formed, as we have just seen, are

those of unimportant people. They have nothing in common with those which the irksomeness of living develops, in similar lines, in Russia, among the upper classes of the nation. Quite contrary to the sects born in the aristocracy, the schisms among the common people take their rise in the need of existence. They serve the instinct which impels the creature to seek not only life, but the best form of life. That is why they act so powerfully on the masses; that is why they cross time and space, making proselytes, apostles, martyrs.

The surprising thing is that the rich and aristocratic Count Tolstoï should become the apostle of such a religion. Like the sectaries of the rustic class, he builds a complete religious, political, and social system upon a new interpretation of the Gospels.

His religion, properly speaking, takes as its foundation the maxim of the Evangelist, "Resist not the one that is evil." And it is not in an allegorical sense, it is by the letter, that these words of Jesus must be understood. The law laid down by Jesus' disciples is precisely the opposite of that of the disciples of this world, which is the *law of conflict.* This doctrine of Jesus, which is sure to give peace to the world, is contained wholly in five commandments:—

1. Be at peace with everybody. Do not allow yourself to consider any one as low or stupid.

2. Do not violate the rights of wedlock. Do not commit adultery.

3. The oath impels men to sin. Know that it is wrong, and bind not yourselves by any promise.

4. Human vengeance or justice is an evil. Do not, under any pretext, practise it. Bear with insults, and render not evil for evil.

5. Know that all men are brothers, the sons of one father. Do not break the peace with any on account of difference of nationality.

By putting this doctrine into practice, man can realize a happiness in life, and there is no happiness in life except in this path. There is no immortality. The conception of the resurrection of the dead, according to Tolstoï, is the greatest piece of barbarism.

The political doctrine derived from this religious doctrine admits of no tribunals or armies or national frontiers.

The social doctrine to which we must be led by this religious and political dogma is the suppression of property, and the proclamation of communism. Man is not put into the world that others should work for him, but that he himself should work for others. He alone who works shall have daily bread.

The most dangerous enemy of society is the Church, because it supports with all its power the errors which it has read into its interpretation of Jesus' doctrine. In place of this false light of Church dogma, which misleads believers and lets them "go into the pit," must be substituted the light of conscience; one's whole conduct must be irradiated by it, by submitting each of his acts to the approbation of the judge which we feel within us, "in our inner tribunal."

To succeed in leading the life which conscience may approve, what is, above all, necessary? "Do not lead a life which makes it so difficult to refrain from wrath, from not committing adultery, from not taking oaths, from not defending yourself by violence, from not carrying on war: lead a life which would make all that difficult to do." Do not crush at pleasure the very conditions of earthly happiness; do not break the bond which unites man to nature: that is to say, lead lives so as to enjoy "the sky, the sun, the pure air, the earth covered with vegetation and peopled with animals;" become a rustic instead of being the busy, weary, sickly urban. Return to the natural law of labor, — of labor freely chosen and accomplished with pleasure, of physical labor, the source of appetite and sleep. Have a family, but have the joys of it as well as the cares: that is, keep your children near you; do not intrust their education to strangers; do not imprison them; do not drive them "into physical, moral, and intellectual corruption." Have free and affectionate intercourse with all men, whatever their rank, their nationality. "The peasant and wife are free to enter into brotherly relations with eighty millions of working-men, from Arkhangel to Astrakhan, without waiting for ceremony or introduction. A clerk and his wife find hundreds of people who are their equals; but the clerks of higher station do not recognize them as their equals, and they in their turn exclude their inferiors. A wealthy man of society and his wife have only a few score families of equal distinction, all the others are unknown to them. The cabinet minister and the millionnaire have only a dozen people as rich and as important as they are. For emperors and kings, the circle is still narrower. Is it not like a prison, where each prisoner in his cell has relations only with one or two jailers?" Finally, live in a community, in hygienic conditions, with moral habits, which bring you the nearest possible to that ideal which is the very foundation of happiness, health as long as you live, death without disease, when existence has reached its limit.

The higher one rises in the social scale, the farther one departs from this ideal. The picture which Tolstoï paints of the physical pains and tortures of the wealthy and of the aristocratic, of those whom he calls "the martyrs of the religion of the world," is remarkably vigorous. Rousseau's declamation against the pretended benefits of civilization here finds a powerful interpreter.

Does that mean that Tolstoï declaims? No

one is more in earnest. It is not only in words that he declares war on the organization of society recognized and defended by the government of his country. He puts the doctrine into practice; he is ready to suffer all things to affirm the cause of Jesus. His refusal to take an oath, which is one of the articles of his creed, has already brought upon him a condemnation from one of those tribunals which he himself condemns in the name of the maxim of the Gospels, "Judge not." It is not credible that the old hero of the wars of the Caucasus and Crimea compels his son to refuse military service, as was done once by the son of Sutaïef, the *raskolnik* of Tver. He would have liked to strip himself of his property, in order to conform to the socialistic dogma forbidding inheritance and property. He was hindered only by the fear of trampling upon the liberty and the conscience of others. But amid the luxury of his family Count Tolstoï lives the life of a poor man. He has dropped his pen as a novelist.[1] Clad like a *muzhik*, he

[1] At last accounts, the reports about Count Tolstoï's vagaries were found to be idle exaggerations: he is living on his estate, like a reasonable man, studying Greek and Hebrew, and writing short stories. — N. H. D.

wields the scythe or drives the plough; between seedtime and harvest, he preaches his evangel.

I do not wish either to spread or to confute his teaching: for me it is sufficient to have given the reader an idea of it. Let him not show the characteristic behavior of a French reader; let him not hasten to see in Count Tolstoï's latest attitude a sign of aberration. This attitude in his country is shared by a multitude of men. The single religious sect of *Shalaputui* (Extravagants), preaching and practising a communistic gospel like Tolstoï, has, within a score of years, won over all the common people, all the rustic class, of the south and south-west of Russia. Judicious observers, well-informed economists, foresee the complete and immedate spread of the doctrine in the lower classes throughout the empire.[1] The day when the work of propagation shall be finished, the *raskolniks* of a special socialistic dogma will be counted: their number will

[1] In 1882 a Russian writer, Mr. Abramof, published, in The Annals of the Country, a very curious study of the *Shalaputui*. Turgénief was greatly struck by it. He said in regard to it: "There is the peasant getting up steam; before long he will make a general up-turning." — *Author's Note.*

suffice to show their power. That day, if they take it into their heads to act, will only have — using the popular expression — "to blow" on the old order of things, to see it vanish away.

APPENDIX.

As M. Dupuy does not pretend to give any thing more than a hasty *résumé* of biographical facts, the reader may like to have for reference a more definite and fuller account of the lives of the three great authors whose literary work has been analyzed. The main authority which I have consulted has been P. Polevoï's "History of Russian Literature, in Sketches and Biographies" [*Istoriya Russkoï Literaturui f Otcherkakh i Biografyakh*, fourth edition, published in 1883.] Some of his dates differ slightly from those commonly accepted. How far a man's judgment is to be accepted who writes with the fear of the censor in his eyes, is a question; but there are a few quotations in Polevoï which are surprising in their liberality. The work is a valuable compound of literary fact and criticism, and it is illustrated with capital woodcuts.

Nikolaï Vasilyévitch Gogol-Yanovsky was

born on the 31st of March, 1809 (N.S.), in the little town of Sorotchintsui, in the Government of Poltava. His father, Vasíli Afanasyévitch Gogol, was the son of a regimental clerk: at the time when the Zaporog Cossacks were still in existence, this position was considered highly respectable. Only two generations separated Gogol from the time of the Cossack wars; and his grandfather, the regimental clerk, used to relate to his family a great many stories of that time. Gogol was surrounded from his earliest childhood by a life that was hardly freed from its mediæval, warlike, half-wild character. It was full of fresh recollections of the olden times, of legends and war-songs; it was a life in which religious fervor was intermingled with a swarm of popular prejudices. Gogol's grandfather was a lively representative of the just vanishing past, and not in vain does Gogol speak about him often in his *Vetchera na Khutoryé* (Evenings at the Farm). Gogol was indebted to his grandfather for at least half of his Malo-Russian tales. "My grandfather," he says, in his sketch in his *Vetcher Nakanunya Ivána Kupála* ("The Eve of Ivan Kupalo's Day").

"My grandfather (may he prosper in heaven! may he eat in the other world little wheaten rolls, with poppy seeds and honey!) was able to tell stories in a wonderful way. When he told stories, I would sit the whole day without moving from my place, and never cease to listen. . . . It was not so much the marvellous tales of the olden time, about the invasions of the Zaporozhtsui (Cossacks) and the Poles, about the brave deeds of the old heroes (Polkova, Poltor-Kozhukh, and Sagaidatchnui), that interested us, as the legends about some olden deed, which used to make the shudders run down my back, and my hair stand on end. Sometimes my fear would be so great from them, that every thing would appear to me like God knows what monsters."

While his grandfather was a representative of the vanishing past, his father, Vasíli Afanasyévitch, appeared as the representative of modern times. He was a well-read man and full of experience, was fond of literature, subscribed to magazines, and at the same time was endowed with a gift of relating stories, and of enhancing them with Malo-Russian humor. His farm,

Vasilyevka, was the centre of society for the district. Among the varied festivals in this farm, Gogol's father used often to get up private theatricals. At these spectacles they used to give Kotlyarevsky's just published comedy *Natalka Poltavka* ("The Girl from Poltava"), and *Moskal Tcharivnik* ("The Charming Muscovite"). Thus Gogol was early attracted to the stage.

Gogol's father wrote, in imitation of Kotlyarevsky, several comedies which were played at Vasilyevka. Gogol was taught to read at home by a hired seminarist. Afterwards he was taken, with his younger brother Ivan, to Poltava, where he was taught by one of the teachers of the gymnasium. While the children were at home on their vacation, Ivan died; and Gogol was not sent back to Poltava, but remained for some time at home. Meantime, the governor of Thernígof, the *prokuror* (attorney-general) Bazhánof, informed Gogol's father about the opening at Niézhin, of a gymnasium for higher learning, founded by Prince Bezborodko, and advised him to place his son in the boarding-school connected with the gymnasium. This was done in May, 1821. Gogol entered as a paying pupil, and at the end of a year he received the government scholarship. It cannot be said that Gogol was much indebted to this gymnasium of the higher education, or that he gained there any solid knowledge of any kind whatsoever, even in the very elementary branches. He studied his lessons very superficially; but as he had a good memory he got a smattering of the lectures, and, by studying hard just before the examinations, he was promoted in due time. He especially disliked mathematics, and he had a very slight inclination even for the study of languages. After graduation he could not read a French book without a dictionary. Against German and English he had a curious spite. He used to say, in jest, that he did not believe that Schiller or Goethe knew German; "surely they must have written in some other language."

The slight progress made by Gogol in the modern languages was more than rivalled by his backwardness in the classic tongues. "He studied with me three years," says Kulzhinsky, Gogol's Latin teacher at the Niézhin gymnasium, in his "Reminiscences," "and he could not learn any thing except the translation of the first sentence of the "Chrestomathie" by means of Koshansky's grammar, 'Universus mundus plerumque distribuitur in duas partes, cœlum et terram' (for which he was nicknamed *universus mundus*). During the lectures, Gogol used to hide some book or other under his desk, paying heed neither to *cœlum* nor *terram*. I must confess that neither under me nor under my colleagues did he learn any thing. The school taught him only some logical formality and directness of understanding and thought; and, more than that, he learned nothing with us."

Not even the Russian language was accurately learned by Gogol in the gymnasium of the higher sciences, according to the testimony of his biographer. "His school letters," says he, "can be distinguished by the absence of all rules of orthography. To make them plainer, I used to arrange the punctuation-marks as it was necessary; I used to change the capital letters, of which he was very extravagant; and I often corrected his blunders in the endings of adjectives."

The only thing that Gogol acquired in the gymnasium was the art of drawing, and his letters to his relatives prove that he took great pleasure in spending much time in this art.

As he was towards the bottom of his class in his studies, he was at the same time greatly distinguished by his love of mischief; and he was a great favorite with every one. His comrades were especially drawn to him by his inexhaustible humor. Even in childhood could be seen in him his spontaneous wit; and at the same time, no one could copy or imitate a character as well as the little Gogol.

He was an indefatigable reader. He especially liked Pushkin and Zhukovsky. His parents subscribed to the *Vyestnik Yevropui* ("Messenger of Europe"), and the reading of this and the almanacs aroused in him a desire to write. At first this came in the form of parodies. While he was at Niézhin, a certain scholar showed some signs of poetical passion; and Gogol collected this fellow's verses, and put them in the form of an almanac, which he called *Parnassky Navoz* ("Manure from Parnassus"). These parodies suggested to him to publish a serious written journal, and his enterprise cost him great trouble. He had to write articles on all subjects, and then copy them, and, what was more important, to make a volume out of them. He spent whole nights trying to decide upon his titlepage, on which was ornamented the name of his journal "The Star" (*Zvyezdá*). It was all done stealthily, without the knowledge of his friends. Early in the month, the journal made its first appearance. In "The Star" were published Gogol's story, "The Tverdislavitch Brothers," which was an imitation of contemporary fiction, and some of his poems. In Gogol's lofty style, which he now affected, he also wrote a tragedy, "The Murderers" (*Razboiniki*) and a ballad, "Two Little Fish" (*Dvé Ruíbki*), touching on the death of his brother. He also wrote at this time "Hans Küchel-Garten," a rhymed idyl, which tells how an ideal young man leaves his sweetheart through his thirst for grandeur, but, after vain wandering, returns again to his home, and shares with his love happiness under a straw thatch. Gogol's comic talent, however, in spite of his belief in a lofty style, began to find means of expression. Thus, among other things, he wrote a satire on the inhabitants of the town of Niézhin, under the title "Something about Niézhin; or, no Law for Fools," in which he depicts the typical people of the town. It was divided into five parts, — "The Dedication of the Church in the Greek Cemetery," "The Election to the Greek Magistracy," "Swallowing-all Fair," "The Dinner to the *Predvodítel* of the Nobility," and "The Coming and Going of the Students."

On returning once to the gymnasium after his vacation, Gogol wrote a comedy in Malo-Russian, which was played in his father's theatre; and thus he made his *début* as a director and actor.

Blackboards served as scenes, and the insufficiency of costumes was made up by imagination. Then the schoolboys clubbed together, and got scenery and costumes, copying what Gogol had seen in his father's theatre, the only one that he had ever attended. The direction of the gymnasium, wishing to encourage the study of French, introduced pieces in that tongue; and the repertory of the little school theatre soon was composed of comedies by Moliére, Florian, Von Vizin, Kotzebue, Kniaznin, and Malo-Russian authors. The townspeople heard about the theatre, and it soon became very popular; and a few years ago people were still living in Niézhin who could remember how successfully Gogol took the *rôle* of old women.

Towards the end of his course, Gogol and his comrades subscribed quite a sum of money, and bought a library, which contained the works of Delvig, Pushkin, Zhukovsky, and other distinguished contemporaries, and subscribed to several journals. Gogol was made librarian. He was so indefatigable that he made every person who took a book finish it, and so careful of their cleanliness that he used to wrap up the fingers of his readers in paper.

Gogol graduated in 1828, with the rank of the fourteenth *tchin*. Even at this time he was very religious, as can be seen in his correspondence with his relatives. "After the death of his father, in 1825, he writes to his mother, 'Don't be worried, my dearest *mámenka*. I have borne this shock with the strength of a Christian. It is true, at first I was overwhelmed with this terrible tidings. However, I did not let anybody see that I was so sorrowful; but, in my own room, I was given over mightily to unreasonable despair. I even wanted to take my life. But God kept me from it. And towards evening, I noticed only sorrow, but not a passionate sorrow; and it gradually turned into an uneasy, hardly noticeable melancholy, mingled with a feeling of gratitude to Almighty God. I bless thee, holy faith! In thee only I find a source of consolation and compensation for my bitter grief.'"

At the same time he was a fiery enthusiast; he imagined himself a great benefactor of his fatherland. For this reason he felt inclined to a governmental situation. He wrote his mother in 1828 that he was not understood: some, he said, took him to be a genius; others, to be a stupid. He tried to be one of the romanticists; and, like all of those budding geniuses, he thought that he had a great deal to put up with from people. In the same letter he writes his mother how much ungratefulness, coldness, vexation, he had been obliged to bear without complaint and without grumbling. He writes one of his friends that the people of Niézhin, not excepting "our dear instructors," have heaped upon our genius the pressing heaps of their earthiness, and crushed us." Two features of Gogol's life at this time are interesting as showing his development, — a tendency to asceticism, which led him to a stern self-restraint, turning all the pleasures and interests of his life to a spiritual and intellectual sphere. "My plan of my life," he writes to his mother in 1829, "is wonderfully stern and exact. Every *kopek* has its place. I refuse myself even very extreme necessities, with a view of being able to keep myself in the position which I am now, so that I can satisfy my desire of seeing and feeling the beautiful (*prekrásnoe*). With this view I lay up all my annual allowance, except what is absolutely necessary."

In 1829 Gogol first went to Petersburg, where, in spite of his vivid dreams of success and glory, he found the hard realities of life, and met with discouraging failures. He wrote his mother: "Everywhere I met with disappointments; and, what is strangest of all, I met them when I least expected them. Men entirely incapable, without any letters of introduction whatever, easily succeeded where I, even with the aid of my patrons, failed." He also fell in love with a girl of high rank; and in his letter to his mother he speaks about it, but does not mention her name: "For God's sake, don't ask her name. She is very, very high. . . . No, it is not love: I, at least, never heard of such a love. Under the impulse of madness and horrible torments of the soul, I was thirsty to intoxicate myself only with the sight of her, only the sight of her I looked for. To look upon her once more was my only desire, which grew stronger with an unspeakable, gnawing anguish. I looked upon myself with horror, and I saw all my horrible situation. Every thing in the world was strange to me, life and death were equally intolerable, and my soul could not account for its impulses."

His mental state arising from all these disappointments became so serious that he went abroad with money that his mother sent him to pay a mortgage on their estate, and told his mother to take his portion of the estate in exchange for it. He went to Lübeck by sea, staid there a month, took a few baths, and returned to Petersburg without seeing any thing more of Europe. At all events, he returned, sobered, refreshed, and strengthened, in September, 1829. In April, 1830, Gogol found a very insignificant place in the ministry of Appanages. The whole outcome of this year of servitude was the knowledge of tying up papers, and a vivid memory of various types of *Tchinovniks* which he used to advantage in his works later on.

In 1829 he wrote his poem "Italy," and sent it anonymously to the publisher of *Suin Otetchestva* (Son of the Fatherland.) Soon afterwards he published "Hans Küchel - Garten," which had been written while he was in the gymnasium. It was signed *Alof*, and brought a review full of unmerciful ridicule. This review cut Gogol so keenly that he immediately withdrew the story from circulation. Buying up all the copies that he could get hold of, he hired a room in a hotel, and made a grand holocaust of them. The last tendencies of his immature, imitative romanticism went up with the incense of the fire and smoke. He soon saw that a new spirit was invading Russian literature: historical novels were becoming fashionable. So Gogol writes to all his friends and relatives in Malo-Russia to send him every possible scrap about the history of that region, about the habits, manners, customs, legends, games, songs, of the Cossacks. "It is very, very necessary for me," he would add. He was working over his "Evenings on the Farm near Dikanka." In February, 1830, there appeared anonymously in the *Otetchestvennuie Zapiski* one of Gogol's tales, entitled "Bassavriuk; or, Ivan Kupala's Eve." In 1831, in "Northern Flowers," appeared a chapter of his historical novel "Hetman," signed with four zeros. In the first number of the "Literary Gazette" he published a sketch from his Malo-Russian story, *Strashnui Kaban* (The Terrible Boar). He also wrote serious articles and translations.

In March, 1831, he was made teacher of Russian in the Patriotic Institute. Here, instead of teaching Russian, he taught history, geography, and international history; and when he was called to account for his vagaries, and was asked when he was going to teach the Russian language, he smiled, and said, "What do you want it for, gentlemen? The main thing in Russian is to know the difference between *yé* and *yat* [two similarly sounding, but differently written, letters], and that I perceive you know already, as is seen by your copy-books. No one can teach you to write smoothly and gracefully. This power is granted by nature, but not by instruction."

Indeed, Gogol himself, to his dying day, was not able to spell correctly. He cared more for the spirit than the form. The publication of "Evenings on the Farm," especially the second series, which are marked by the purest humor, without a shade of melancholy, immediately placed him in the front rank of the authors of his day; and this was the happiest epoch of his life. Soon afterwards he began to feel a re-action. In 1833 he wrote to Pogódin: "Let my stories be doomed to oblivion till something really solid, great, artistic, shall come out of me. But I stand idle, motionless. I don't want to do any thing trivial, and I can't think of any thing great." He then betook himself to historical investigation, and determined to write the history of Malo-Russia and of the Middle Ages. He laid out the work on a colossal scale. He wrote to Maksímof, "I am writing the history of the Middle Ages, and I think it will fill eight volumes, if not nine." He never finished these histories, but his study of Malo-Russia led him to the composition of his great epos "Taras Bulba."

There happened to be a vacancy in the university of St. Vladímer in Kief. Some one suggested Gogol, and he was invited to apply. He came, he saw, and he conquered the man in whose hands the appointment lay, by his wonderful flow of brilliant conversation; but he brought no documents. He was requested to come again, with his documents and application. Again he appeared, and again he dazzled by his wit; but when he was asked for his documents he pulled from his inside pocket his certificate of graduation from the gymnasium, which gave him the right to a *tchin* of the fourteenth class, and an application for the chair of Ordinary Professor. He was told that it was impossible, with such credentials, for him to be given any thing more than the chair of adjunct. Gogol was obstinate, and absolutely refused to take that position. Shortly after, he was appointed professor at Petersburg, where he gave the one lecture which was so beautiful. "We awaited the next lecture with impatience," says Ivanitsky, who was a pupil at that time; "Gogol came in very late, and began with the phrase: 'Asia was a volcano belching forth people.' Then he spoke a few words about the emigration of nations; but it was so dull, lifeless, and desultory that it was tedious to listen to him, and we could not believe that it was the same Gogol who had spoken so beautifully the week before. Finally he mentioned a few books where we could read up the subject, and bowed and left. The whole lecture lasted twenty minutes. The following lectures were of the same stamp; so that we became entirely cool to him, and the classes became smaller and smaller. But once, — it was October, — while walking up and down the hall of assembly, and waiting for him, suddenly Pushkin and Zhukovsky came in. They knew, of course, through the Swiss, that Gogol had not yet come; and so they only asked us in which room he would read. We showed them the auditorium. Pushkin and Zhukovsky looked in, but did not enter. They waited in the hall of assembly. In quarter of an hour the lecturer came; and we, following the three poets, entered the auditorium and sat down. Gogol took his chair, and suddenly, without any warning, began to read the history of the Arabians. The lecture was brilliant, exactly in the manner of the first. Word for word it was published in the 'Arabesques.' It was evident that he knew beforehand the intention of the poets to come to his lecture, and therefore he prepared himself to treat them like poets. After the lecture Pushkin said something to Gogol, but the only word I heard was 'fascinating' (*uvlekátelno*). The rest of his lectures were very dry and tedious. Not one historical personage caused any lively and enthusiastic discussion. . . . He looked upon the dead nations of the past with dreary eyes, as it were; and it was doubtless true that it was tedious to him, and he saw that it was tedious to his hearers. He used to come and speak half an hour from his platform, and then leave for a whole week and sometimes for two. Then he would come again and repeat the same proceeding. Thus went the time till May."

He gave up his thoughts of the nine-volume history of the Middle Ages; and of this year of disappointment there remained only a few articles in the "Arabesques," and the sketches of a tragedy entitled "Alfred," which show that he had not a trace of talent for tragedy. In 1835 he resigned, and devoted himself entirely to literature.

About this time he began to develop a great passion for the supernatural, which is best illustrated in his sketch "Vii." It is an interesting fact that the poet Pushkin, whose influence over Gogol was considerable, suggested to him the subject of "Dead Souls." He also told him the story which he afterwards worked up into the "Revizor." Pushkin himself at one time intended to use both of these subjects. Gogol attended the first production of the "Revizor" on the stage, and was greatly disgusted. He trained the actors, however, giving them the meaning of every inflection, and showing what gesticulation was needed. "All are against me," he wrote to M. S. Shchepkin in 1836, "all the decent *tchinovniks* are shouting that I hold nothing sacred, since I dared to speak so about people who are in the service. The police are against me, merchants are against me, literary men are against me: they berate me, yet they go to see the play. At the fourth act it is impossible to get tickets. Had it not been for the mighty protection of the emperor, my play would never have been put on the stage; and people even now are doing their best to have it suppressed. Now I see what it means to be a comic writer. The least spark of truth, and all are against you, — not one man, but all classes. I imagine what it would have been if I had taken something from Petersburg life, with which I am even more acquainted than provincial life. It is very unpleasant for a man to see people against him whom he loves with brotherly affection."

Gogol wrote another comedy, entitled "The Leaving of the Theatre after the Production of a New Comedy." It was founded on the various criticisms of his "Revizor," but it was not very successful. In 1836 Gogol went abroad. He lived the most of the time in Rome, though he wandered all over Europe, and occasionally returned for short visits, renewing his acquaintance with his old friends. Like Turgénief, while he was in Russia he was disgusted with the state of affairs, but when he left there his soul began to turn with intense yearning for his native land. In 1837 Gogol wrote "Dead Souls." He said in his "Confessions of an Author," "I began to write 'Dead Souls' without laying out any circumstantial plan, without deciding what the hero should be. I simply thought that the bold project, with the fulfilment of which Tchitchikof was occupied, would of itself lead me to various persons and characters, that the natural impulse in me to laugh would create many scenes which I intended to mingle with pathetic ones. But I was stopped with questions at every step, why and wherefore? What must express such and such a character? What must express such and such a phenomenon? Now I had to ask: What must be done when such questions arise? Drive them off? I tried, but the stern question confronted me. As I felt no special love for this character or that, I could not feel any love for the work to bring it out. On the contrary, I felt something like contempt: every thing seemed strained, forced; and even that which made me laugh became pitiable."

Charles Edward Turner, English lector in the University of St. Petersburg, says in his "Studies in Russian Literature:" "In the year 1840 Gogol came to Russia for a short period, in order to superintend the publication of the first volume of the "Dead Souls," and then returned to Italy. With the appearance of this volume we may date the close of his literary career; for though in 1846, at which period he again settled in Russia, he published his "Correspondence with my Friends," the work can only be regarded as the production of a disordered and enfeebled intellect. . . . Describing his final illness and death in 1852, he says, "One of his last acts was to burn the manuscript of the concluding portion of 'The Dead Souls,' and to write a few sad lines in which he prays that all his works may be forgotten as the products of a pitiable vanity, composed at a time when he was still ignorant of the true interests and duties of man." At the end of his article on Gogol he says, "What ultimately became of Tchitchikof, we do not know; for, as has been already stated, the concluding portion of his adventures was destroyed by Gogol in a fit of religious enthusiasm. A certain Dr. Zahartchenko of Kief thought fit to publish, in 1857, a continuation of Gogol's inimitable work. The stolid complacency which alone could encourage an obscure and talentless novelist to undertake such a task is in itself a sufficient standard of the success he could achieve; and his book must be regarded with the same mingled feeling of astonishment and pity an Englishman would experience on having put before him a continuation of Thackeray's "Denis Duval" or Dickens's "Mystery of Edwin Drood."

In 1848 Gogol made a pilgrimage to Jerusalem, and returned to Russia by way of Odessa. The last years of his life were passed in Moscow in an ever-deepening state of fanatical mysticism. His death, in March, 1852, was probably due to his insane attempt to keep the strict fast. His last days were troubled by strange hallucinations. His life-long disorder was an acute derangement of the nerves caused by self-abuse.

As an example of Gogol's early style, the opening scene of "Taras Bulba," which has been mentioned by M. Dupuy, may be read with interest:—

"'Ah! turn around, little son. How funny you look! What kind of a parson's garment have you got on? Is that the way you go in your academy?' With such words the old Bulba met his two sons, who had been studying in the theological school in Kief, and who just came home to their father.

"His sons have only just dismounted from their horses. They were a couple of hearty fellows, who looked from under their brows like just graduated seminarists. Their strong, healthy faces were covered with the first downy hair, as yet untouched by a razor. They were very much confused at such a reception by their father, and stood motionless, with their eyes fixed on the ground.

"'Hold on, hold on, children!' he continued, turning them around and around. 'What a long *svitkas* you've got on! Those are fine *svitkas*. *Nu, nu, nu*, such *svitkas* as these were never yet seen! Well, now, both of you try to run; I'll see if you don't trip up.'

"'Don't you make fun of us, don't you make fun of us, father!' at last said the eldest of them.

"'*Fu*, what a dandy you are! Why not laugh?'

"'Simply because [*Da tak*]; I suppose, you are my father; yet, if you keep on making sport of us, by Heaven, I'll give to you!'

"'*Akh!* a fine kind of a son you are. What's that you say to your father?' said Taras Bulba, falling back a little in surprise.

"'Yes, though you are my father. I don't regard anybody, or have any respect for anybody, who insults me.'

"'How do you want to fight with me, — with fists?'

"'It makes no difference to me.'

"'*Nu!* let us fight with fists,' said Bulba, rolling up his sleeves.

"And the father and son, instead of saluting each other after their long separation, began to beat each other angrily.

"'The old man must be crazy,' said the pale, thin, and kindly mother, who was standing on the threshold, and who has not yet had a chance to embrace her beloved children. 'By Heaven, he is crazy! Here the children have come home. For more than a year he has not seen them, and now he is doing, God knows what! To fight with fists!'

"'Yes, he fights gloriously,' said Bulba, stopping. [*Êï Bogu!*] 'Capital! . . . So, so!' he continued, adjusting himself a little. 'There won't be any need of trying. He will make a good Kazak. — *Nu*, how are you, little son? Give us a kiss.' And the father and son began to kiss each other.

"'Excellent, little son; pound everybody just as you have thrashed me; don't give in to anybody. Yet you have on a funny rig. What kind of a rope is that hanging down? — And, you dog, what are you there for with your hands by your sides?' said he, addressing the younger one. 'Why don't you thrash me, you son of a dog?'

"'Now he is talking nonsense again,' cried the mother, at the same time throwing her arms around the younger one. 'And what nonsense gets into his head! How can a child beat his own father? As though that was all he had to tend to now. He is a little child; he has travelled such a long way, he must be tired' (this child was more than twenty years old, and exactly a *Sazhen*, almost seven feet high). 'He must need to rest now, and have something to eat; and yet he compels him to fight!'

"'*Ey!* you are a little dandy [*mazuntchik*], I see,' said Bulba. 'Don't listen, little son, to your mother: she is a *baba* [woman], she doesn't know any thing. What kind of petting do you want? Your petting is the clear field and a good horse; that is your petting. And do you see this sabre? That is your mother. All they are stuffing your heads with is nonsense: the academy and all those little books —primers and philosophies—are the Devil knows what. I spit at it all. I am going to send you away next week to the Zaporozhe. That is the school for you. It is there only where you will learn reason.'

"'Won't they stay at home with us but one week?' asked the thin old mother pitifully, with tears in her eyes. 'Poor fellows, they won't have time to enjoy themselves. They won't get any good out of their own home, and I sha'n't look at them half enough.'

'That'll do, that'll do, old woman! A Kazak's got something better to do than spend his time with women [*babas*]. Hurry up, and put on the table every thing you've got, — poppy-seed cake [*pampushek*], gingerbread, and such like; *puddings* we can get along without. But fetch us a whole ram for dinner, and then whiskey; and let's have more whiskey than any thing else: not the kind with different kinds of stuff in it, — raisins, and other such things, — but straight whiskey, the unadulterated, such as'll hiss like the devil!'

"Bulba took his sons into the small room. Every thing in the room was arranged according to the taste of that time; and that time was about the sixteenth century, when the idea of the union had just begun to be discussed. Every thing was clean and whitewashed. The whole wall was adorned with sabres and guns. The windows in the room were small, with round panes of ground glass, such as can be found at the present time only in old churches. On the shelves, which occupied the corners of the room, and which were made triangular in shape, were standing earthen pitchers, blue and green bottles, silver cups, gilded wine-glasses, of Venetian, Turkish, and Circassian workmanship, which had found their way into Bulba's room in different ways, — third and fourth hand, a very ordinary thing in those bold days. The linden benches around the whole room, the huge table in the middle of it, the stove occupying half of the room, like a fat Russian merchant's wife, and adorned with tiles with designs of cockerels, — all these things were very familiar to our two young fellows, who used to walk home almost every year to spend their vacation; they used to walk because they had no horses, and because it was not customary to allow scholars to go on horseback. They had only the long forelocks which every Kazak who carries weapons felt that he had a right to pull. Bulba, just as they were about to leave school, sent them from his stud a pair of good horses.

"'Well [*nu*], little sons, before all let us have some whiskey. God bless you! to your health, my little sons; yours, Ostap, and yours, Andriĭ! May God grant you be always successful in battle, that you may beat the Busurmans (Mahometans), beat the Turks, beat the Tatars, and when the Poles begin to do any thing against our religion, beat the Poles too! *Nu!* hold up your glass. Is the whiskey good? And what is whiskey in Latin? That's it [*to-to*], little son. The *Latuintsui* [Latins] were fools; they did not know there was such a thing as whiskey in existence. What was the name of that fellow who wrote Latin verses? I don't know much of reading and writing, and therefore I do not remember. Wasn't it Horatsii?'

"'That's a fine father,' said the older son, Ostap, to himself. 'The dog knows every thing, but he makes believe that he doesn't.'

"'I don't believe the *arkhimandrit* allowed you even to smell whiskey,' continued Bulba. 'Well, now, little sons, tell the truth: did they lash you with cherry and maple sticks over the back, and everywhere else? Or maybe, being as you are so mighty smart, they used straps on you! I reckon that; besides Saturdays, they used to thrash you on Wednesdays and Thursdays too.'

"'Father, there's no need of bringing up all

that,' said Ostap, in his usual phlegmatic voice. 'What's past is gone.'

"'Now we shall pay everybody off,' said Andriĭ, 'with sabres and bayonets. Just let the Tatars come in our way!'

"'That is good, little son. By Heavens, that's good! If that's the case, I shall go along with you. By Heavens, I'll go! What the devil is the good of staying here! What! must I look after the grain and swine-herds, or to fool with my wife? I stay at home for her sake? I am a Kazak. I do not want it! Well, even supposing there is no war, I am going with you to the Zaporozhe. We'll have a good time. By Heavens, I'm going!" And the old Bulba, little by little, grew excited, and finally became entirely fierce. He got up from the table, and, trying to look dignified, stamped his foot upon the ground. 'To-morrow we'll go! Why put it off? What in the devil should we sit here for? What good does this hut do us? What do we want all these things for? What's the good of these pots?' And, while saying this, Bulba began to smash and throw about the pots and the bottles.

"The poor old wife, who was long wonted to such tricks of her husband, looked on sorrowfully as she sat on the bench. She did not dare to say a word; but after hearing this resolution, so terrible to her, she could not refrain from tears. She looked up at her children, from whom such a quick separation threatened her; and no one could describe the whole speechless force of her sorrow, which seemed to quiver in her eyes and in the tremblingly compressed lips.

"Bulba was terribly stubborn. He was one of those characters which could spring up only in the rough sixteenth century, and especially in the half-nomadic Eastern Europe, when ideas were both right and wrong as to the possession of lands which were a disputed and undecided property. At that time, the Ukraïna was in this state. The everlasting necessity of defending the border against three different nations, — all this added a sort of free and broad character to the actions of its sons, and it trained in them a stubborn spirit. This stubbornness of spirit was imprinted with full strength in Taras Bulba. When Batori raised regiments in Malo-Russia, and roused in them that warlike spirit which at first marked only the inhabitants of the Rapids, Taras was one of the first colonels; but at the first opportunity he quarrelled with all the others, because the booty obtained from the Tatars by the united forces of the Polish and Cossack armies was not equally divided between them, and because the Polish army received a greater share. He, in the presence of all, resigned his rank, and said, 'When you colonels don't know your own rights, then let the Devil lead you by the nose. And I am going to recruit my own regiment; and whoever will attempt to take away what belongs to me, I shall know how to wipe off his lips.' And, in fact, in a short time he collected from his father's estate quite a good number of men, made up of both farm-laborers and warriors, who gave themselves up entirely to his wish. He was generally a great hand for taking part in invasions and raids; he heard with his nose, as it were, where and in what place an uprising was taking place. Like snow upon the head, he would appear on his horse. '*Nu*, children, what is it? How is it? Who is to be beaten? What is the reason?' was what he generally asked, and then took a hand in the affair. First of all, he would sternly analyze the circumstances, and he would take a hand only in cases when he saw that those who seized the weapons had really a right to do so; and this right, according to his opinion, was only in the following cases. If the nation in the neighborhood had been carrying off cattle, or cutting off a portion of land; or if the commissioners had been putting on heavy taxes, or had not respected their elders, and had spoken in their presence with their hats on; or if they had left the Christian religion,—in such cases it was inevitably necessary to take up the sabre; but against the Busurmans, Tatars, and Turks, he considered it just to use the weapon any time, in the name of God, Christianity, and Kazatchestvo (Cossackdom). The position of Malo-Russia at that time, having no system whatever, and being in perfect uncertainty, brought into existence many entirely separate partisans. Bulba led a very simple life; and it would have been impossible to distinguish him from any ordinary Kazak in the service, if his face had not preserved a certain expression of command, and even grandeur, particularly when he used to make up his mind to defend something.

"Bulba comforted himself beforehand with the thought of how he should appear now with his two sons, and say, 'Just look what nice fellows I have brought to you.' He thought about how he should take them to the Zaparozhe, to that school of war of the Ukraïna of that day, how he should introduce them to his comrades, and superintend their advance in the science of war and making raids, which he considered at that time one of the first qualities of a knight. At first he intended to send them off alone, because he deemed it necessary to give himself up to the enlistment of a new regiment which demanded his presence; but at the sight of his sons, who were well built and hearty, all his warrior-spirit suddenly awoke in him, and he made up his mind to go along with them on the following day, though the necessity of this was only his stubborn will.

"Without losing a minute, he began to give orders to his *csaul*, whom he called Tovkatch, because he was really like some kind of a cold-blooded machine: during battle he would pass indifferently along the enemy's ranks, sweeping them down with his sabre as though he was mixing dough, like a boxer clearing his way. The orders were to the effect that he should stay on the farm till orders came for him to set out to the war. After this, he went around the village, giving orders to some of his people to accompany him, to water the horses, to feed them with wheat, and to saddle his own horse, which he used to call Tchort, or the Devil. '*Nu*, children, now we must go to sleep, and to-morrow we shall do what God may instruct us to do. Don't give us any bedding! We don't need any bedding: we shall sleep in the *dvor!*'

"The night had just embraced the heaven; but Bulba always retired early. He made himself comfortable on the carpet, covered himself up with a sheep-skin *tulup*, because the night air was rather fresh, and because Bulba was fond of covering himself warmly when at home. He was soon snoring, and his example was followed by the whole court. Every thing that was lying in its various corners was snoring and singing.

Before anybody else the watchman fell asleep, because he drank more than anybody else, in honor of the arrival of the young lords.

"The poor mother only was not sleeping. She leaned towards the heads of her dear sons, who were lying side by side; with a comb she straightened their young, carelessly disordered locks, and moistened them with her tears. She gazed at them with her whole soul, with all her feelings; she *metamorphosed herself into one gaze*, and she could not satisfy herself in looking at them. She had nursed them with her own breast; she had brought them up, caressed them, — and now only for one moment does she see them before her. 'My sons, my precious sons! what will become of you? what fate awaits you there? If only for one week more, I might look upon you both,' said she; and her tears stood in the wrinkles, which had changed her once beautiful face. And indeed she was pitiful, like any other woman of that bold age. She saw her husband two or three days a year, and then for several years there would be no tidings of him. And if she did see him, when they lived together, what kind of a life was hers?

She suffered insults, even blows. Only out of mercy at times she felt his caresses. She was like a strange creature in this assemblage of wifeless knights, upon whom the dissolute Zaparog life threw its stern shadow. The joyless days of her youth flashed before her, and her cheeks were covered with premature wrinkles. All her love, all her feelings, all that is tender and passionate in a woman, all turned with her into one motherly feeling. She, with heat, with passion, with tears, like the gull of the steppe [*step-tchaïka*], looked upon her children. Her sons, her dear sons, are taken away from her: they are taken away, never to be seen again. Who knows? Maybe at the first battle the *Tatarin* will chop off their heads, and she would not even know where their bodies lie: the ravening birds may pick them up; and for every little piece of their flesh, for every drop of blood, she would have given up her all! As she wept, she looked straight into their eyes, which all compelling sleep began to close, and she thought to herself, 'Maybe Bulba, after having a good sleep, will postpone the journey for a couple of days. Maybe he decided to go so soon because he drank too much.' The moon from the height of the heaven was already shining over the whole *dvor*, filled with sleeping people, with the thick mass of willows and tall steppe grass, in which the fence around the yard was drowned. She was still sitting at the heads of her dear sons, without for a moment taking off her eyes from them, and not thinking of sleep.

"The horses, anticipating the dawn of day, lay down on the grass, and ceased eating. The upper leaves of the willows began to rustle, and little by little the rustling stream descended down over them to the very bottom. She sat till the very morning: she was not at all tired, and she inwardly wished that the night might last as long as possible. From the steppe was heard the loud neighing of a young colt.

"Ruddy stripes brightly gleamed in the heaven. Bulba suddenly awoke and jumped up. He remembered very well every thing that he had ordered the day before. '*Nu*, fellows, you've slept long enough: it is time. Water the horses. And where is the old woman? [Thus he generally called his wife]. Be lively, old woman, have something for us to eat, because there is a long journey before us.'

"The poor old woman, who was deprived of her last hope, gloomily dragged herself to the hut. While with tears in her eyes she was preparing every thing for breakfast, Bulba gave his orders, busied himself in the stable, and he himself selected for his sons his best adornments. The seminarists were suddenly transformed: instead of their old soiled boots, they wore red leather ones with silver rings on the heels; pantaloons as wide as the Black Sea, with a thousand folds and pleats, were fastened tight around the waist with a golden belt; to the belt were attached long straps, with tassels and other little ornaments for the pipe. The *kazakin* (a little Russian garment), of gay color, of cloth as bright as fire, was tightened with an embroidered belt. Silver-mounted Turkish pistols were stuck behind the belt; the sabre clattered under their feet. Their faces, which were a little burned by the sun, it seemed, became handsomer and whiter; their young black mustaches brought out now in somewhat more striking contrast their whiteness and the healthy, robust color of youth. They looked well under their sheepskin hats with golden tips.

"The poor mother! As soon as she looked up at them, she could not utter a word, and the tears were checked in her eyes.

"'*Nu*, little sons, every thing is ready! There is no need of wasting time,' cried Bulba at last. 'Now, according to the Christian style, all of us must sit down before setting out.'

"All of them sat down, not excepting even the serfs, who were standing respectfully at the door. 'Now, mother, bless your children,' said Bulba. 'Pray to God that they may fight with courage, that they may always keep the honor of knights, that they may always stand up for the Christian faith; else rather may they sink, so that their spirits perish from the world. — Go over, children, to your mother. A mother's prayer saves in fire and water.' The mother, weak as a mother, embraced them, took out two small holy images, put them on their necks, all the time weeping bitterly. 'May the

Mother of God — preserve you. — Don't forget, little sons, your mother. — Send me some little word about you.' Further she could not speak.

"'*Nu*, let us start, children,' said Bulba.

"At the steps their horses were standing. Bulba mounted his *devil*, who wickedly began to back on feeling a weight of twenty *puds* (nearly eight hundred pounds), for Bulba was exceedingly heavy and fat.

"When the mother saw that her sons were already on the horses, she hurried after the younger one, whose face expressed more of tenderness. She caught the stirrup, clung to his saddle, and, with desperation in all her features, would not let it out of her hands. Two strong Kazaks took her gently and carried her into the hut. But as soon as they left her, she, with all the rapidity of a wild goat, though it was not in accordance with her age, ran out of the gate, and with an incomprehensible strength stopped the horse, and threw her arms around one of them in a sort of a mad and senseless excitement.

"They took her away again.

"The young Kazaks rode on gloomily, but

kept their tears, fearing their father, who, however, on his part, was also somewhat melancholy, though he tried not to show it. It was a gray day; the green fields gleamed brightly, the birds were singing somehow in discord. After going some distance, they looked back. Their farm seemed as though it was swallowed up by the earth; only two chimneys of their humble house stood on the earth; only the tops of the trees, on the branches of which they used to climb like squirrels. Only the distant prairie remained before them, that prairie which reminded them of the whole history of their life, since the days when they used to ride over its dewy grass. And now there is only the sweep over the well, with a *telyega* wheel attached to its top, standing out by itself against the sky; already the level over which they have passed looks, in a distance, like a mountain, and it has covered every thing. Farewell, childhood, and games, and all, and all, farewell."

TURGÉNIEF.

AMONG the historical characters belonging to Turgénief's family were Piotr, who exposed the character of the False Dmitri, and who in consequence was executed on the Lobno Place in Moscow; and Yakof Turgénief, the well-known jester of Peter the Great, who, in the year 1700, had to shear off the *boyars'* beards. Still more worthy of mention among those who bore the name of Turgénief was his cousin Nikolaï Ivanovitch, who was implicated in the celebrated Dekabrist conspiracy of 1825, and was exiled by Nicholas. He wrote a large work entitled "Russia and the Russians." He was a passionate advocate of the emancipation of the serfs.

Ivan Turgénief's father served in a regiment of cuirassiers stationed at Orel, and there he married Várvara Petrovna Lutovinova. His father resigned with the rank of colonel, and died in 1835. Ivan's mother lived till she reached the age of seventy. In 1820 the whole Turgénief family went abroad and visited Switzerland. At Berne the little four-year-old Ivan Sergéyevitch narrowly escaped falling a prey to the bears. His father caught him by the leg just as he was pitching headlong into the pit. When the family returned to Russia, they lived in the Government of Orlof; and Ivan Sergéiyevitch had tutors of every nationality except his own. His first acquaintance with Russian literature came from a serf named Kheraskof, belonging to his mother. The first Russian book that he ever read was the "Rossiada." In 1828 the family moved to Moscow, and six years later Ivan Sergéyevitch entered the University of Moscow; but the year following he left for Petersburg, where he graduated as *kandidat* in philology. His first attempts at writing were made before he graduated; and his teacher, Pletnef, was able to discover in him signs of future greatness. Turgénief says, in his "Reminiscences," "At the beginning of 1827, while I was a student in the third course of the University of St. Petersburg, I handed the professor of literature, P. A. Pletnef, one of the first 'fruits of my muse,' as they used to say in those days. It was a fantastic drama, in iambic pentameters, entitled 'Stenio.' In one of the following lectures, Pletnef, without mentioning any names, analyzed, with his usual kindness, this absolutely stupid piece of work, in which, with childish incapability, was shown a slavish imitation of Byron's 'Manfred.' After leaving the university building, and finding me on the street, he called me to him, and caressed me like a father, remarking at the same time that there was something [*tchto-to*] in me. These two words gave me sufficient assurance to take to him some more of my poetical productions. He picked out two of them, and a year later published them in 'The Sovremennik,' which he inherited from Pushkin. I don't remember the title of one; but "The Old Oak" was the subject of the other, and it began thus: —

'The forests' mighty tsar with curly head,
The ancient oak, bent o'er the water's sleeping smoothness.'"

In 1838 Turgénief went to Berlin. On his way the ship took fire, and he narrowly escaped with his life. He afterwards embodied the recollection in his story, or sketch, "A Fire at Sea." "I was then nineteen years old," he says, in his "Reminiscences," "and I had been dreaming about this trip. I was convinced that it was possible to acquire in Russia only elementary knowledge, but that the source of real knowledge was abroad. Among the number of the professors in the St. Petersburg University at that time, there was not one who could have shaken that conviction in me. Moreover, they themselves felt the same way. Even the ministry itself, including its chief, Count Uvarof, was convinced of this same thing; and the latter used to send at his own expense young men to the universities of Germany. I was at Berlin (at two different times) for about two years. I studied philosophy, the ancient languages, history, and with special eagerness I devoted myself to Hegel under the guidance of Professor Werder. As proof of the insufficiency of the knowledge to be gained at our own colleges, I am going to quote this fact: I studied Latin antiquity with Zumpt, the history of Greek literature with Beck; but at my own home I was compelled to learn by heart Latin and Greek grammar, of which I had a very slim acquaintance, and I was not one of the worst candidates."

In his "Reminiscences" he throws further light on the causes which induced him to live abroad. He says that there was nothing to keep him in Russia. Every thing around him was calculated to fill him with indignation, contempt, and scorn. "I could not hesitate long. It was necessary either to submit to humiliation, and calmly make up my mind to follow the general rut over the beaten road, or boldly to push away 'every thing and all,' even at the risk of losing much that was dear and near to my heart. And so I did. I threw myself head first into the 'German sea,' which should purify and regenerate me; and, when at last I emerged from its billows, I became a *Zapadnik*, — a Western man, and such I remained for all my life."

In 1841 Turgénief returned to Russia, going directly to Moscow, where his mother was living. Here he became acquainted with the

Slavophiles Aksákof, Khomiakof, and the Kiriyevskys, who at this time were just beginning to promulgate their ideas. But Turgénief found them hopelessly in the "general rut."

He tells in his "Reminiscences" how he first thought of "Fathers and Sons." "I was taking baths at Ventnor, a little town on the Isle of Wight, in August, 1860, when the first thought of 'Fathers and Sons' entered my mind, —that narrative which checked, as it seems to me, forever the kindly disposition of the Russian younger generation. More than once I read in journals, and heard that 'I was off the track,' or was 'bringing in new ideas.' Some praised me; others, on the contrary, blamed me. On my part, I must confess that I never attempted to 'create a figure.' I always had for my starting-point, not an idea, but a living person, to whom I would gradually add and join suitable elements. The same thing happened in 'Fathers and Sons.' As the foundation of the main figure, Bazarof, the person of a young provincial doctor, who surprised me very much at the time, was chosen. He died just before 1860. This remarkable man appeared to me to contain all the elements of what has since received the name of Nihilism, but which at that time was just beginning to rise, and had not yet been formulated. The impression made upon me by this person was very strong, and at the same time not very clear. At first I could not account for him very well; and I used my utmost endeavors to hear and see every thing about me, with a view of vivifying the truthfulness of my own impressions. This fact confused me. In no book of our literature could I find a single hint of what seemed to me to be everywhere. Reluctantly the doubt arose in me whether I was not hunting for a shadow."

What he found at last was Bazárof, in which type he predicted the spirit of a new epoch, and showed "the new man" at the very moment of his appearance. No one understood it, and hence arose the storm which assailed the author.

"I experienced impressions," says Turgénief, "of different kinds, but all equally disagreeable to me. I noticed coolness, even going so far as indignation, in many who had been near and dear to me. I received almost fulsome congratulations from people who belonged to the camp of my enemies. This confused me: . . . it grieved me. But my conscience did not reproach me. I knew well that I had been true to the type which I had described."

M. le Vicomte E. Melchior de Vogüé, in a capital study of Turgénief's life and works, thus speaks of the reason for the novelist's popularity and influence in Russia: "We read books as the passer-by glances at a painting in a shop-window, for an instant, from the corner of the eye, as he goes to his business. If you knew how differently they read their poets there [in Russia]! What for us is only a feast for enjoyment is for them the daily bread of the soul. It is the golden age of lofty literature, which all very youthful peoples in Asia, in Greece, in the Middle Ages have seen flourishing. The writer is the guide for his race, the master of a multitude of commingling thoughts; still in a measure the creator of his language, poet in the ancient and complete meaning of the word *vates*, poet, prophet. Simple-hearted and serious readers, new-comers into the world of ideas, eager for direction, full of illusions about the power of human genius, ask their intellectual guide for a doctrine, for a reason for life, for a perfect revelation of the ideal. In Russia the few members of the aristocratic *élite* long ago reached, and perhaps went beyond, our dilettanteism; but the lower classes are beginning to read: they read passionately, with faith and hope, as we read 'Robinson' at twelve. . . . For the Moscow merchant, the son of the village priest, the small country proprietor, to whom a few volumes of Pushkin, of Gogol, of Nekrásof represent the encyclopædia of the human mind, this novel ["Virgin Soil," or "Fathers and Sons," or "A Nest of Noblemen"] is one of the books of the national Bible: it assumes the importance and the epic significance which the story of Esther had for the people of Judæa, the story of Ulysses for the people of Athens, the romance of 'The Rose' or of 'Renart' for our ancestors.

"Three years ago, in dedicating the statue of Pushkin at Moscow, Turgénief quoted a characteristic remark made by a peasant standing near the monument. In reply to a comrade who asked the name of this gentleman in bronze, the *muzhik* said, 'He was a schoolmaster.' The orator appropriated the remark, and developed it, saying rightly that the peasant in his ignorance had hit upon the true name of the hero of the celebration. The first Russian poet had been the schoolmaster of his countrymen, he had given new life to their language and their thought. The day, not far distant, doubtless, when Turgénief's statue will be erected at Moscow, the *muzhik* will be able to repeat his saying: he also was a schoolmaster.

"His generation listened to him more willingly than to any other. It would be a mistake to seek solely in what we call talent for the reasons of this popular adoption. How many among his primitive and passionate readers troubled themselves about the question of talent, of devices of form, delicacies of thought? In literature, as in politics, a people follow instinctively the men whom they feel belong to themselves, made of their flesh and their genius, marked by their virtues and their failings. Ivan Sergeyévitch personified the master qualities of the Russian people, — their simple-hearted goodness, simplicity, and resignation. He was, as it is said popularly, *une âme du bon Dieu:* that mighty brain was ruled by a child's heart. Never did I approach him without better comprehending the magnificent meaning of the gospel saying about the "simple in spirit," and how this state of soul can be allied to the artist's exquisite gifts and knowledge. Devotion, generosity of heart and of hand, brotherly kindness — all were as natural to him as an organic function. In our cautious, complicated society, where every one is armed for the rough struggle of life, he seemed like a person from another sphere, from some pastoral and fraternal tribe of the Ural; — some grand, self-forgetful child, following his thoughts under the sky, as a shepherd follows his flocks in the steppe.

"Physically, likewise, this tall, calm old man, with his somewhat coarse features, his *sculpturesque* head, and his thoughtful gaze, brought to mind certain Russian peasants, — the elder who sits at the head of the table in patriarchal families, — but ennobled and transfigured by the labor of thought, like those peasants of old who became monks, were worshipped as saints, and are seen represented on the *ikonostas* with the aureole and the majesty of prayer. The first time that I met this good giant, the symbolical statue of his country, I had great difficulty in making my impression clear: it seemed to me that I saw and heard a *muzhik* upon whom had descended the fire of genius, who had been raised to the pinnacles of mind without losing any of his native candor. He would assuredly not have been offended by the comparison, he who so loved his people."

M. de Vogüé goes on to speak of Turgénief's work. "The public," he says, referring to the "Annals of a Sportsman," "did not at first perceive their hidden significance: the watchful censor was deceived. All that was seen in them was a literary manifestation of the first order, a new note in Russia. Doubtless Gogol's influence was apparent in the young writer's style, in his comprehension of nature: the 'Evenings at the Farm' set the model for the class. It was always the grand and melancholy symphony of the Russian land; but this time the interpretation by the artist was quite different. No longer were seen Gogol's sharp humor, the frankly popular character of his paintings, his warm outbursts of enthusiasm suddenly checked by touches of irony: in Turgénief, no jests or enthusiasm; a soberer note, a more subdued emotion; landscapes and men are seen in the pale twilight, through an idealizing mistiness, yet clearly outlined and focussed, as it were, under the eyes of the ever watchful observer.

"The language, also, is richer, more flexible, more graceful; no Russian writer had ever carried it to such a degree of expression. It is not the clear and limpid prose of Pushkin, who had read much of Voltaire, and did not forget it. Turgénief's periods run slow and voluptuous, like the surface of the mighty Russian rivers, without haste, harmonious, amid the reeds, bearing water-lilies, floating nests, wandering perfumes, showing luminous vistas, and long mirages of sky and land, and suddenly reappearing in shady depths. His discourse stops to gather up any thing, — the humming of a bee, the call of a night-bird, a passing, caressing, dying breeze. The most elusive accords of the grand register of nature it translates with the infinite resources of the Russian keys, flexible epithets, words welded together with poetic fancy, popular joinings of sound to sense.

"I dwell on that which makes the power of this book: it is only a song of the earth, and a murmur of a few poor souls directly heard by us. The writer takes us to the heart of his native land; he leaves us face to face with this country; he disappears, it seems: yet, if not he, who then has drawn from things, and condensed on their surface, that mysterious poetry which they hide within them, but which so few can see, and which we clearly see here? The 'Annals of a Sportsman' have charmed many French readers; yet how much they lose in color across the double veil of the translation and the common ignorance of the country! . . .

"When these fragments were brought together into a volume, the public, till then uncertain, saw the significance of the work. Some one had appeared with courage to develop the meaning concealed in Gogol's sinister jest about "Dead Souls." What other name can be given to that gallery of portraits gathered by the sportsman, — small country proprietors, selfish and hard; sneaking overseers, idle and rapacious functionaries; beneath this cruel society, wretched helots, fallen, as it were, from the state of humanity, touching by force of misery and submission? The process — however well disguised it be, there is always a process — was invariably the same. The author causes a ludicrous being to pass again and again in his lantern, showing all its phases, laughable and pitiable, in turn, without wants, without resources, condemned to crepuscular life. By the side of the serf appeared the master, a half-civilized marionette, a good devil, after all, unconscious of the harm he was doing, led astray by the fatality of his environment. This painting, which would otherwise be ugly, repulsive, the writer clothed with grace and charm, in some sort contrary to his desire by the inborn virtue of his poetry. Why were all the mainsprings of life broken in all the heroes of the book? Whence came this malaria over the Russian land? What was the name of this pest? The reader was left the trouble of answering.

"It is not very exact to say that Turgénief *attacked* serfage. Russian writers, in consequence of the conditions under which they work, as well as by the peculiar turn of their genius, never attack openly; they neither argue nor declaim: they paint without drawing conclusions, and they appeal to pity rather than wrath. Twenty years later, when Dostoyevsky will publish his "Recollections of a Dead House" (*Zapiski Mertvava Doma*), his terrible memoirs of ten years in Siberia, he will proceed in the same way, without a word of mutiny, without a drop of gall, seeming to find what he describes as quite natural, only a trifle sad. It is the national trait in all things. . . . The public understands by a hint.

"It understood this time. The Russia of serfage looked at itself with horror in the mirror which was held before its eyes: a long shudder shook the country; between night and morning the author was famous, and his cause was half gained. The censorship was the last to comprehend, but finally it also comprehended. Possibly its sensitiveness will be wondered at: I have said that serfage was condemned even in the Emperor Nicholas's heart. You must know that the wishes of the censorship do not always coincide with the emperor's wishes; at least, it is backward, it is sometimes a reign behindhand. It gave up launching its thunder against the book, but it kept its eye on the author. Gogol being dead in the interim, Turgénief dedicated a warmly eulogistic article to the dead author. This article would seem inoffensive enough, as it appears in Turgénief's complete works,[1] and we should have difficulty in discovering the crime if the criminal had not revealed the secret in a very gay note: '*Apropos* of that article, I remember that one day at Petersburg, a lady of very high rank criticised the punishment inflicted upon me, judging it to have been undeserved, or at least too severe. As she was warmly speaking in my defence, some one said to her, "Is it possible that you don't know that in this article he called Gogol *a great man?*" — "It is impossible." — "I assure you that it

[1] Ten volumes, published by Salaïef, in Moscow: his poetry, in one volume of two hundred and thirty pages, bears no publisher's imprint, simply the title, Stikhotvoreniya I. S. Turgénieva, S. Peterburg, 1885.

is so." — "Ah! in that case, I have nothing more to say. I am sorry, but I see that they had to be severe upon him."'

"This impertinent epithet, given to a simple writer, cost Turgénief a month of arrest; then he was advised to go and meditate in his domain. I imagine that he found that society was very ill arranged, so unfair are we to the power that wills our best good. It must be confessed, however, that this power sometimes serves our interest better than we ourselves, and *lettres de cachet* are generally in accordance with the views of Providence. Thirty years earlier an order of exile saved Pushkin by tearing the poet from the dissipations of Petersburg, where he was wasting his genius, and by sending him to the sun of the East, where his genius was to ripen. If Turgénief had remained at the capital, the warmth of youth and compromising friendships, perchance, might have brought him into some barren political quarrel: sent into the solitude of the woods, he lived there laborious years, studying the humble provincial life of Russia, and gathering materials for his first great novels."

An anonymous writer, who knew Turgénief intimately, contributed, shortly after his death, to "The London Daily News," an article, some of the details of which are worthy of preservation: "Turgénief hated luxury. The more he advanced in life, the more he prized simplicity in all things. His bedroom at Les Fresnes[1] had an almost austere aspect. The bed and toilet-stand were in iron; and the desk, drawers, and a large bookcase, in mahogany, of a plain design. Some photographs and engraved likenesses of literary and other friends broke the monotony of the wall. Portrait-cartes, many of which had autographs of those whom they represented, were stuck into the frame of the chimney glass.

"Turgénief was the youngest of three very distinguished brothers. Were the eldest of the trio now living, he would be almost a centenarian. He remembered Buonaparte, Bernardin, St. Pierre, Talleyrand, Sir Walter Scott, — of whom he was for some weeks a guest at Abbotsford, — Miss Edgeworth when she was in the zenith of her fame; visited Mme. de Staël at Coppet, and fell in with Byron as he was mak-

[1] The summer home of his friends the Viardots, at Bougival.

ing a tour on the Rhine. The eldest Turgénief was a many-sided man. Though not a professional author, he had great literary qualities. His political insight and sagacity were no less remarkable, and he had a wider experience of human nature than perhaps any other European of his time. Though he belonged to a family which stood well with the Court and high in the administration, he enjoyed close intercourse with his 'unmasked countrymen.' He thus designated the serfs, who had learned to be patient and resigned, but were unable to dissimulate. Nevertheless, he was accomplished in every polite art, and, if he had chosen, might have risen to the highest diplomatic position. His education was French on Russian soil. Voltaire and Diderot were his early schoolmasters. When he grew up, he made wide incursions into English literature, and came to the conclusion that Maria Edgeworth had struck on a vein which most of the great novelists of the future would exclusively work. She took the world as she found it, and selected from it the material that she thought would be interesting to write about in a clear and natural style. It was Ivan Turgénief himself who told me this, and he modestly said that he was an unconscious disciple of Miss Edgeworth in setting out on his literary career. He had not the advantage of knowing English;[1] but, as a youth, he used to hear his brother translate to visitors, at his country house in the Uralian, passages from 'Irish Tales and Sketches,' which he thought superior to her three-volume novels. Turgénief also said to me, 'It is possible, nay, probable, if Maria Edgeworth had not written about the poor Irish of the County Longford, and the squires and squireens, that it would not have occurred to me to give a literary form to my impressions about the classes parallel to them in Russia. My brother used, in pointing out the beauties of her unambitious works, to call attention to their extreme simplicity, and to the distinction with which she treated the simple ones of the earth.'

[1] Mr. Henry James, in his Atlantic Monthly article upon Turgénief, says: "He had read a great deal of English, and knew the language remarkably well, — too well I used often to think; for he liked to speak it with those to whom it was native, and, successful as the effort always was, it deprived him of the facility and raciness with which he expressed himself in French."

"Turgénief's stature was far above the average. He was admirably proportioned, and, when young, could walk as far in a day as a tough horse would amble, and that without any oppressive sense of fatigue. The big bones supported tremendous muscles, which at no time of his life were clogged with adipose tissue. When I knew him, his thick, long hair and flowing beard were white as snow; but as the complexion was fresh, the eye bright, the carriage upright, the voice resonant, I never thought of him as an old man. This giant wrote a neat and almost delicate hand. I have before me a book of his with an autograph inscription which he sent me last winter. . . . This autograph, though almost ladylike in its delicacy, is very free and unconventional. Turgénief felt what was beautiful in minute and lowly things. He was one of those who are happy in admiring flowers in the valley of humiliation. In some respects he was a big child. Nobody was more easy to amuse. He used to say that Providence was so kind in throwing in his way the kind of persons who exactly suited him. Liking fine arts and music, and disliking fashion and worldly frivolity, he deemed it a piece of rare good luck to fall in with Louis Viardot and his gifted wife (*née* Garcia), and to be allowed to enter their family circle. . . .

"Turgénief's conversation was analogous to his handwriting. It was light, delicate, of a free and quite original style, and abounded in picturesque traits. Nothing was forced or far-fetched. His ideas came in the bright, easy flow of a quick-running and well-fed streamlet. It was all the same to him whether he was brought forward or unnoticed in society, for he was neither shy nor vain. He rarely, in talking, broached a subject; but there was no subject on which he could not talk with ease. The politician, philosopher, artist, poet, novelist, intelligent or simple, woman or child, found him good company. Whatever interested mankind appeared to concern him, and to be a thing to study. At the Universal Exhibition of 1878 I found Turgénief in the United States Agricultural Department studying horse-shoes and horse-shoe nails with as much zest as he afterwards showed in comparing the works of the

English, Russian, and German schools of pictorial art. The person who explained to him the peculiar merits of the horse-shoe nails was a character; and his peculiarities, which were racy of the soil of Texas, acted as a stimulant on the Russian novelist."

"Theoretically, there was no depth of human degradation with which the Russian novelist was not acquainted; but it was said that personally no vice ever touched him. '*Gros innocent*' was a term which M. Viardot often applied to him in their intimate conversation. The giant was '*naïf*.' He preserved until old age the impressionable eyes of childhood, and a freshness of nature which to those who did not know him must seem incompatible with his extensive knowledge of human nature, which he studied as a student at Moscow and Berlin, as a functionary at St. Petersburg and in other parts of Russia, and as an exile in Paris. Although an old bachelor, he was free from crotchets and angles. He was glad to oblige, often obliged, sometimes was heartily thanked; and, when he met with ingratitude, he did not think about it. Flaubert was the French novelist whom he best liked as a man and a writer. But he was of opinion that he travelled too far south when he went to Carthage[1] to look for a heroine. His eyes were not used to the glaring landscape of North Africa. They discerned better the cool tints of the Normandy landscape. Plots, he thought, spoiled novels, which were *peintures de mœurs;* and he was glad to see that the taste for them was dying out. Dickens, in his opinion, was at his best in the 'Pickwick Papers,' because he had not to be thinking about a plot, instead of letting his pen run on according to the humor of the moment. The plot was necessary for a drama, but in the way of a novelist, who should, above every thing else, keep truth in view. . . .

"Turgénief was of opinion that a splendidly picturesque country was a bad soil for literary or artistic production. Strong emotions or sensations tended to dethrone the faculty of exact observation upon which we are dependent for æsthetic enjoyment in flat districts. We console ourselves for the prose of a landscape in looking with an almost microscopic eye at the plants and insects, and come to see a world

[1] Referring to Salammbo.

replete with beauty and animation in a tangle of gorse, brambles, and humble field-flowers. In expressing to me this theory, he asked, 'Did you ever see a mountaineer who was sensible to the beauty and song of a small bird? He watches the flight of game and birds of prey. But, for my part, I have found him indifferent to the lark and swallow. My first acquaintance with the skylark was precisely in looking about for compensation for the ugliness of a flat near Berlin. I shall never forget the broadening out of the æsthetic faculty on this occasion. The little creature rose almost from under my feet, and went up singing her joyful song, which I heard long after she was invisible. I then remarked the beauty of the sky and of many other things which I should not otherwise have noticed.' "

A few sentences from the "noble discourse" spoken by M. Renan at Turgénief's tomb, on Oct. 1, 1883, will fittingly bring this note to a close.

"Turgénief was an eminent writer. He was, above all, a great man. I shall speak to you only of his soul as it always appeared to me in the pleasant retreat which an illustrious friendship had provided for him among us.

"Turgénief received, by that mysterious decree which makes human avocations, the noblest gift of all: he was born essentially impersonal. His consciousness was not that of an individual more or less finely endowed by nature: he was in some sort the consciousness of a people. Before his birth he had lived thousands of years; infinite series of visions were concentrated in the depths of his heart. No man has been to such a degree the incarnation of an entire race. A world lived in him, spoke by his lips; generations of ancestors lost in the sleep of ages, without voices, through him came to life and to speech.

"The silent genius of collective masses is the source of all great things. But the masses have no voice. They can only feel and stammer. They need an interpreter, a prophet, to speak for them. Who shall be this prophet? Who shall tell their sufferings, denied by those who are interested in not seeing them, their secret aspirations which upset the sanctimonious optimism of the contented? The great man, gentlemen, when he is at once a man of genius and a man of heart. That is why the great man is least free of all men. He does not do, he does not say, what he wishes. A God speaks in him; ten centuries of suffering and of hope possess him and rule him. Sometimes it happens to him, as to the seer in the ancient stories of the Bible, that, when called upon to curse, he blesses; according to the spirit which moves, his tongue refuses to obey.

"It is to the honor of the great Slav race, whose appearance in the world's foreground is the most unexpected phenomenon of our century, that it was first expressed by a master so accomplished. Never were the mysteries of an obscure and still contradictory consciousness revealed with such marvellous insight. It was because Turgénief at once felt, and perceived that he felt: he was the people, and he was of the elect. He was as sensitive as a woman and as impassive as a surgeon, as free from illusions as a philosopher and as tender as a child. Happy the race, which, at its beginning a life of reflection, can be represented by such images, simple-hearted as well as learned, at once real and mystical.

"When the future shall have brought to their real proportions the surprises kept in reserve for us by this wonderful Slav genius, with its ardent faith, its depth of intuition, its individual idea of life and death, its martyr spirit, its thirst for the ideal, Turgénief's paintings will be priceless documents, something, as it were, like the portrait of a man of genius, if it were possible to be had, taken in his infancy. The perilous solemnity of his duty as interpreter of one of the great families of humanity, Turgénief clearly saw. He felt that he had souls in his charge; and, as he was a man of honor, he weighed each of his words. He trembled for what he said, and what he did not say.

"His mission was thus wholly that of the peacemaker. He was like the God of the Book of Job, who 'makes peace upon the heights.' What everywhere else caused discord became with him a principle of harmony. In his great bosom, contradictions united. Cursing and hatred were disarmed by the magic enchantments of his art.

"That is why he is the common glory of schools, between which so many disagreements exist. This great race, divided because it is great, finds in him its unity. Hostile brethren separated by different ways of interpreting the ideal, come all of you to his tomb. All of you have the right to love him; for he belonged to all of you, he held you all in his heart. Admirable privilege of genius! The repellent sides of things do not exist for him. In him all finds reconciliation. Parties most opposed unite to praise him and admire. In the region whither he carries us, words which stir irritation in the vulgar lose their sting. Genius accomplishes in a day what it takes centuries to do. It creates an atmosphere of higher peace when those who were foes find that in reality they have been co-laborers; it opens the era of the grand amnesty when those who have been battling in the arena of progress sleep side by side and hand in hand.

"Above the race, in fact, stands humanity; or, if you prefer, reason. Turgénief was of a race by his manner of feeling and painting. He belonged to all humanity by his lofty philosophy, facing with calm eyes the conditions of human existence, and seeking without prejudice to know the reality. This philosophy brought him sweetness, joy in life, pity for creatures, for victims above all. Ardently he loved this poor humanity, often blind, in sooth, but so often betrayed by its leaders. He applauded its spontaneous effort towards well being and truth. He did not reprove its illusions; he was not angry because it complained. The iron policy which mocked at those who suffer was not for him. No disappointment arrested him. Like the universe, he would have begun a thousand times the ruined work: he knew that justice can wait; the end will always be success. He had truly the words of eternal life, the words of peace, of justice, of love, and of liberty."

COUNT LYOF N. TOLSTOÏ.

Count Tolstoï traces his ancestry back to Count Piotr Andreyévitch Tolstoï, a friend and companion of Peter the Great. In all probability the unnamed *atavus* who lurks in the patronymic *Andreyévitch* was merely distinguished by his size, — Andrew the Stout. Many Russian family names, just as is the case with our own English appellations, are derived from characteristics or resemblances. The great Speransky was a hopeful foundling; Soloviéf recalls our nightingales; Pobyedonovtsof means "of the victorious;" the name of Katkof may refer to the proverbial rolling stone; Gogol is a species of duck called the golden eye; the report of cannon may be heard in Pushkin's name; the ancestor of Griboyédof was probably an eater of mushrooms.

Tolstoï's father was a retired lieutenant-colonel, who died in 1839. His mother, the Princess Marya Nikolayevna Volkonskaïa, died when Count Lyof was only two years old, and he ·was brought up by a distant relative, Mme. Yergolskaïa. At Yasmaïa Polyana his education was desultory. In 1840 the five children were taken in charge by a relative of their mother, Pelagia Ilinishna Yushkovaïa, who lived at Kazan. It was thus that Lyof Tolstoï happened to enter the university of that city in 1843. After a few years of study, he suddenly determined to leave the university without graduation. The *rektor* and the professors argued with him, but in vain; and he went back to his ancestral estate, where he lived till 1851, very rarely visiting the capital. A visit from his beloved brother Nikolaï, who was an officer in the army of the Caucasus, inspired him to see "cities of men and manners, climates, councils," though least of all the cities of men. Especially strong was his desire to be with his brother in the *Kavkaz*, where Russia's greatest poets had won their proudest laurels. The impressions made on him by the splendid scenery of the 'white mountains,' and by the rough, half-savage life, were so strong that in 1851 he entered the service, like Olénin, as a *yunker*, or ensign-bearer in the Fourth Battery of the Twentieth Artillery, the same in which his brother was an officer.

Here in the Caucasus Count Tolstoï first began to write fiction. He planned to weave his recollections of family life and old traditions into a great novel. Fragments of this work were written and afterwards published in the "Sovremennik." "Infancy" (*Dyetstvo*) came out in 1852. "Adolescence" (*Otrotchestvo*) was also written then, and several of his brilliant sketches of wild life, — "The Invasion," "The Felling of the Forest," and, as has been said, "The Cossacks." "The Cossacks" is translated into English by Mr. Eugene Schuyler. A very little polishing would make it a brilliant piece of literary work: in its present form it is crude and rough.

Count Tolstoï lived two years in the Caucasus, taking part in various guerilla expeditions, and enduring in common with the soldiers all the hardships of frontier warfare. Here on the spot he made his powerful and life-like studies of the Russian soldier, which are seen in his "War Sketches" (*Voyennuié Razskazui*). At the breaking out of the Crimean War, Count Tolstoï was transferred to the army of the Danube, and served on Prince M. D. Gortchakof's staff. At Sevastópol, whither he went after the. Russian army was driven from the principalities, he was attached to the artillery. His literary work had attracted attention in high quarters, and orders were sent to the front to see that he was not exposed to danger. In May, 1855, he was appointed division commander: he took part in the battle of the Tchernaïa, was in the celebrated storming of Sevastópol, and after the battle was sent as special courier to Petersburg. At the end of the campaign Count Tolstoï retired, and the next winter he spent at Moscow and Petersburg. This was a period of great literary activity. Besides his stories, "Sevastópol in December," and "Sevastópol in May," there appeared in the magazines "Youth" (*Yunost*), "Sevastópol in August," "Two Hussars" (*Dva Gusári*), and "Three Deaths" (*Tri Smerti*).

After the liberation of the serfs, Count Tolstoï, like many conscientious Russian proprietors, felt it his duty to live on his estate. He was profoundly interested in agronomic questions, and in the application to the Slavic commune of Occidental methods, which he studied abroad for himself. He was still more interested in popular education; and a school journal, called "Yasnaïa Polyana," which he established, discussed all pedagogical questions. He also published a series of primers, readers, spellers, in paper covers and large type. It was about this time that a Russian journalist met Count Tolstoï; and his account of the interview is interesting, as showing the novelist's views a quarter of a century ago. He says, —

"In 1862 I became acquainted with him in Moscow. I saw before me a tall, wide-shouldered, thin-waisted man, about thirty-five years old, with a mustache, but without a beard, with a serious, even gloomy expression of face, which, however, was softened by a gleam of kindliness whenever he laughed. Our conversation turned on the occurrences which at that time were exciting Russian life. Count Tolstoï immediately showed that he lived outside of this life, that the interests of the class which regards itself as cultured were foreign to him. He seemed to be opposed to progress, which, in his opinion, was only advantageous for the smaller portion of society, having plenty of time to spend, and which was absolutely injurious for the majority, for the people; and for them it was just as disadvantageous as it was profitable for the minority. . . . Those present argued angrily with him: he himself sometimes was drawn away, sometimes he spoke ironically. I listened more than I spoke. At the time when all were infatuated with progress, such original boldness of thought was remarkable; and I felt an involuntary sympathy for this Rousseau, who began to contrast the products of nature with the products of civilization, — forests, wild creatures, rivers, physical development, purity of morals, and other such things. It seemed that this man was living the life of the peasantry, sharing their views, that he was devoted to the welfare of the people with all the strength of his soul, though he understood the people in different way from others. The proof was his school, — those *maltchiks*, of whom he spoke with evident love, praising their talents, their powers of comprehension, their artistic sense, their moral virginity, which was so far from being the case with children of other nationalities."

The latter years of Count Tolstoï's life, since the publication of "War and Peace" and "Anna Karénina," are somewhat wrapped in mystery. Various wild stories, founded on the evident bias of "My Confession" and "My Religion," have assumed almost the proportions of myth. It may be that at the present day, that we of the calm, rational, sceptical, Western world are granted the privilege of seeing the actual evolution of a myth, as a boy may see a chrysalis unfold.

The Russian race, standing with its Janus face towards the sunset and the more mystical sunrise, a link, as it were, between Occidental fact and Oriental fancy, might well allow us the spectacle. "My Religion" declares that titles, emoluments, dignities, and all such things, are vain. Next we hear that Count Tolstoï is only a *muzhik*. No man has a right to wealth. We hear that the opulent aristocrat has stripped himself to give to the poor. All must earn their bread by the sweat of the brow. The young sons of the count are next heard of as crossing-sweepers. The truth probably is, that Count Tolstoï has in reality changed little from the Olénin of "The Cossacks," praying for occasion of self-sacrifice, for chance of renunciation, changed little from the threefold manifestation of himself in "War and Peace," working for the same end, or from the twofold and simpler manifestation of himself, morally in Levin, socially in Vronsky, of "Anna Karénina." The little picture of him given by the Russian journalist casts a flood of light on the man; and therefore it was but a fulfilment of prophecy to read that Count Tolstoï, instead of beggaring his children, instead of deserting the pen of the writer for the awl of the cobbler, was brave and cheerful and healthy in body and mind, superintending his schools, cultivating his ancestral *desyatins*, and writing stories when the mood was on him.

This brief sketch of Count Tolstoï's life may fitly come to a conclusion with an acute bit of criticism from a Russian writer. It is very possible that his marriage to Sofia Andreyevna

Beers, the daughter of a Muscovite professor, which took place in 1862, may have cast a back gleam, and inspired the thought of creating the gracious forms that move through Count Tolstoï's later novels. At all events, this is what the critic said when "War and Peace" appeared, at the end of 1860, "It is remarkable, that in all Tolstoï's works, until the appearance of "*Voïna i Mir*," there is not a single female figure brought out in strong relief; but here were seen a whole *pleiad*, wonderfully clear, psychologically true, and beautifully described. The richness and variety in the figures of the men, the splendid description of the battles, a perfect mass of marvellously described scenery, in which persons of all classes appear, beginning with emperors, and ending with *muzhiks* and *babas*, make this work one of the greatest ornaments of our literature."

Note to P. 145 — Tchernuishevsky.

It is commonly reported in Russia, that Tchernuishevsky wrote yet another novel besides *Tchto Dyélat*, entitled *Prolog Prologof* (a Prologue of Prologues), which may possibly be still in existence in manuscript.

Note to P. 202. — Dostoyevsky.

Feódor Mikhaïlovitch Dostoyevsky's father was a doctor. The boy, who was one of a large family, grew up pale and thin. He had a nervous and impressionable nature, with some tendency to hallucination. He was very fond of the woods. He tells in his recollections of his childhood, that his "special delight was the forest, with its mushrooms and wild cherries, with its beetles and birds, its porcupines and squirrels, with its delicious damp of the flying leaves." He had all the books that he desired. By the time that he was twelve, he had read all of Sir Walter Scott's and Cooper's novels, besides some Russian authors, including Karamzin's great history. At fifteen, Dostoyevsky was sent to Petersburg, where he entered the main engineering school. Notwithstanding his passion for literature, which was shared by many of his school-mates, he distinguished himself in mathematics, and graduated number three in a class of thirty. About this time he was deprived of both father and mother.

"While he was living in Petersburg," says Mr. S. S. Skidelsky, "he visited all the slums and haunts of poverty, for the sake of collecting materials for his future literary work." Dostoyevsky tells in his recollections, quoted by Polevoï, that in the winter of 1845 he began his first story, "Poor People" (*Byédnuië Liudi*). "When I finished the tale, I did not know what to do with it, or where to place it. I had no literary acquaintances, except possibly Grigoróvitch, who at that time had written nothing except 'Petersburg Organ-grinders,' in a magazine. . . . He came to me one day in May, and said, 'Show me the manuscript: Nekrásof is going to publish a magazine next year, and I want to show it to him.' I took it over to Nekrásof. We shook hands; I became confused at the thought that I had come with my writing, and I quickly beat a retreat without saying another word. I had very little hope of success; for I stood in awe of the party of 'the Country Annals,' as the literary men of that day were called. I read Byélinsky's criticisms eagerly, but he seemed to me too severe and cruel; and 'he will make sport of my "Poor People,"' I used to think at times, but only at times. 'I wrote it with passion, almost with tears. Is it really possible that all these minutes spent with pen in hand over this story, that all this is falsehood, mirage, untrue feeling?' But I had these thoughts only now and then, and immediately the doubts returned again.

"On the evening of the very day that I handed him the manuscript, I went a long way to see one of my former classmates. We talked all night about 'Dead Souls,' and we read it again, — I don't know how many times it made. At that time it was fashionable, when two or three young men met, to say, 'Hadn't we better read some Gogol, gentlemen?' and then to sit down and read late into the night. . . . I returned home at four o'clock, in the white Petersburg night, bright as day. It was a beautiful warm time; and when I reached my room I could not go to sleep, but opened the window, and sat down by it. Suddenly the bell rang: it surprised me greatly; and in an instant Grigoróvitch and Nekrásof were hugging me in a glory of enthusiasm, and both of them were almost in tears. The evening before they had returned home early, took up my manuscript, and began to read it for a trial: 'By ten pages we shall be able to judge.'

But after they had finished ten pages they decided to read ten more. And afterwards, without budging, they sat the whole night through till early morning, taking turns in reading aloud when one got tired. 'He read about the death of the student,' said Grigoróvitch, after we were alone; 'and suddenly I noticed, that, when he reached the place where the father runs after his son's coffin, Nekràsof's voice broke once, and a second time, and all at once it failed entirely. He pounded with his fist on the manuscript: "*Akh*, what a man!" That was said about you; and so we spent the whole night.'

"When they finished the manuscript, they exclaimed, simultaneously, 'Let us go and find him right away. Suppose he is asleep, this is more important than sleep.' . . . They staid half an hour. For half an hour we talked about, God knows what, understanding each other by half words, by exclamations, so eager were we. We talked about poetry, about prose, about the 'situation of affairs,' and of course about Gogol, quoting from the 'Revizor' and 'Dead Souls,' but chiefly about Byélinsky. . . . Nekrásof took the manuscript to Byelinsky that very day. 'A new Gogol has appeared,' shouted Nekrásof, entering with 'Poor People.' 'Gogols with you spring up like mushrooms,' remarked Byélinsky severely; but he took the manuscript. When Nekrásof returned that same evening, Byélinsky met him in perfect enthusiasm. 'Bring him, bring him as soon as you can!'"

On the next day an interview took place between Dostoyevsky and the great Russian critic. Dostoyevsky thus describes it: "He began to speak with me ardently, with flashing eyes. 'Do you understand yourself what you have written?' he shouted at me several times, in his own peculiar way. 'Only by your own unassisted genius as an artist, could you have written this. But have you realized all the terrible truth which you have presented before us? It is impossible that you, at the age of twenty, could understand it. . . . You have touched the very essence of the matter, you have reached the most vital inwardness. We journalists and critics only argue; we try to explain it with words: but you are an artist, and with a single stroke put the very truth into shape so that it is tangible, so that the simplest reader can understand instantly. Here lies the secret of the artistic, the truth of art. Here is the service that the artist performs for truth. The truth is revealed and imparted to you; it is your gift as an artist. Value your talent, and be true to it, and you will be a great writer.'

"I went from him in a state of rapture. I stopped at the corner of his house, looked up at the sky, at the bright sun, on the passing people, and all; and with my whole body I felt that a glorious moment had come into my life, — a most important crisis; that a new life had begun, such as I had never anticipated in my most passionate dreams (and at that time I was a great dreamer). 'Is it really true that I am so great?' I asked myself, full of shame, full of timid glory. — Oh, do not laugh! — Never again did I have an idea that I was great. But at that time was it possible to bear it calmly? Oh! I will be worthy of this praise."

His name from this time began to stand with Turgénief's, Byélinsky's, Iskander's (Herzen's), and others, in the pages of the Russian magazines. This period, which began so auspiciously, was clouded by a catastrophe which greatly affected his whole life. In 1849 he was arrested and imprisoned on the charge of being engaged in a secret political society. His older brother, a married man, the father of three children, was also arrested on the same charge. Dostoyevsky knew that his brother's family was almost penniless, that his brother had taken no active part in the Petrashevsky Society, and had only borrowed books from the general library. The brother, however, was soon released by the interposition of the Emperor Nicholas. While he was in prison, Feódor Mikhaïlovitch wrote his beautiful story, "The Little Hero." He was condemned to death; but the sentence, without his knowledge, was commuted to transportation to the mines. He wrote his brother on the 3d of January, 1850: "To-day we were taken to the Semyónovsky Place. Here the sentence of death was read to us, we were given the cross to kiss, the sabres were broken over our heads, and our death-toilet was prepared, — white shirts. Then three of our number were placed at the 'disgraceful post,' ready for execution. I was the sixth. Three were summoned at a time: consequently my turn came next, and I had only a second to live. I remembered thee, my brother, and all of thy household; at the last moment thou alone wert in my mind; here, only, I learned how I loved thee, my dear brother! . . . At last the drums sounded a retreat. Those who were fastened to the 'disgraceful post' were taken down, and it was announced that his Imperial Majesty had granted us our lives."

"Dostoyevsky, as a thoroughly religious and highly moral man," says Polevoï, "endured all the deprivations of his life in the mines with remarkable firmness and undisturbed equanimity. His faith was strengthened, not by the Bible alone, which was the only book allowed him in prison, but by his love for 'Poor People,' to whom he had sworn to be true till he died."

After he spent a number of years in the mines, he entered the military service, and was quickly promoted to be an officer. He says, "I remember that soon after leaving the Siberian prison, in 1854, I began to read all the literature written during the five years since my imprisonment. The 'Annals of a Sportsman' had just begun to be published; and Turgénief's first stories I read at one draught. The sun of the steppe shone upon me, spring began, and with it an entirely new life, an end to prison, — freedom!"

His passion for literature, so long restrained, broke out with energy and strength; and even before he quitted military service and returned to Petersburg, he wrote a few little trifles. In Petersburg he took part in the journal, "The Times" (*Vremya*), edited by his brother Mikhaïl Mikhaïlovitch. In 1860 appeared the first collection of his works, and shortly after appeared his great novel, "The Degraded and Insulted" (*Unizhónnuie i Oskorblonnuie*). At this time Turgénief, Gontcharóf (author of "Oblómof"), Grigoróvitch, and Count Lyof Tolstoï were in the full bloom of production, and Dostoyevsky's book was not warmly received. But the most antagonistic critics were silenced when "The Recollections of a Dead House" appeared. It immediately gave him the reputation as one of the greatest lights of Russian literature.

In 1863 Dostoyevsky's wife died; and in the following year he lost his beloved brother, whose journal, "The Times," passed into his hands. But he was entirely unused to business, and was placed in a very embarrassing situation, which was intensified by a strange public impression that it was the novelist who was dead. Consequently its circulation was greatly reduced, and Feódor Mikhaïlovitch had to give it up. As a distraction for all these tribulations, Dostoyevsky devoted himself to literary work, and wrote his great story, "Crime and Punishment," which established his reputation as a psychological analyst. In 1867 he married again, and lived abroad for four years. He also, looking from the "beautiful distance" upon the pitiful side of Russian social life, wrote his two stories, "Idiot" and "Devils." After he came back he wanted to analyze the abnormal relationship between the rising generation and the older writers; and he founded a new journal, and wrote a novel entitled "Podrostok" (The Adult). The journal was given up at the end of 1877; but Dostoyevsky, who had new novels in view, promised ultimately to continue the journal at some future time. He died on the 9th of February, 1881; and on the day of his funeral the first number of the long-looked-for journal, which he did not live to see, was issued. All Petersburg escorted the beloved remains to the tomb; tens of thousands of people were counted in the procession. Dostoyesky's faith in humanity is summed up in his own words: "I never could understand the reason why one-tenth part of our people should be cultured, and the other nine-tenths must serve as the material support of the minority and themselves remain in ignorance. I do not want to think or to live with any other belief than that our ninety millions of people (and those who shall be born after us) will all be some day cultured, humanized, and happy. I know and I firmly believe that universal enlightenment will harm none of us. I also believe that the kingdom of thought and light is possible of being realized in our Russia, even sooner than elsewhere maybe, because with us, even now, no one defends the idea of one part of the population being enlisted against the other, as is found everywhere in the civilized countries of Europe.'

Note to P. 203.

The *Banya* (from "The Recollections of a Dead-House").

"In the whole city, there were only two public baths. The first, which was kept by a Hebrew, was numbered, with an entrance-fee of fifty *kopeks* for each number, and was designed for high-toned people. The other *banya* was pre-eminently common, old, filthy, small; and to this *banya* our prisoners were going. It was cold and sunny. The men were already rejoicing because they were going to get out of prison, and have a glimpse of the city. Jests, laughter, did not cease during the walk. A whole squad of soldiers escorted us with loaded guns, to the wonder of the whole city. At the *banya* they immediately divided us into two detachments. The second had to wait in the cold ante-room while the first detachment soaped themselves, and this was necessary on account of the smallness of the *banya;* but, notwithstanding this fact, the *banya* was so small, that it was hard to imagine how our half could find accommodation in it. But Petrof did not leave me: he himself, without my asking him, hurried to help me, and even offered to wash me. Bakliushin, as well as Petrof, offered me his services. He was a prisoner from a special cell, and was known among us as the pioneer, and him I remembered as the gayest and liveliest of the *arestants*, as indeed he was. We had already become somewhat well acquainted. Petrof helped me undress myself, because, as I was not used to it, it took me long; and the dressing-room was cold, almost as cold as the street. By the way, it is very hard for a prisoner to undress if he has not had some practice. In the first place, it is necessary to know how to unfasten quickly the shin-protectors.[1] These shin-protectors are made of leather, about seven inches long; and they are fastened to the underclothes directly under the iron anklet which encircles the leg. A pair of shin-protectors are worth not less than sixty kopeks; but, nevertheless, every prisoner gets himself a pair, at his own expense of course, because without them it is impossible to walk. The iron ring does not encircle the leg tightly, and it is easy to thrust a finger between the ring and the leg. Thus the iron strikes the leg, chafes it; and a prisoner without shin-protectors would in a single day have bad wounds. But to take off the shin-protectors is not the hardest thing of all. It is much harder to learn to get off the clothes when one wears the rings (*kandalui*). This is the whole trick: Suppose you are taking off the drawers

[1] *Podkandalniki.*

from the left leg, it is necessary first to let the garment slip through between the leg and the ring. Afterwards you have to put it on again the same way. The same process must be gone through with when you put on clean clothes. For a newcomer it is even hard to guess how it is accomplished. The first one who ever taught us how to do it was the prisoner Kóryenef in Tobolsk, who had once been atamán of a gang of cut-throats, and had been fastened to a chain five years. But the prisoners get used to it, and do it without any difficulty. I gave several kopeks to Petrof to get soap and scrubbers. To be sure, the authorities furnished the prisoners with soap. Every one would get a little piece about the size of a two-kopek coin, and as thick as the slice of cheese served at evening lunch by middle-class people. Soap was sold here in the dressing-room, together with *sbiten* [a kind of mead], twists, and hot water. Every prisoner would get, according to the agreement made with the proprietor of the *banya*, a single pail of hot water. Whoever wanted to wash himself cleaner could get for a *grosh*, or half kopek, an extra pail, which was handed into the *banya* itself through a window made for that purpose from the dressing-room. After helping me to undress, Petrof led me by the hand, observing that it was very hard for me to walk in the rings. "Pull them up a little higher over the calf," he added, supporting me as though he were my uncle (*dyadka*). "Be a little careful here, there is a door-sill." I even felt a little ashamed. I wanted to assure Petrof that I could get along by myself, but he would not have believed me. He treated me just like a young and incapable child, whom everybody was obliged to help. Petrof was far from being a servant, by no means was he a servant. Had I insulted him, he would have understood how to behave to me. I did not offer him any money for his services, and he did not ask for any. What, then, prompted him to take such care of me?

"When we opened the door of the *banya*, I thought that we were going into Gehenna. Imagine a room about twelve feet long, and as wide, stuffed with probably a hundred men at once, and, at the very least, surely eighty, because the prisoners were divided into two detachments, and the whole number of us who went to the *banya* were two hundred men; the steam blinding our eyes, the sweat, the filth, such a crowd that there was no room to get a leg in. I was alarmed, and wanted to go back, but Petrof immediately encouraged me. Somehow, with the greatest difficulty, we squeezed ourselves through to the benches, over the heads of those who were sitting on the floor, asking them to bend down so that we could pass. But all the places on the benches were occupied. Petrof told me that it was necessary to buy a place, and immediately entered into transactions with a prisoner who had taken a place near the window. For a kopek the prisoner surrendered his place, immediately took the money from Petrof, who had it tight in his fist, having foreseen that it would be necessary to bring it with him into the *banya*. The man threw himself under the bench, directly under my place, where it was dark, filthy, and where the slimy dampness was almost half a finger in thickness. But the places under the benches were also taken; even there, the crowd clustered. On the whole floor, there was not a free place as large as the palm of the hand where the prisoners would not be sitting doubled up, washing themselves in their pails. Others stood upright among these, and, holding their pails in their hands, washed themselves as best they could. The dirty water ran down directly on the shaven heads of those who sat beneath them. On the platform, and on all the steps leading to it, were men washing themselves, bent down and doubled up. But precious little washing they got. Plebeians wash themselves very little with hot water and soap: they only steam themselves tremendously, and then pour cold water over them, and that's their whole bath. Fifty brooms or so on the platform were rising and falling in concert: they all broomed themselves into a state of intoxication. Every instant steam was let in. It was not merely heat, it was hell let loose. It was all one uproar and hullaballoo (*gogotalo*), with the rattling of a hundred chains dragging over the floor. . . . Some, trying to pass, entangled themselves with the chains of others, and they themselves bumped against the heads of those sitting below, and they tumbled over, and scolded, and dragged into the quarrel those whom they hit. The filth was streaming on every side. All were in an excited, and as it were intoxicated, state of mind. Shrieks and cries were heard. At the dressing-room window, where the water was handed through, there was a tumult, a pushing, even fighting. The hot water ordered was spilt on the heads of those sitting on the floor, before it reached its destination. Now and then, at the window or in the half-opened door, a soldier with mustachioed face would show himself, with gun in hand, ready to quell any disorder. The shaven heads and red, parboiled bodies of the prisoners seemed uglier than ever. On their parboiled shoulders clearly appeared, oftentimes, the welts caused by the strokes and lashes which they may have received in days gone by; so that now all these backs seem to be freshly wounded. Horrid welts! A chill went through my skin at seeing them. "Give us more steam;" and the steam would spread in a thick hot cloud over the whole *banya*. From under the cloud of steam gleamed scarred backs, shaven heads, disfigured arms and legs. And as a fit climax Isaï Fomitch (the Jew) would roar with all his throat, from the top of the platform. He steams himself into insanity, but it seems as if no heat could satisfy him. For a *kopek* he hires a washer (*parilshchik*); but at last it gets too warm for him, and he throws down the broom, and runs to pour cold water on him. Isai Fomitch does not give up hope, but hires a second, a third: he makes up his mind, on such occasions, not to grudge any expense, and he has as many as half a dozen washers. "You are tough, Isai Fomitch, you are a fine fellow," shout the prisoners from below. And Isai Fomitch himself feels that at this moment he stands above them all, and could thrust them all under his belt; he is in a glory; and with a sharp, crazy voice he shouts out his aria *lya-lya-lya-lya*, drowning all other voices.[1] The thought entered my mind, that,

[1] At the beginning of the chapter Isaï Fomitch assures Dostoyevsky, "under oath, that this song and the same motive was sung by the six hundred thousand Hebrews, from small to great, when they crossed the Red Sea: and that every Hebrew has to sing this song at the moment of glory and victory over his enemies."

if we were ever to be all in hell, then it would look very much like this place. I could not refrain from imparting this thought to Petrof: he only looked around, but said nothing."

INDEX.

www.ingramcontent.com/pod-product-compliance
Lightning Source LLC
Chambersburg PA
CBHW031055110726
47900CB00003B/937